Wild Wolves We Have Known

STORIES OF WOLF BIOLOGISTS' FAVORITE WOLVES

EDITED BY

Richard P. Thiel,
Allison C. Thiel
and
Marianne Strozewski

International Wolf Center
Teaching the World about Wolves

International Wolf Center, 3410 Winnetka Ave N, Minneapolis MN 55427 USA

ISBN 978-0-615-86002-2

Wild Wolves We Have Known: Stories of Wolf Biologists' Favorite Wolves

1. Wolves. 2. North America. 3. Europe. 4. Stories of individual wild wolves.

Layout and Design by Tricia Austin www.Designaloona.com

Illustrations by Richard P. Thiel, maps by Tricia Austin

Front cover photograph by permission of John Vucetich

Back cover photograph by permission of Linda Nelson

Printed in the United States by
Suttle-Straus, Inc.
1000 Uniek Drive
Waunakee, Wisconsin 53597 USA

CONTENTS

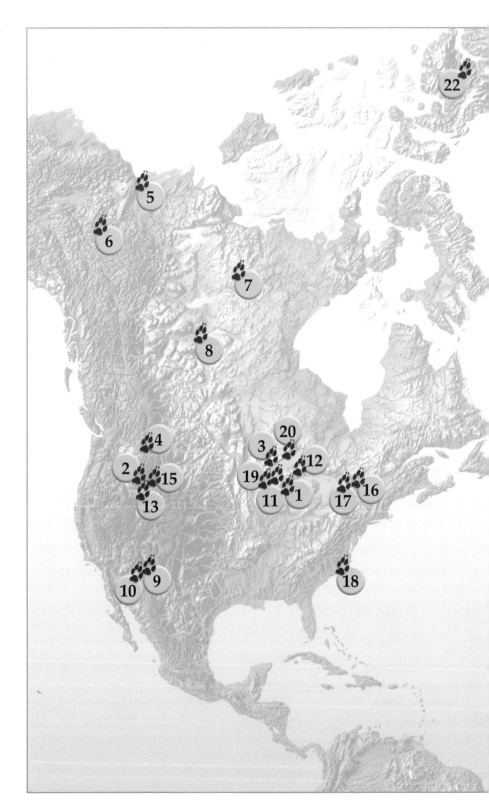

EDITORS' FOREWORD

OF ALL THE BOOKS AND ARTICLES published on wolves none to our knowledge have focused on stories by wolf biologists about their favorite wild wolves. Such stories exist around campfires and dinner tables, but would biologists be willing to share them in a published collection? In October of 2012 we determined to find out. Over forty inquiries were sent to wolf biologists from around the world, inviting their participation in this project. The response—this book—was overwhelming.

As editors we have strived to ensure that authors should be free to express their experiences in their own words. Sometimes we had to abandon standard editorial protocol that stresses uniformity, to introduce the reader to unique individuals—both wolves and wolf biologists. And individuality is what this collection of stories is all about.

So, for instance, because all biologists are trained to measure things, you will find stories reporting weights, distances traveled, etc. We made no attempt to "standardize" these. Some scientists in their everyday work lives use the metric system while others use English rule. Still others use combinations of the two! These preferences reflect differences between scientists. Welcome to their world!

Some authors actually named their wolf. Others used scientific identification numbers as formal names. Still others used numbers without attaching any significance to it. We realized most readers prefer names to numbers and find it very frustrating tracking "numerous" life-forms in a story known only by a number. To resolve this, we embarked in some editorializing by encouraging authors to use occasional euphemisms such as "...the old gray girl, 635." Some authors remained immovable and stuck to their scientific intransigence. We honored this occasional stubbornness since it reflects an adherence to scientific protocol, therein revealing the variety of personalities present among wolf biologists!

Most authors completed the story by either summarizing or highlighting the significance of their wolf's life, at least as known to the wolf biologist. As editors we presented the concluding remarks in italics to separate this portion from the actual story.

Overall, we meddled little as editors. As the scripts came in we discovered they fell into one of three broad categories: (1) experiences of the wolf biologist as these related to their wolf, (2) stories that focused on some type of conflict (mostly human-centered), and (3) chronicles of the resilience of individual wolves. We therefore assembled these stories along those defined lines, realizing, of course, that nearly every one of these stories touches on all three of these elements.

These stories reveal that wild animals like wolves live individual lives. As you will learn, life is often a struggle. In sharing these stories we wish to acknowledge that the wild creatures inhabiting our world are every bit as much the sentient beings we humans are. Therein lies a dodgy scientific hazard—explored further in John Vucetich's fine Introduction.

We hope you will find this collection of stories enjoyable and inspiring.

Richard P. Thiel
Allison C. Thiel
Marianne Strozewski

Wolves and Their Place in the Great Hierarchy of Life

John A. Vucetich

MOST WOLVES ARE GRAY, but some are white and others are black. The simplest observations sometimes have remarkable explanations. Quite a few thousand years ago, before black wolves existed, the relationship between humans and wolves rose to a new level. Our lives grew entwined, and humans began to influence wolves' reproduction and evolutionary trajectory. A result was *Canis lupus familiaris*, the domestic dog. By some chance mutation to their genes, some dogs were born with black fur. They were probably born before humans had even learned to write or live in cities. Those dogs did well—perhaps because humans liked that color in a canid companion, or perhaps because blackness conferred some fitness advantage. Still many thousands of years before today, some of those dogs bred with wolves, and, shortly afterward, the gene for black fur became established in wolves.

Observation from Isle Royale, a remote wilderness island in Lake Superior, during the 1960's and 70's indicated pretty clearly that wolf predation had been exerting considerable pressure on the moose population. Now, if a place had been studied so carefully for a couple of decades and revealed a strong and simple signal, you might think we'd pretty much come to understand that place—unless you continued observing. In 1980 disease struck, and wolf abundance dropped by about eighty percent. Moose were released from the pressure of predation. The wolves eventually recovered from the disease, but the ecosystem did not return to its previous state. For the next two decades, wolves exerted only a minor influence on fluctuations in moose abundance. That role had been replaced by the influence of climate. Wolf populations rise and fall like the feverish notes in a symphony written by some French Romantic. Sometimes they seem to be architects of the ecosystems in which they live. Other times they flourish and languish at the mercy of the ecosystems they inhabit.

Wolves, like all creatures, have lives that exist at several different levels—there are stories to be told of their genetic evolution, population dynamics, and ecosystem interactions. This book is about wolves, but it is not about wolf genes, or wolf populations, or the role of wolves in ecosystems. This is a book of stories about *individual* wolves, at least insomuch as the story of any life can be disentangled from its genes, or ecological relationships, or the people who tell their stories.

A wolf on Isle Royale once shared her story with me. I knew her throughout most of her adult life. But I never knew more than shadows of fragments of the life that she knew. It is probably better to say, with much effort I knew her better than I have known most of the wolves I have studied. I won't share with you here so much about her life.[1] Instead, I'll share how knowing about her life changed mine.

In some ways the life of a wolf is easy to understand. If you like to walk, eat meat, and hang out with your family, then you have a great deal in common with wolves. In other ways, their lives lie at the very murky edges of our imaginations—panting every time you're just a little bit too warm, learning more about the world through your nose than your eyes, killing prey ten times your size with your teeth, losing one-in-four family members to death every year of your life. Trust me – just as your family dog knows when you're gone for the weekend, so too does a wolf experience a missing sibling or parent.

Understanding the life of a wolf—how it is the same and how it is different—helps us understand ourselves and our humanity. The most remarkable lesson to learn from stories of individual wolves is also the simplest. The most important similarity between you and a wolf is that you both experience a life. The lesson is so simple and easy to overlook it merits being repeated—wolves are experiencers of life.

Life breathes and respires. It is created, transformed, and recreated. Life is complicated, interconnected, and contingent beyond our imagination. It is material, energy, and experience flowing across landscapes, over time, and through the hierarchy of life—genes, organisms, populations, and ecosystems. Understanding that hierarchy of life is critical for understanding our relationship with nature.

Ecosystems emerge from interactions—predation, herbivory, parasitism, symbiosis, and so on—between populations of various kinds of creatures living together in one place. Populations rise from the actuarial manifestation of more births and deaths than you could ever bear to know, the births and deaths of individuals belonging to the same species living together in the same place, sometimes competing with one another and other times cooperating. Populations are comprised of individual organisms, and organisms rise from their genes. This is life's hierarchy or "order of holy beings," as the word hierarchy is derived from the Middle English word *ierarchie* which carries that meaning. This hierarchy represents the diversity of life's manifestations. This is the skeleton to which the flesh of biodiversity is attached.

Developing a healthy relationship with this "order of holy beings" is quite a challenge. One great development in this relationship was the widespread realization, during the twentieth century, that humans are not the only kind of organism that deserves our moral consideration. A second great development of the twentieth century was the widespread realization that other positions in the hierarchy of life—populations, species, and ecosystems—also deserve our moral consideration. Not so much because it serves us to treat the non-human world well, but for its own sake.

Great as those developments were, too often we pit our concern for the welfare of species and ecosystems against concern for the welfare of animals. We kill thousands of individual cowbirds to save endangered populations of warblers. We kill Burmese pythons to save the Everglades. We are planning to kill hundreds of barred owls to save endangered populations of spotted owls. This page and the next could be filled with more examples of the same.

A common approach to resolving this conflict is to deny that individual organisms have any significant value. Another approach is to deny that populations and ecosystems have any significant value. An example illustrates the tragedy of this infantile nay-saying. In southern British Columbia, abundant moose support healthy wolf populations. The wolves also kill caribou; but the caribou are rare. While they are an incidental component of wolves' diet, the caribou losses are crippling to the caribou population. And these caribou populations are important beyond themselves. In particular, Canadian law makes the presence of endangered caribou an effective way to protect the rare old growth forests that they inhabit from logging. To protect caribou and old growth, we kill wolves. Many scientists don't even think it is possible to kill enough wolves to save caribou, but we kill them anyway. While wolves are the immediate cause of the problem, they are not the ultimate cause of the problem. Wolves are abundant because moose are abundant, and moose are abundant because we log the forest for timber and mineral exploration; these logging activities favor abundant moose.

Too often, we create circumstances where we feel we must kill individuals of one species to protect some aspect of ecosystem health, harming innocent manifestations of life to pay the price for our having harmed some other manifestation of life. Do two wrongs really make it right? This relationship with the great hierarchy of life is perverse, and our humanity depends on discovering a healthier relationship.

I do not know precisely what that relationship should look like, but I'm pretty sure it involves greater respect for life at each level in the great hierarchy. And the solution almost certainly involves better understanding the lives of individual organisms. This book is an opportunity to develop such an understanding, in this case for wolves. Understanding the life of an organism from its perspective should generate not so much respect, but empathy. Empathy is vivid, knowledge-based imagination about another's circumstances, situation, or perspective. Empathy tends to generate care, sociopaths excluded. Empathy and care for wolves, as individuals, does not mean we will never find occasion to kill a wolf. But it will prevent us from saying the life of an individual wolf is without significant worth or value. It will prevent us from thinking it doesn't matter if we kill, or even hate, wolves. It will prevent us from thinking it is okay to kill a wolf—or any creature—for fun or convenience. It will force us to re-consider what counts as "convenience." If we understand the life of an organism from its perspective, we will be unable to disenfranchise it, to cover for problems that humans have caused, and do little to remedy, without indicting ourselves.

Knowing about individual wolves, meditating on their lives from their perspective, engaging that knowledge-based imagination—each of these requires considerable care. One risk is anthropomorphism, which involves mistakenly attributing some human trait or capability to a nonhuman. Understanding this collection of essays requires some understanding of the capabilities a wolf does and does not possess. Consider a few:

- Sensory consciousness is the bundling together of sensory perceptions to create a unified, indivisible scene of the world around us at this present moment[2]. Some aspects of that scene capture our attention and of other aspects we have only a vague awareness. What most captures our attention is sometimes a conscious decision, sometimes it is unconsciously determined; sometimes we learn to focus attention on various aspects, sometimes we focus on an aspect out of instinct or habituation. Consciousness is the scene you have in your head right at this moment as you read this sentence. If fruit flies possess sensory consciousness, as recent research suggests[3]; then it's a safe bet that wolves do.

- Memories are information about ourselves or the world around us that is stored, in part, by being encoded in the physical structure of the neurons in our brain, and subsequently retrieved, decoded, and re-presented to our conscious mind. Remember the excellent dinner you had last night, who your closest friend is, and that great scare you had last week? Wolves can do that, too.

- Dreams are involuntary sensations and scenes that occur in the brain during sleep. The medulla oblongata portion of your brain prevents the rest of your body from acting out or responding to your dreams. Researchers have found a way to inhibit that brain function. This technique has been used to observe cats prowling and pouncing while completely asleep[4]. If cats dream about hunting mice, it's not difficult to accurately imagine some of the things that a wolf dreams about.

- Intentionality involves belief, desire, and expectation. Learning —even the simplest kinds of learning, like associative learning—may require intentionality. The kind of mental states required for a creature to be capable of intentionality is hotly debated among scholars. Nevertheless, behavioral ecologists believe that male cuttlefish communicate their intention to fight another cuttlefish by changing color prior to fighting[5]. Some research even suggests that the foraging behaviors of the sea slug exhibit intentionality[6]. It's a safe bet that wolves have intentionality.

- Emotions are a certain kind of stimulus (e.g., the sight of your big brother approaching with an angry expression) that causes a certain kind of automatic chemical or neural reaction (e.g., elevated heart rate, dilated pupils, sweaty paws). If you possess a thalamus and amygdala you are capable of basic emotions like fear, joy, and love[7]. Wolves certainly qualify. Group-living mammals also experience more complicated emotions that also involve the brain's cortex, where higher thought processes and memories occur. Behavioral ecologists have documented, what is by all accounts, post-traumatic stress disorder in young elephants whose parents were murdered by humans[8]. It should be no surprise that wolves (like dogs) are capable of social emotions like pride and embarrassment. Granted, you cannot know exactly how a wolf feels when it is proud, just as you cannot know exactly how another human feels when she is proud. The private nature of how an emotion feels does not prevent you from making a reliable guess as to when another is experiencing a certain emotion.

- Personalities are distinct patterns of behavior that vary consistently among individual organisms—such as being consistently aggressive or risk averse. Behavioral ecologists have identified and studied the genetic causes and population consequences of personality types among hermit crabs[9]. It's a safe bet that wolves have personalities.

The similarities we share with wolves are considerable. Many arise from a central nervous system that we inherited from a common ancestor that lived some forty to sixty million years ago, during the early days of mammalian evolution. Other similarities rise from the adaptations associated with living intensely social lives[10].

The idea of anthropomorphism, which literally means "turn into a human," raises another concern. Wolves are certainly not human, and we possess capabilities that they do not[11]. But it is an entirely separate concern to ask, is a wolf a person? The etymological root of person is a Greek word that means "mask," referring to the mask an actor would wear on stage. A person is an actor in the world. And so Shakespeare wrote, "All the world's a stage, and all the men and women merely players." Possessing those traits mentioned above—sensory consciousness, memory, dreams, intentions, personality, emotions—certainly qualifies as being an actor in the world, as the experiencer of a life. It is perfectly right to treat our dogs as people. Native Americans were certain that wolves and many other creatures were people[12].

The essays in this book present us with two basic opportunities. After hearing the stories of a few individual wolves, then you will be only a tiny step away from realizing that every wolf that has ever lived has a story to tell. When you see a wolf track, hear a wolf howl, or if you are lucky enough to catch a glimpse of a wolf as it slips over the hill or into the forest's shadow—you will know that wolf has a story. You just won't know the details of that story. Wolves are like all the people we brush past in our own lives; people whose names we never learn. They all have a story. With some knowledge we can imagine those stories, and they are true. Some are tragic and others triumphant. We just don't know who is living which life.With that realization, you will be only a step away from realizing that all mammals experience lives—elk, deer mice, leopard seals… Imagine, if you can, the life of a leopard seal. Each has a story to tell and a life with which to empathize. It is true of all vertebrates—all creatures, in fact. If you think, for example, it is impossible to empathize with the life of a plant, then you might pick up (after reading this book) a copy of Shel Silverstein's *The Giving Tree*. If you think it is impossible to empathize with individuals and ecosystems at the same time, you might consider Aldo Leopold's *Thinking Like a Mountain*.

The second opportunity provided by these essays is occasion to reflect on the idea that some humans have expended considerable life energy to reflect on the lives of some individual wolves enough to know and share their stories. While these people are privileged with life circumstances that permit such a possibility, no one is excused from the fundamental obligation to know the life around us. These essays are an encouragement to embrace that obligation more fully. You may not be able to know the life of a wolf through your own direct observations. But you can use these essays as inspiration to know the creatures that live near you—the gray squirrel that nests in your neighbor's tree, the house sparrow that feeds outside your window, or the moth that comes to your porch light at nightfall. They have lives, and you will flourish when you reflect on those lives and take the time to share their stories.

These essays also provide occasion to reflect on how the various authors tell their stories. The diversity of voice and perspective is rich. Each perspective reflects a personal relationship with nature. With such a diversity of thoughtful voice, there is great value in imagining yourself in each author's position, wondering, How would I tell that story? The value of doing so is not the prospect for critique, but the occasion to become the story-teller of the life that best reflects you and your relationship with nature. It is from your own story-telling that your relationship with nature grows.

Genes, individuals, populations, and ecosystems—these are the manifestation of biodiversity. They deserve our care. This motivation lies at the heart of conservation, stewardship, and environmentalism. The obligation to care runs deeper than caring only when our human welfare benefits. And the obligation does not stipulate caring for some manifestations of life, while not others. This obligation comes with conflict. But the conflict does not dissolve the obligation, in the same way that your obligation to share time with your family is not dissolved by your need to stay at work later than you'd promised. Similarly, our obligation to protect ecosystems does not dissolve our obligation to care for individuals. The hierarchy of life is an indivisible package. Wolves, like all organisms, cannot be separated from the ecosystems into which they are embedded or the genes they carry.

I am not sure that anyone has learned to navigate this conflict well. However, I believe that skill can begin with understanding the stories of a few individual wolves and, being inspired by those stories, to develop and share the stories of life that we can discover in our midst—the stories that make us human. These concerns are vital for another reason. In particular, they lie near the heart of sustainability—nearer than may at first be apparent. Sustainability is meeting human needs without disenfranchising ecosystem health or social justice, which is the wise balance of fairness, equality, and need[13]. Justice for whom? People, I believe. People, the experiencers of life. When we become good at telling the stories of other creatures and manifestations of life, then we will be one important step closer to living a sustainable life.

ENDNOTES:

1   You can read about, for example, her last year of life in John Vucetich's *Notes from the Field* (CreateSpace, 2010). You can read about her father in Rolf Peterson's essay of this volume.

2   See F. Crick's *The Astonishing Hypothesis* (Simon & Schuster, 1994) and G. Edelman and G. Tononi's *A Universe of Consciousness* (Basic Books, 2000).

3   Swinderen, Bv. 2011. Attention in Drosophila. *International Review of Neurobiology* 99:51-85.

4   Jouvet, M. 1979. What does a cat dream about. *Trends in Neurosciences* 2:280-282.

5   Adamo, SA and RT Hanlon. 1996. Do cuttlefish (Cephalopoda) signal their intentions to conspecifics during agonistic encounters? *Animal Behavior* 52: 73–81.

6   A. Proekt et al. 2004. Dynamical basis of intentions and expectations in a simple neuronal network. *Proc. Nat'l Acad Sci.* 101:9447-9452.

7   Panksepp, J. *Affective Neuroscience: Foundation of Human and Animal Emotions* (Oxford, 2004). See also M Bekoff and SJ Gould's *The Smile of a Dolphin: Remarkable Accounts of Animal Emotions* (Discovery, 2000).

8   Bradshaw et al. 2005. Elephant Breakdown. *Nature* 433: 807.

9   Watanabe, N.M., Stahlman, W.D., Blaisdell, A.P., Garlick, D., Fast, C.D. & Blumstein, D.T. (2012). Quantifying personality in the terrestrial hermit crab: Different measures, different inferences, Behavioural Processes, DOI: 10.1016/j.beproc.2012.06.007.

10 Being social creatures, wolves have what some scholars consider proto-ethical behaviors. Living social lives is considered an important evolutionary explanation for why humans are ethical creatures. See Marc Bekoff, M and J Pierce. 2010. *Wild Justice: The Moral Lives of Animals* (University Chicago Press).

11 Aside from grabbing objects with an opposable thumb or walking upright, there are other capabilities that humans possess, but wolves do not. For example, while wolves have a complicated means of communicating among themselves and other species, including ravens and humans, they probably do not have what most linguists would consider language, which involves grammar and syntax. The best available research suggests that wolves do not have much in the way of reflective consciousness, such as self awareness, theory of mind, an understanding of their own mortality, or religious beliefs.

12 Callicott, JB and MP Nelson (2004). *American Indian Environmental Ethics: An Ojibwa Case Study* (Upper Saddle River, NJ: Prentice-Hall).

13 For details on this definition of sustainability, see Vucetich, J. A. & Nelson, M. P. 2010 Sustainability: Virtuous or vulgar? *BioScience* 60:539–44. For a scholarly, but accessible, treatment of justice, see D. Miller's *Principles of Social Justice* (Harvard University Press, 1999).

Experiences of the Biologist

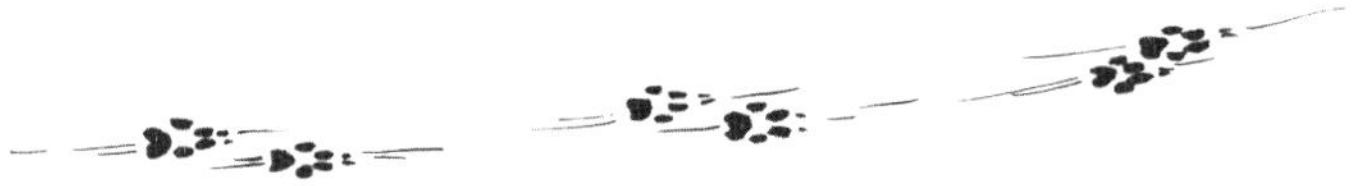

CHAPTER ONE

Old Two Toes and the Willow Wolf Pack[1]

Richard P. Thiel

IT WAS THE TWENTY-FIRST OF MAY in the year 1946. Here, firmly imprinted in the sand of the remote fire lane in western Oneida County, Wisconsin were the fresh tracks of two wolves. This was Dan Thompson's first encounter with the Willow Wolf Pack since his return from the Pacific, having served in the U.S. Coast Guard throughout much of World War II. But where was the celebrated two-toed wolf, believed to be the leader of this pack, one of the few family groups of timber wolves remaining within the state?

Upon his return home to Madison, Dan was rehired to work with the Wisconsin Conservation Department's Deer Research Project. Back in the winter of 1941–42, Dan had worked briefly with a half-dozen other temporary biologists on this start-up project, hiking over 200 miles on snowshoes throughout northern Wisconsin, documenting starvation and poor conditions of winter browse within northern Wisconsin deer yards.

Following his discharge Dan visited his undergraduate professor at the University of Wisconsin. During the War he had carried out correspondence with the professor, relating observations on birdlife at scattered locations throughout the far Pacific. His desire was to take advantage of the GI Bill. Would his former professor accept Dan as a candidate for a master's degree in wildlife management?

Professor Aldo Leopold was delighted and, unlike some professors, didn't seem concerned that Dan intended to work while attending school. As a commissioner of the Wisconsin Conservation Department during the War years, Leopold had been drawn into deer management debates. Not long after his first encounter with the Willow Pack wolves, Dan had decided on his thesis topic. He would investigate the timber wolves' food habits. Leopold approved.

By the 1940's wolves were nearly gone. The public, and practically every single employee within federal and state game agencies, resolutely believed that wolves had no place in the world because they depredated on livestock and preyed on hoofed mammals, coveted by an emergent hunting

---

1 As gleaned from Daniel Q. Thompson, University of Wisconsin M.S. Thesis (1950), field notes of Thompson and Felix Hartmeister, and interviews with Dan Thompson and Walt Rosenlaf.

public. Positively no one of sound mind sympathized with the wolves. In his role as a Wisconsin Conservation Commissioner, Leopold had convinced the State Legislature to repeal their wolf bounty bill during a brief period in 1944. Owing to intense public fury, the State reinstated the twenty-dollar bounty. Perhaps the political fallout stirred something within Leopold because in this same year he penned his now famous "Thinking Like a Mountain" essay. It would not see print until 1949, the year following his death.

Also in 1944 Adolf Murie's epic pioneering wolf ecology study "The Wolves of Mount McKinley" was published by the National Park Service. Only the third scientific study on wolves, it was the first comprehensive look at the social lives of wild wolves. It was also the first impartial view of the effect of wolves on big game animals. Murie reasoned that wolves performed a role in maintaining prey populations more in balance with vegetative conditions, but his viewpoint was accepted by only a minority of biologists working in the profession. This view was rejected as academic nonsense by the masses of outdoor-minded individuals and organizations.

It just so happened that while Aldo Leopold was a commissioner, the Wisconsin Conservation Department was itself in the midst of a huge deer management debacle. Agency biologists had instituted the first-ever doe hunting season in the state in an effort to quell starvation problems in the northern forests. Their nascent deer research project, studying the effects of overbrowsing, had revealed widespread starvation patterns among white-tailed deer occupying the northern forests. Funded through the federal Pittman-Robertson program, this first-ever research was paid for by taxes placed on the sale of hunters' sporting goods equipment.

As a falconer, program leader Bill Feeney admired predators. At the height of the War, and with the personal backing of Leopold, Feeney had instructed his field men to document the presence or absence of wolves within deer yards. Where and when encountered they were to plot wolves' movements, inspect wolf-killed deer, and determine prey remains in wolf scats. In essence, these government men were studying wolves—and all of this was to be conducted with the strictest secrecy.

Studying wolves in forested terrain was a logistical nightmare. These creatures were far-ranging, highly mobile and, because of the decades of intense human persecution, exceedingly wary. In that era biologists did not have the array of gadgets we have at our disposal today: radio telemetry, 4-wheel drive and all-terrain vehicles, global positioning systems, computers, links to satellites, digital trail cameras, and genetic testing technologies. These technologies wouldn't become available for another twenty-five to fifty years. Their automobiles were limited to the few passable roads and trails. They walked, using compasses and

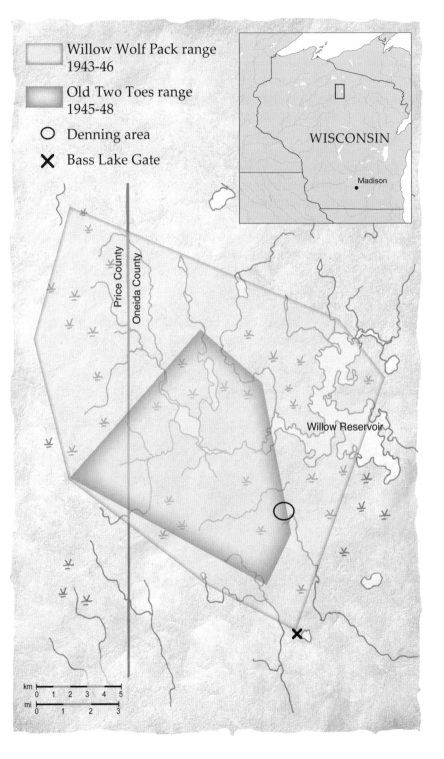

Willow Wolf Pack range
1943-46

Old Two Toes range
1945-48

O Denning area

X Bass Lake Gate

WISCONSIN

Madison

Price County

Oneida County

Willow Reservoir

km
0 1 2 3 4 5
mi
0 1 2 3

3

topographic maps, binoculars, Kodak photography, and notebooks in which field notes were scribbled with stubby pencils by hands that needed to be inserted frequently into pockets to avert frost-bite. Back at the office they were faced with reams of paper on which calculations were performed manually, and reports were typed on messy triple carbon-copy forms. It was laborious and the data was hard to come by.

Standing beside Dan that day in May back in 1946 was one of Feeney's field men. Felix Hartmeister looked down at the large, elongated tracks coming onto the lane from the old sandpit and remarked, "I wonder where Old Two Toes is?"

Toes were missing from two of the wolf's feet due to narrow brushes with fate at the hands of bounty trappers. Felix had first encountered the tracks back in March of 1945 near the very spot they were now standing. At first glance the tracks appeared normal, but something confused him.

Throughout that winter he had snow-tracked the Willow Pack and each encounter yielded a count of three or four individuals. All tracks appeared normal. But that day he detected something odd in the trails of the two wolves sauntering up the fire lane heading towards Gobbler Lake. One of the wolves had a peculiar gait—the first two steps averaged around 22 inches while the third consistently spanned 37 inches. Felix wondered if this animal was using only three legs.

He returned the next day but found tracking difficult because of the melting snowpack. Limiting his search to scattered sandy stretches along the lane, he nonetheless found enough tracks to realize this wolf was actually missing some toes from one of its great paws. Apparently, this wolf had pulled free from a bounty trapper's set, leaving a few toes behind in the process. This left Felix with a question: was this maimed wolf just drifting through, or was it a pack member with a freshly injured paw?

Either way, Felix knew this wolf with the missing toes could supply him with the means of estimating movement patterns, associations between pack members, and perhaps even the size of the pack's territory. Here, he recognized, was a marked wolf that could be identified on the basis of his track. Provided, of course, the wolf stayed alive or wasn't simply passing through. He explained to Thompson that, in order for all of this to work, he needed to intercept the crippled wolf's paths repeatedly over the course of several winters to get sufficient information to determine with confidence the size of the pack's territory. That didn't seem likely given the intensity of bounty trappers' efforts to catch and kill these wolves.

His concerns weren't unfounded. A few weeks later, and before Hartmeister got back out in the field, two wolves had been turned in for the twenty-dollar state bounty, trapped on the north side of the Willow reservoir. This was within the area where Felix had frequently snow-tracked the Willow wolves. He worried that one of them may have been his sore-footed wolf.

On April 10 he found a trail that appeared to have been made by two wolves. But the crippled wolf was not present. Nor did the cripple show up on five return trips Felix made to the western Oneida County wolf range. Finally, on a warm day in mid-May, Hartmeister's luck changed. He had been conducting surveys in a number of vegetative study plots within a remote deer yard inside the Willow Pack's usual haunts. He was in a hurry, racing against the emergence of foliage that would soon shut down his surveys for the season. Twice during that day he had driven by wolf tracks on the lane past Willow Springs while moving between survey plots, but he didn't have time to stop to inspect them. As he was driving out of the woods that evening he finally examined them and was surprised to see a pair of fresh wolf tracks clearly imprinted on top of his tire tracks made earlier that day. Amazingly, one of the wolves was the cripple-foot!

A few weeks later Felix again encountered the crippled wolf's trail while passing through the area. That evening he scribbled into his field notebook, "...Old two toes showed up again." The name stuck. Returning to their vehicle Felix told Dan that Old Two Toes had lost yet more toes this past winter.

As they drove the eight miles out towards a blacktop highway, Thompson got a taste of what this small family group of wolves was up against in their struggle for survival. On a rise in the middle of the lane they encountered a spot that had been greatly disturbed. Obviously a coyote had stepped into a trapper's set. Boot tracks and bloody sand revealed the fate of this smaller cousin to the wolves, whose tracks ambled past the site. Destiny had perhaps ordained the coyote to move down the lane before the wolves did. The trap and coyote were gone.

Appalled by the all-out war being waged on wolves, Dan decided right then and there to wage his own very private war against the bounty trappers. On return visits henceforth, as Dan confided thirty-five years later, he kept "...a can of ripe human urine for my return trips to Oneida County. There was an excellent roadside trap site on the west side of the fire lane (near the sand pits). Someone had taken a wolf or a coyote in this set in the spring of '46—signs of the struggle were still visible in the sand. It was a high traffic area (rendezvous?) for wolves—so thereafter I always anointed the set with a pint or so of old urine. In the interest of wolf preservation, I 'marked' [it]."

On the following day Dan returned with Felix to the sandpits beside the fire lane. Overnight a pair of wolves had left the lane, crossed through the sandpits and entered the forest. Felix was interested in this spot. The previous summer the wolves had frequented this area, entering or exiting the lane at these same sand pits.

Standing here and peering down at the tracks, both suspected a den lay somewhere beyond, within this large, forested tract. They split up that day, each walking miles along random transects through the brush, hoping to trip into the wolves' den. Though they collected some wolf scats encountered along deer trails, they emerged from the forest that evening empty-handed. They remained convinced the Willow Wolf Pack's den site lay somewhere east of these sand pits. On September 17 Dan finally confirmed that the pack had pups; he found pup tracks with that of three adult-sized wolves. Old Two Toes was among them.

Snow arrived in late November, but Thompson saw no wolf tracks until February 3, 1947. On that day he found tracks made by three or four wolves working their way south from the sand pits to the locked Bass Lake fire lane gate maintained by the Wisconsin Conservation Department. The tracks of Old Two Toes were not among these. At this same gate he also encountered the tracks of a trapper who parked his car at the gate and walked north on the fire lane. That trapper was Walt Rosenlaf.

Many years earlier, as a youngster, Rosenlaf had caught his first coyotes while walking home from school, checking his newly established trap line. Arriving home with his forty dollars in bounty money, he was greeted at the door by an older brother who had just returned from having spent the entire winter in a remote logging camp in Michigan's Upper Peninsula where he had worked for a wage of one dollar per day!

It was the twenty-dollar state bounty that got Rosenlaf's attention. In those days wolf and coyote hides were nearly worthless. Most trappers preferred catching coyotes because a 25 pound coyote could be hauled out of the woods with infinitely more ease than an 80 pound wolf—especially considering that each was worth twenty dollars in bounty money. But Walt enjoyed the challenge of trapping the big wolves. They were rare, extremely wary of people and were far more difficult to trap. And there was a certain prestige that came with being recognized as a timber wolf trapper. By the mid-1930's Walt was consistently catching three or four wolves annually out of the Willow Wolf Pack.

Each autumn he parked his car at the gate along the Bass Lake fire lane, placed a number of eight-pound wolf traps in his wicker basket, hoisted it over his shoulders onto his back and walked the eight miles up to the flowage, setting traps along the way. Near the flowage he sheltered the night beneath a scrap of tin that had once been the roof of an old shack.

The next morning he would arise and check his traps on his return trip. Once his trap line was established, it was just a matter of checking the sets, skinning and rolling up the hides of animals killed, or in the case of wolves, coyotes and bobcats, hauling their carcasses out so that he could collect the state bounty.

Hartmeister never knew Rosenlaf, but their paths crossed often as they each pursued the trails of Old Two Toes and his Willow Wolf Pack for very different reasons.

One day in the winter of 1946 Rosenlaf was inspecting traps along the Bass Lake fire lane when he noticed a greatly disturbed patch of snow and brush right where one of his sets was located. A wolf had managed to pull free, taking the trap with it. He followed. It didn't take long to figure out the trap's drag, or anchor, had been bent straight, caused by repeated thrusts as the wolf lunged where the drag had temporarily ensnared root clumps or saplings. Each time, with gargantuan strength, the wolf managed to pull out, eventually bending straight the curved iron anchor. It now dangled uselessly, cutting a furrow through the snow.

About mid-morning Rosenlaf finally caught sight of the wolf. Swiftly mounting his 30-30 he got off a shot just as the wolf turned to flee. He missed, but the blast shocked the wolf. It lunged forward crashing headlong into a poplar tree so forcefully that the trap and two toes snapped off. In an instant the wolf was gone.

Rosenlaf knew this wolf was not Old Two Toes. Earlier that same winter, Old Two Toes had been snagged in one of his traps, managing yet again to leave a few toes behind for Rosenlaf.

By chance Felix encountered the tracks of the trapped wolf and the trapper who parked beside the Bass Lake fire-lane gate in pursuit of the wolf. He returned over three successive days following the trapped wolf's trail, finally convinced this was not Old Two Toes. Later in winter Felix realized Old Two Toes was missing still more toes!

In the months leading up to Dan's arrival Felix was confident that Old Two Toes was the Willow Pack's leader. Old Two Toes was often accompanied by two or three other wolves. Over the two winters Felix noted the pack's range extended beyond the gate on the Bass Lake fire lane, some ten miles north. The wolves frequented the northern and western arms of the Willow Flowage. From here they ranged west eight miles across a blacktop county highway into Chequamegon National Forest lands. By his calculations the Willow Pack's territory was some 150 square miles.

Felix left the Department's Deer Research Project the summer of Dan's arrival. At about the same time project leader Bill Feeney called his men off the secret wolf study. Dan left the Department too, leaving him free to continue his Master's project studying the wolves' food habits, but on his own time.

His trips north from Madison were more infrequent now. During that time he found scats, but rarely encountered tracks. In early February 1948, Thompson encountered tracks of Old Two Toes, accompanied by three other wolves. The snow was lightly crusted. Thompson noted that Old Two Toes "...was evidently handicapped under these particular snow conditions, for his maimed pads would frequently break through the light crust. The three wolves accompanying him trotted along easily on the surface of the snow."

Thompson gave a detailed description of Old Two Toes maimed feet. "Tracks of this animal showed the central toes missing from both rear feet and the inner toe missing from the right front foot. The left front foot had a normal number of digits, but field sketches and photographs showed that even this foot did not make a symmetrical spoor."

On one trip to western Oneida County in the spring of 1948 Dan was reassured that all was well with the Willow wolves, finding tracks of three wolves. Among them was Old Two Toes. He had managed to survive yet another winter.

The long summer daylight periods allowed Dan more time to walk and drive miles of fire lane deep within the Willow Pack's territory, searching for wolf scats. He had heard stories from other members of the Deer Research Project that they had once located a wolf's den quite by accident while working at night when the wolves revealed the den's presence through howling.

While not interested in actually locating the Willow Pack's den, he was curious to learn whether any pups were produced. On June 26 he orchestrated his scat-collecting route so that he would pass by the sand pits just at dusk. Was the pack back in their suspected denning ground?

He arrived at the sand pits around dark and lingered. An hour passed. Nothing. Suddenly, around 11:25 p.m. two adult wolves began serenading some distance off to the east. The voices of these two wolves then mingled with a series of high, shrill yipping and yapping, quite different from that of coyotes. All came from the direction of the Little Rice River drainage. These could only be pups!

That September a local hound hunter reported seeing tracks of two adult and four pup wolves on a sandy stretch of fire lane south of the reservoir. Thompson was relieved to know the pups had survived. Then, in October, another local trapper caught a wolf in the vicinity of the reservoir. Walt Rosenlaf began laying traps in early December.

Toward the end of December 1948, Dan Thompson made the six-hour journey from Madison to Tomahawk with the intention of searching for droppings. It was night by the time he arrived. He had heard of Walt

Rosenlaf, so he decided to visit him with the intent of asking Walt to notify him should he finally capture Old Two Toes.

The Rosenlafs invited him into the farmhouse. They talked for awhile about the wolves, and then Thompson asked Walt to let him know in the event that he should catch the old crippled wolf. Walt's response stunned Dan. "Why he's hanging up in the pine tree just outside. I got him today!" It was too dark for Dan to inspect the dead Willow Pack wolves so he returned the following morning.

Thirty-five years later Dan related, "I can still recall the ghoulish shock of driving into Walt's yard and seeing the Oneida Wolf Pack hanging by wires from the trees. It was as though some of my own family were hanging over the bright snow."

Earlier in the month Rosenlaf caught and killed an adult male and a female pup up near the reservoir. He then pulled sets, returning a half month later with more sets. A few nights later a little female wolf stepped into one these. Rosenlaf noticed several beds where Old Two Toes had lain near the pup. After dispatching it, Walt placed out a second series of sets hoping to entice Old Two Toes in. He did just that but once again this powerful and ornery old patriarch pulled free.

A few days later Walt found fresh tracks of Old Two Toes on a game trail four miles to the south near the denning grounds. Setting out some traps, he returned early the next morning. He saw something move ahead of him in the brush. Approaching a bit closer Walt finally looked into the eyes of Old Two Toes, the wolf that had repeatedly managed to elude him over the past four or five years. As he pulled up his rifle the old patriarch raised his head and gave one long, last howl.

And before the echo of his howl died away, the Willow Wolf Pack ceased to exist.

Before that fateful day in the spring of 1945 wolves, like all other forms of wildlife, had been devoid of any recognition of individuality. Felix Hartmeister had the presence of mind to carefully document encounters with Old Two Toes. In so doing, he and Dan Thompson became exposed to a different level of understanding wild animals. They possessed individual lives. As a consequence they came to relate to this animal.

Dan and Felix were among the first biologists to winter-track wolves inhabiting deep forested terrain, counting wolves in this pack each winter over a four-year period, accounting for those removed by bounty, and marveling at the tenacity of the survivors that repeatedly produced litters. They were among the first to employ passive howling to locate denning and rendezvous sites. And droppings scooped up among the miles of fire lanes verified what the public already knew and hated about wolves: their diet consisted primarily of white-tailed deer. Dan's scat study, published in the Journal of Mammalogy in 1952 would be the standard for a generation of wolf biologists who launched the science of wolf ecology in the 1970's and beyond. Thompson's exposure to the year-to-year struggles of Old Two Toes' pack deeply affected him. He was the first wildlife biologist to write about the need for limiting public road access to preserve some space for wolves. These efforts had little immediate effect. Wolves were extirpated from Wisconsin and neighboring Upper Michigan within a decade. But through their efforts these biologists and others like them elsewhere devised methodologies that would be refined and employed by a future generation of wolf biologists who would later drive the wolf's return to the Upper Great Lakes states and beyond.

CHAPTER TWO

The White Wolf of Yellowstone: Bechler 192 Male

Dan Stahler

"ONE, TWO, THREE ... FOUR, FIVE," I recorded into my Dictaphone. I was zoomed in to full power on a hole in the earth about half a mile away at the base of a large glacial erratic. A slight aberration of light at the hole beneath the boulder had caught my eye. A litter of four-week-old wolf pups poured out from beneath the rock onto the hard-packed dirt mound, as if a gate had just been opened from deep below. They wriggled and writhed as one, until the first three pups to emerge came tumbling down the entrance mound onto the grass below, pushed by their littermates who continued to boil out from the den hole.

"Six, seven, eight—oh boy!" I was mesmerized—bound by the excitement of my first sighting of wild Yellowstone wolf pups. They appeared utterly vulnerable, and undeniably cute. Ironic to think these tiny creatures were the new generation of top predators on the Yellowstone landscape. With all the commotion, it didn't take long for the pups' mother, female 18 of the Rose Creek Pack, to rise from her napping spot at the base of a nearby Douglas fir tree, trot over to the pups and quickly gather them back up. Mobbed and seemingly agitated, the young black female, known to us as 18F, nosed over her squirming offspring as if taking count. Nearly overtaken, she graciously nuzzled them out of her way and disappeared down the hole, dragging her litter back into the darkness. I glanced away from my scope to rest my eyes, staring at the distant south-facing slope of sagebrush, rock and scattered trees to locate the den boulder unaided by optics. As quickly as they had appeared, they were gone, leaving the hillside quiet but for a few ravens that flew in to investigate.

Observed only a brief minute, it marked the beginning of a magnificent journey. Not only was this journey mine, through which I was entering the world of field biology with the awe and eagerness of youth, it was also the journey of a young wolf that had emerged from the dark cavern of his birth into that Yellowstone morning light. One of these small gray pups would become known to us as male Wolf 192.

He would not receive his official moniker until several years later when first captured and radio collared, but from this day on throughout the next twelve years, we would share more minutes, even hours, of our lives connected by the threads of science.

"Happy Birthday," I whispered to myself. It was May 5, 1997, the day I turned 23. The very day I first saw him emerge from his birthplace beneath that boulder I was just a young pup myself. Born and raised in the wild lands of Vermont's Northeast Kingdom, I grew up nurturing the grandiose idea that I would someday live and work among wild animals, imagining a career containing the essence of Jack London, Marlin Perkins, Louie L'Amour, and Tolkien's Bilbo Baggins. In college, I had recalibrated to the more practical, but no less fantastical, inspirations of scientific pioneers like Charles Darwin, Aldo Leopold, E.O. Wilson, and Michael Soule. But throughout it all, I still craved the simplest desire of my youth—to spend my days in the out-of-doors, following the lives of wild animals that did not know I cared.

Like many others who studied wolves, I had gained experience working for L. D. Mech trapping and radio collaring wolves in northern Minnesota. Despite arduous months of canoe portages laden with heavy traps, an ever-present smell of rotting bait, few successful trap nights, and even fewer sightings of wild wolves, I was living a dream. Being let loose into the Boundary Waters with the task of finding and live-catching wolves as part of a historic ecological study was too good to be true for any aspiring young biologist.

A week later I was perched on a hilltop peering into a spotting scope, watching the den from a safe distance. After a couple hours with no activity, the mother wolf climbed out of the hole followed by her litter. Stretching, squinting, and yawning in the morning sun, mom and her pups were greeted by a cacophony of sandhill crane chatter and coyote yips sounding from the west. The she-wolf walked away to nap in the sun and immediately all eight pups started wrestling in the den entrance. This drew the attention of a group of ravens that had been cruising sporadically all morning. Several perched in a Douglas fir above the den while three others strutted around like pickers at a flea market, sifting through bones and scats that lay strewn about. The four-week-old wolf pups were quite vulnerable and still physically smaller than ravens. As a couple of the ravens sidled up to two gray pups, the mother wolf rushed to flush. "Never discount a raven's capacity to secure a meal, no matter how seemingly unlikely," I reminded myself, my eye to the scope.

No sooner had mom re-bedded than two ravens returned, following a lone pup that had wandered off. The closest raven reached out with its bill and grabbed onto the pup's tail. The pup tried pulling away and, after a brief hold, the raven released its grip. A second time, the raven grabbed the pup's tail, causing it to struggle. The raven released its grip once again

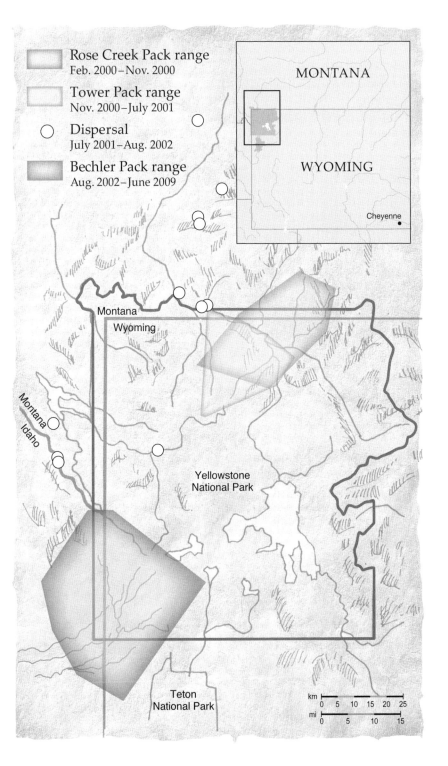

Rose Creek Pack range
Feb. 2000–Nov. 2000

Tower Pack range
Nov. 2000–July 2001

Dispersal
July 2001–Aug. 2002

Bechler Pack range
Aug. 2002–June 2009

MONTANA

WYOMING

Cheyenne

Montana
Wyoming

Montana
Idaho

Yellowstone
National Park

Teton
National Park

km
0   5   10   15   20   25
mi
0   5   10   15

and easily dodged the mother wolf's incoming charge by flying up to a branch just beyond her reach. This little gray pup may well have been the future Wolf 192. Regardless, the entire litter would become quite familiar with ravens, one of the many constants I quickly realized a wolf would face throughout its life, along with summer thunder, violent blizzards, the smell of blood and rumen, polarized perceptions of mankind, and a persistent struggle to survive in an environment under constant change.

I spent the rest of the morning catching up on notes in my field journal. My first day in Yellowstone I retrieved the body of female Wolf 19 who was the mother wolf's sister. She had been killed at her den by the neighboring Druid Peak Pack in a territorial assault. This wolf's small litter perished within a few days. A few days later I watched the Rose Creek Pack chase and kill a coyote near a fresh elk carcass in Lamar Valley east of their den. I also had observed a grizzly bear lying spread-eagle, napping on a bison carcass while the Leopold Pack's alpha male waited patiently on the sidelines.

Only one week into my journey and I could already sense it would be grand and unique. With radio collars, distinctive pelages, and even personalities that leached through generic wolf prototypes, I began to connect with each wolf I was observing in short order. Seduced by the prospects of each new day, I went into the field to connect with wild individuals in wild places. This was just the opportunity I had been seeking.

As my first summer rolled on, I observed almost daily the development of the Rose Creek litter along with the daily routines of other denning packs as part of a den study led by Linda Thurston, who was assembling data on adult attendance and pup provisioning at home sites. I was eager to find patterns in what I was observing, and in my spare time read others' research on wolves, writing down ideas, and framing questions about wolves on my own. I leaned heavily on my observations of specific individuals, drawn to the stories unfolding each day in the field. I had been inspired by the insight of University of Vermont professor, Bernd Heinrich, noted raven researcher, nature writer, bumblebee economist, and, eventually, my graduate advisor. Wondering how tiny, golden-crowned kinglets survived winter in the Maine woods, he wrote "I do not yet want to form a hypothesis to test, because as soon as you make a hypothesis, you become prejudiced. Your mind slides into a groove, and once it is in that groove, has difficulty noticing anything outside of it. During this time, my sense must be sharp; that is the main thing... to be sharp, yet open." Placing credence in Heinrich's approach, inspired by my observations of the pups and their mother interacting with ravens, I developed a graduate project with Heinrich and Yellowstone National Park's Wolf Project Leader, Doug Smith, to evaluate the relationship between wolves and ravens.

Wolves are perhaps the most studied large mammals in the world. The ability to readily and repeatedly observe Yellowstone's wolves is unique among wolf studies. As Yellowstone wolves continued to perform almost daily their wild ways for all to see, a new trajectory for wolf research was underway. Under the guidance of first Mike Phillips and later Doug Smith, the Yellowstone Wolf Project embraced a research environment where collection of data occurred on multiple levels. Predator-prey research was established almost immediately, along with the traditionally essential task of counting wolves. But soon it became apparent that unprecedented behavioral research could be conducted, and the importance of individual-based behavioral questions gained momentum. It was easy in the early years of wolf restoration in Yellowstone to appreciate the importance of individuals from a conservation perspective, despite the nagging template in a biologist's mind to care only about populations. In the initial stage every individual was important to recovery; documenting each wolf's territorial establishment, movements, reproduction, and survival in their new ecosystem was critical. Biologists, young and old, contemporary and veteran, were caught up in the excitement of Yellowstone wolves and the anticipation and potential to learn.

Over the next several years, Wolf 192 remained an uncollared member of the Rose Creek Pack, unknown to us. Like most young wolves, he likely participated in various duties expected of any wolf family member—hunter, warrior, babysitter, meal ticket for his younger siblings—his anonymous presence contributing to the Yellowstone Wolf Project's growing datasets on predation, population dynamics, and behavior. Then, on February 4, 2000, a tranquilizer dart fell from the sky, delivering its liquid dissociative compounds into the bloodstream of this wolf, rendering him helpless at maintaining a more mysterious lifestyle. Blood was drawn, measurements taken, a collar fitted.

At nearly three years of age, still climbing the male wolf growth curve, he was already an impressive 120 pounds. He had a relatively generic-looking gray coat, although slightly lighter than other grays in his pack. A mere thirty minutes of careful handling by biologists transformed the uncollared gray male into the one hundred and ninety-second individual to formally enter the wolf research database. This transition meant that his patterns of growth, reproduction, and survival, as well as knowledge of his innermost genetic code, would enter the annals of science, bringing everlasting recognition to a creature with no such aspirations.

For the rest of the winter, summer and fall of 2000 this newly-collared male wolf remained part of his natal Rose Creek Pack, ranging between the Hellroaring Creek drainage, Buffalo Plateau, and Tower Creek drainage on the Northern Range of Yellowstone. The Rose Creek Pack at the time numbered eleven wolves and was still a dominant force on the landscape, nestled between the Druid Peak and Leopold Packs. But by the following winter, this young male wolf splintered off with a group of his siblings and a couple of individuals from the neighboring Leopold Pack to form the Tower Pack. This pattern of group dispersal appeared to be advantageous in the increasingly competitive environment of Yellowstone. Not only was the risk of death higher for lone dispersers, successfully hunting large ungulates and defending newly carved territories improved considerably if you had friends. But in the summer of 2001, Wolf 192 disappeared, ditching his siblings and vanishing from our radar for a bit of time. He was a wolf in his prime with no mate. We had an idea what he was up to.

As a wolf biologist, one learns to appreciate and admire the feat of animal dispersal. For a typical wolf, dispersing from one's natal group is a common, and often necessary, life history phase to gain reproductive success. Undeniably risky leaving the safety net of one's family, as is often the case in embracing life's risks, it is also ripe with opportunity. The adventurer in me envied the essence of 192's life at this stage. I wondered if he experienced the same neural stimuli at the reward center of the brain as I did while venturing through the wilderness, free from the restrictions of routine, social rules and boundaries.

Collared, dispersing wolves are a challenge to stay connected with. During airplane telemetry flights, I would be ever vigilant for the faint ping of missing collars whose frequencies I'd keep running through the radio receiver as I traversed the park. There is jubilance that accompanies rediscovery of wolves gone missing—a genuine relief that your study animal is still alive, the admiration that they have succeeded in a world of uncertainty, and the mystery of their journey. When we finally relocated our wayward male Wolf 192 in the fall of 2001, after months of unknown movements, we learned that he had traveled about fifty miles from his home on the northern range to the west side of the park. He spent the fall poking around the Montana/Idaho border seemingly alone, disappearing again for much of the winter. He eventually reappeared the following spring up north near his natal grounds and further north into the Paradise Valley, all the while eking out an existence as a lone wolf. In April 2002, he was observed alone, chasing a group of thirty mule deer on Deckard Flats at the park line outside of Gardiner, Montana, before vanishing once again.

A little over five years after I first saw him emerge from the den, my journey with this wolf took a more meaningful turn. I was several months into my new job as Project Biologist for the Yellowstone Wolf Project, having become fully integrated into a National Park Service position. Like male 192, I had spent the previous five years learning about the Yellowstone ecosystem and establishing myself a bit more in the wolf world. I, too, was seeking maturity and new territory while negotiating the risks of becoming an adult. In my new job I was responsible for much of the aerial tracking of Yellowstone's wolves, which meant spending heavenly hours in a Piper Super Cub flying over the park with one of the best wildlife pilots in the world—Roger Stradley. It is hard to find one more excitable when it comes to tracking wolves than Roger. When I met him at the Gardiner airport on September 21, 2002 to fly the park's wolves, he immediately shouted from the plane as I approached, "we gotta go figure out what wolves are in the Bechler today!"

Two days earlier, Roger and the park ornithologist had seen a collared gray wolf with a black adult and two pups chasing a spike bull elk while conducting a swan survey in the southwest corner of the park on the edge of a lake north of Bechler Meadows. Up to this point, we had no records of wolves in the Bechler region, so I was eager to figure out who the collared individual was and to confirm if there was indeed a new pack in Yellowstone. So off we went, flying the fifty-odd air miles to the Bechler.

The Bechler River flows through vast meadows in the remote southwest corner of Yellowstone. Named after Gustavus Bechler, a chief topographer on the 1872 Hayden survey, the namesake river and surrounding landscape features are stunning, with a magical combination of diamond-hued waterfalls splashing off forested benches into lush green meadows accented by hidden, steaming hotpots. Moose, elk, beaver, black bears, cutthroat trout, mosquitoes, and huckleberries are some of the prominent species frequenting this relatively wet area of the park. If a pack of wolves had indeed established a territory here, it would be one of the last prominent places in the park that wolves could call home.

Soaring off the Martian-like landscape of the Madison Plateau, Roger eased the yellow plane over one of the many waterfalls that descended into the valley. Meandering along the Bechler River's twists and sloughs, we approached the lake where the wolves had been two days earlier. "There they are!" shouted Roger through the plane's intercom, "Right where we had them before!"

Glancing down at the lake's edge I saw four wolves, a black and gray adult lying down in the grass and two smaller individuals that appeared to be a black and gray pup, chasing one another along the shoreline. I could clearly see the collar belting through the light gray fur on the neck of the largest wolf as we circled above the pack. Excitedly I began searching through my list of missing, collared gray adult wolves. About four radio frequencies into my search, a loud beep blasted from the receiver through my earpiece. "No way!" I said to Roger, "It's 192 male from the Northern Range!"

"We've got a Bechler Pack—they've got pups!" Roger shouted. The wolves barely gave a glance as we glided above, studying the features of each individual through the windows of the Super Cub. I was impressed with 192's appearance. Well-defined in size and stature, he was now in the prime of his life at over five years old, having made it past the average lifespan of a typical Yellowstone wolf. His pelage was striking in the morning light– it had a silverish-white glimmer that one would expect from a more ancient individual touched by senescence. The black adult was equally striking, with slender female-like features noticeable through a sleek charcoal fur highlighted by silver on her muzzle and legs.

It would be another seven years before we would discover the genetic underpinnings of black and gray coat color in Yellowstone wolves. Using DNA obtained from Wolf 192's blood when he was first captured, along with genetic material from hundreds of other wolves in the Yellowstone pedigree, a team of scientists eventually discovered that a beta-defensin gene called the K-locus ultimately determines gray versus black coat color in wolves through a relatively straightforward inheritance pattern. Our male, 192, was gray because he had received a single gray allele each from his Rose Creek mother, number 18, and his father, number 8. His presumed mate, this sleek black female, was colored so because at least one of her parents contributed a black allele. Astonishingly, our research suggested that this black allele appeared to be a single nucleotide mutation that had originated under dog domestication thousands of years ago in the Old World. The allele's incorporation into North American wolf populations seemingly came later, perhaps through interactions with early nomadic humans and their canine companions traveling through ancient Beringia from Asia. The connection between man and wolf seems more dynamic and complex than we previously understood.

We spent a few more minutes circling the wolves. The two romping pups kicked up mud, leaving dark footprints along the edge of the lake while gray Wolf 192 and his mate watched from the grassy bank. We saw no evidence they had killed the spike bull elk they were chasing just days earlier, but they looked healthy and content. Gazing out the window as Roger banked away from the lake and lifted the plane out of the Bechler meadows, I watched the four wolves turn to tiny dots, smiling widely from the back seat of the plane. That small gray pup I first saw tumbling from his den hole five years earlier on the Northern Range was now a father and leader in a new land. After seventy-some odd years, a family of wolves had returned to the Bechler—one of the last places in the Yellowstone to be recolonized following the famous 1995 and 1996 wolf reintroduction.

For the next seven years, Wolf 192 and the black female, who was never radio collared, raised their family in the Bechler. Given the remote nature of the region relative to our project headquarters in Mammoth Hot Springs, we knew much less of the week-to-week lives of these wolves. We relied largely on aerial observations during routine telemetry flights, with occasional reports from rangers and visitors who would encounter the wolves along the main trail system, or hear their songs broadcasting throughout the various seasons of the Bechler.

At least once a year I would try to explore the Bechler Pack's territory on foot. There are no technologies, experiments, or analyses that will ever provide the crucial knowledge that biologists gain from adventures on the ground in the ecosystems they study. For me, a proper comprehension of our research necessitates that we also appreciate the poetry of ecology obtained only through exposing our most basic animal senses and motions to the touch of wild nature. For instance, there is no better way to appreciate predation then to contemplate its essence up close, by sitting at the remains of a fresh bull elk carcass on the banks of the Bechler River, soaking my walk-weary feet in its cooling waters, swatting the mosquitoes off my arm, smelling the sour rumen baking in the sun, placing my hand over the front pad of 192's massive footprint in the mud.

The size of the Bechler Pack ranged from four to 13 wolves throughout the remainder of 192's life. He and the black female enjoyed high reproductive success throughout their years together, raising to independence 23 of the 26 pups observed at their traditional den and rendezvous sites in the heart of the Bechler. The fate of these offspring was less certain as they grew to adulthood, as relatively few collars were maintained in the pack throughout those years. The pack persisted at healthy numbers, demonstrating that at least some offspring remained in the pack each year to help raise younger siblings, just as 192 had done during his first three years of life with his natal Rose Creek family. Other pack members disappeared, likely dispersing south and west of Yellowstone, perhaps starting packs of their own in Wyoming or Idaho, slipping into vacancies left by the ongoing mortalities that were frequent in wolf societies. Although they spent much of the spring, summer and fall within Park boundaries, the pack would follow migrating prey out along the Bechler and Falls River drainages as the deep winter snows blanketed the land. In search of moose, elk and deer, the pack would even venture occasionally to the edge of Idaho's flat potato country.

The far-ranging movements between Yellowstone and the adjacent private and public land matrix posed considerable challenges to the Bechler wolves. Like all of Yellowstone's wolves, they enjoyed admiration and protection from living within a National Park, but faced animosity and exploitation upon setting foot across an imaginary boundary they did not recognize. With the town of Ashton, Idaho, nearby, ripe with anti-wolf evangelism, there were rumors of routine poaching of wolves just outside the park. Few, if any, of these law enforcement cases were ever closed. Yet despite the risks, Wolf 192 and his mate survived, living well beyond the typical lifespans experienced by fellow Yellowstone wolves.

In his later years, the male 192's gray pelage lightened, resembling an antler shed bleached by the sun. Like a transcended wizard of the wilderness, 192 Male the Gray became 192 Male the White. While common for age to bring lightened pelages in most wolves, few of Yellowstone's gray-colored wolves turned so brilliant a shade. Only the Hayden Valley, Canyon, and Agate Creek Pack lineages had produced similarly white individuals. While the ecological and evolutionary story underlying black and gray colored phenotypes has been described in recent years, I believe that genes within the crisp, snowy white strands of 192's pelt may hold other secrets to the story. With carefully banked aliquots of his DNA and those of his relatives, we may someday be able to pursue such scientific adventures.

In June 2009, a telemetry flight over the southwest corner of Yellowstone discovered a quickened beacon pulse emanating from the old male's collar from within the heart of the Bechler country, indicating that the collar had stopped moving for six consecutive hours—a likely signal that the grand life of our old male, Wolf 192, had come to an end.

Whenever this mortality beacon oscillates through the air, a conflicting sense of both loss and gain emerges from within me. Like heartbeats, the beacons connect us to the lives of the research wolves we follow. Through death, these individual wolves not only represent a loss within their own societies, but also within our own culture as researchers and appreciators of the unique lives we observed. But when we travel to each wolf's final resting place to investigate a death, retrieve a radio collar and collect samples from the remains, there is compensation in the loss. Through the use of rich data contributed by the lives and deaths of the wolves we study, we gain knowledge about the species and ecosystems they inhabit. We watch as their vacancies are quickly filled within the population, but remain irreplaceable in our datasets, our field notes and our memories. From this, they receive eternal reverence from our vocation and the commitment of our science to their stewardship.

A few days later, accompanied by others in the Wolf Project, I ventured into the Bechler to confirm and investigate the death of Wolf 192. Through thick mosquitoes and flooded meadows his signal beckoned us to a dense stand of lodgepole pine near the pack's traditional late summer rendezvous site. The fragrance of pine needles mingled with decomposition as we neared his remains. Between the summer heat, and efforts of flies, beetles, magpies and ravens, little remained of this magnificent wolf except an ivory-colored skeleton surrounded by bleached tufts of fur amidst the deadfall. There was no evidence of trauma, but at twelve years of age, he was ancient. He may have simply lain down in the cool, shaded earth beneath the logs to spend his final hours, tired and weary from living an extraordinary wolf's life. I picked up male 192's skull in my hand, blowing several tiger-striped carrion beetles from the orbits where his eyes once rested, and gazed into the mystical splendor of his immortality.

The legacy of Wolf 192 is one of many which has influenced and enhanced my life as a wolf biologist. There is significance in our mutual transcendence over the course of twelve years from newcomers in Yellowstone, through many interwoven adventures and travails in our personal lives, to fortunate participants in a historical conservation story. To this day, Wolf 192 remains the longest-lived, native-born Yellowstone wolf on record. He contributed to both of my graduate degrees along with those of many other students, to numerous publications, and to stories told to tens of thousands of people each year about Yellowstone wolves. But if there is one major influence 192 male had on my life as a biologist, it is in helping me recognize that in our concrete knowledge of individuals' legacies, not our abstract concepts of populations, lies the key to our understanding of ecology and evolution. More importantly, as I reflect upon our shared time in Yellowstone, an individual wolf reminds me that we must continue to work diligently as stewards of the natural world, our wildlife heritage, and of the lives of wild animals that do not know we care.

In August 2012, three years after the death of male Wolf 192, a white wolf was seen traveling through Bechler Meadows, illuminating the green grasses with its brilliance. It wouldn't know, or care to know, I existed. I, however, would document the continuum of time spanning these generations of wolves. Today, at this moment, I felt an awakening.

CHAPTER THREE

Minnesota Wolf 2407:
A Research Pioneer[1]

L. David Mech

EVER GET THE FEELING that someone is following you? Then just think of how Wolf 2407 must have felt. I had this wolf under surveillance for more than eleven years. My team and I originally captured and radio collared Wolf 2407—named for the number on her ear tag—on October 10, 1971, when she was at least one-and-a-half years old. The only other member of her pack at that time was her mate. The pair occupied an area of at least thirty square miles centering around Harris Lake in the Superior National Forest of northeastern Minnesota and was known as the Harris Lake Pack. I had followed the Harris Lake Pack since I first began a radio tracking study in winter 1968-69, and the pack had varied in size from two to nine members.

Over the years I recaptured and recollared Wolf 2407 seven times. In those early days of radio tracking, wolf collars only lasted a year or so. Thus to maintain contact with a pack, we had to re-trap a wolf several times. Capturing Wolf 2407 grew harder and harder each time as she gained more experience with our trapping methods. Our standard approach was to use a modified steel-jawed foot trap similar to those fur trappers used routinely to catch wolves. In fact, I had learned wolf trapping directly from observing one of Minnesota's top wolf trappers at the time, Bob Himes. I hired Himes a few times in the early days of the project, (beginning in 1968), and, being a trapper myself, readily learned the art from him.

The basic process involved: (1) deciding on a location where wolves likely would pass; (2) carefully burying and camouflaging the trap; and (3) placing a special bait, scent, lure, wolf urine, or wolf scat behind the trap. The wolf would step into the trap as it was sniffing the lure. The trap was attached to an eight-foot long chain and a metal hook. When a wolf was caught, it pulled the trap from the ground and ambled off. Gradually the drag hook would catch on vegetation, leaving a trail we could follow. At some point, usually within one-hundred meters or so, the hook would catch on a tree, log, or stump substantial enough to hold the wolf. We

---

1 Adapted from "A Decade of Data from a Single Wolf." *Endangered Species Technical Bulletin*, Dec. 1981.

would then track the wolf down, jab it with a drug syringe on the end of a stick, and radio collar it.

After being captured once or twice, Wolf 2407 learned what our trap placement, or sets, looked and smelled like and avoided them. The contest between man and wolf then began in earnest. Over the next decade I changed the types of set locations, bait, lures, etc. in my battle to outwit her. One summer it took 5,000 trapnights to recapture her, (one trapnight is one trap out for one night) and the next time 3,000 trapnights. My most bizarre change was to set the trap under water in a shallow ditch, with the lure placed on a tiny island behind it. Lo and behold, 2407 pulled the trap out of the water without springing it and left it for me on the side of the ditch! A deer hoof with just the tips sticking out of the ground finally tripped her up.

Each time we caught 2407 she weighed between 56 and 60 pounds. Because we caught 2407 over a period of eleven years, several of the volunteer wildlife technicians and graduate students who assisted with the project, and thus helped handle her, got to know this wolf. Some of these folks continued to work with wolves and have become well known in the wolf world themselves, such as Fred Harrington, Bill Paul, Rolf Peterson and Mike Phillips.

Wolf 2407 went through at least three mates. Her history of mates reflected a panoply of the peculiarities of the day. The first was Wolf 2499 which we collared on May 5, 1973 when he weighed 73 pounds. We molded radio collars then of a hard dental acrylic to protect the wires and critical electronic elements. Usually that worked very well, but not so with Wolf 2499. On August 27, 1973 we found his collar broken off, with no clues as to what happened. I probably assumed that someone had killed the wolf and had broken the collar off. At that time, though, it had been illegal to kill wolves on federal land in the Superior National Forest since 1970. The Endangered Species Act of 1973 would not further protect wolves until August 1974.

Finding 2499's broken collar left us with a critical uncertainty. Was the wolf alive or dead? If, during the coming winter, the only time we can depend on seeing our radioed wolves and their packs, 2407 still appeared to have a mate, it could mean 2499 was alive, but it could also mean that 2407 paired with a new mate.

In fact, during the next winter, 2407 apparently did still have a mate. On January 28, 1974 my assistant, Jeff Renneberg, saw her copulating. But was the mate 2499 or a new wolf? That question wasn't answered until early 1975, and then the answer came not by any kind of scientific technology, rather, it came via an anonymous message left for me in a lonely bar miles from civilization.

"The Happy Wanderer"[1] was the only commercial establishment along a thirty mile stretch of road through our study area. As such, it sold gasoline, chips, and candy bars, etc. besides the usual array of alcoholic beverages. All the local loggers and other assorted woods folks hung out there. Eventually most of them learned about our wolf research. Although the locals did not look favorably upon our work, they did seem a bit impressed that we could catch wolves, and they were intrigued by our aerial radio tracking technology, which at that time was still quite new.

In any case, in late August 1974, a bartender astounded me by announcing that a patron asked her to pass on to me a deal: he was willing to divulge to her the ear tag numbers of a wolf he had killed, if I would provide background information to her about the wolf. I accepted the deal, and a month later the bartender handed me 2499's ear tags. I wrote a long thank-you letter with the information we had on Wolf 2499, along with a book about wolves and some reprints from our project, as a reward and asked for date and information on the location where it was killed. The typewritten note that I received via "The Happy Wanderer" some time later indicated the wolf had been trapped on January 10, 1974 about ten miles west of 2407's territory. Thus 2407's 1974 mate must have been new.

We will never know which wolf replaced 2499, but each year from 1975 to 1978 Wolf 2407 bore pups. In October 1979, we captured an 85-pound, nine-year-old male in 2407's territory. We knew he was nine years old because he had ear tags. He had been caught as a pup in 1970, only about 18 miles away, as part of another scientist's research study. This male, Wolf 5962, could have been the one that replaced her dead mate, Wolf 2499, because he would have been old enough when 2499 was killed. Whatever the situation, Wolf 5962 accompanied 2407 from November 20 through December 17, 1979. Then the two split up.

By June 25, 1980, 2407 had picked up a new mate, and the two sometimes slept within a meter of each other that winter. However, there was no indication that the pair produced pups that year. We captured 72-pound, three- to- five-year-old, male Wolf 6041 in August 1980. Female 2407's signal indicated she was waiting nearby. These two wolves remained together through at least April 8, 1981, and then we lost Wolf 6041's signal. Did his collar fail, or did he leave 2407? We had no way of knowing, but by December that year female 2407 was running with an uncollared wolf and during breeding season they were sleeping as close as two meters apart. Again, however, she apparently produced no pups that spring.

In November 1982, Wolf 2407 was also running with a presumed mate which may or may not have been Wolf 6041. It was seldom possible at

---

1   Any use of trade, firm, or product names is for descriptive purposes only and does not imply endorsement by the U.S. Government.

that time to see from the air whether wolves were wearing collars or not, because the collars were narrower than they are at present. Wolf 2407's signal disappeared after January 3, 1983, but on September 6, 1983, we recaptured Wolf 6041 in Wolf 2407's territory.

We really hoped that male 6041 would eventually lead us to her, especially during winter when we might be able to see if any wolf was with him. Our hopes soon waned, however, when male 6041 left the territory and began to drift widely like a lone wolf. By November 1983, he was seventeen miles from Wolf 2407's territory.

Our hopes rose again a month later, however, when we spotted Wolf 6041 with another wolf in a territory adjacent to hers. Of course, we dearly wanted to see if the other, smaller wolf wore a collar, thus indicating that it might be Wolf 2407. Our opportunity came on December 20, 1983 when the pair was traveling across a frozen pond in an extensive lowland. The topographical situation was ideal, and the weather was right for us to make a few low passes above the animals so I could get a closer look at their necks. Sure enough, both wolves were sporting collars!

I hardly dared hope that Wolf 6041's mate was our 2407. For one thing, the pair was not in the territory she had roamed these eleven years. Secondly, several wolves with non-working collars roamed our study area, and this could easily be one of them. Still, who knows?

My slim hopes were dashed two days later. The second wolf proved to be one whose signal we had lost, Wolf 6494, a 71-pound female we had collared in June 1983. The pair produced pups during summers 1984, 1985, and 1986. On October 31, 1986, she died of starvation and parasitism.

Wolf 6041 remained in this territory with some offspring, and about December 1, 1986, he paired with two-and-a-half-year-old female Wolf 413 from a pack to the north. This pair produced no pups until summer 1988, when they had at least four.

About December 31, 1988, Wolf 6041 was killed by an invading pack of wolves from the territory to the west. He weighed 81 pounds, plus ten pounds of deer meat was in his stomach. Wolf 413 remained in the territory with at least two offspring, but she produced no pups in 1989. On November 16, 1989, she was shot illegally.

We never learned Wolf 2407's fate. A lost signal could have meant she dispersed or her transmitter failed. The last time we recaptured her, on August 28, 1982, we had used an experimental custom-made, solar-powered transmitter with battery backup that we had hoped would last much longer than standard collars. If it did last long enough, we would not have to trap Wolf 2407 again. This attempt may have been our undoing, for the transmitter may have failed. The fact that her mate, male 6041 stayed in their territory until the following fall is some indication that she also remained there. If so, she may have died that fall, thus explaining why Wolf 6041 left then.

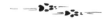

Wolf 2407 was located over 1,300 times during her life; she and her pack mates were observed nearly 500 times. She lived to be at least thirteen years old, the oldest documented wild wolf at that time, and one of the oldest still. She and her various mates held their territory for the entire period during which Wolf 2407 was

radioed, an area varying each year from thirty to seventy square miles, and over the eleven-year period the Harris Lake Pack's territory totaled one-hundred square miles.

Wolf 2407 produced at least five litters totaling at least 13 pups. She watched the local deer population decline to a fraction of its former size, which no doubt accounted for the relatively low number of her pups that survived. One of Wolf 2407's offspring, male Wolf 5465, who was also radioed, dispersed from the Harris Lake Pack, as most wolf offspring do, and formed his own pack adjacent to it, a pack known as the Little Gabbro Lake Pack. Although I was only able to follow him for three years, we had also radioed one of his offspring, female Wolf 5935, and she dispersed from her pack, paired, and set up her own territory. This genetic line of wolves is one of only two lines that I had followed for three generations up to that time. They provided extremely valuable information on the degree of relatedness in the local wolf population.

Wolf 2407 was truly a pioneer in the annals of research wolves. Although both her origin and her fate were obscure, much of her life contributed considerable information about movements, territoriality, mate tenure, longevity, reproduction and many other aspects of wolf ecology and behavior. And, through the young wildlife technicians who handled her during her eight captures, she helped provide some of the important experience and inspiration that encouraged these folks to continue their careers in wolf research and conservation.

CHAPTER FOUR

Sage's Story

Diane Boyd

YES, THERE IT WAS AGAIN, a wolf howl from just outside my cabin. I slowly opened the door and stepped outside. On the opposite river bank stood a huge gray wolf peering at me from the snow-laden willows. I stared back, mesmerized, and we looked at each other for what seemed a very long time. Then he slipped back into the willows and was gone. It was November 1983, and I had spent the previous four years intensively searching for phantom wolves in the North Fork of the Flathead River drainage along the northwest corner of Glacier National Park, coming up with little evidence of their presence. And this wolf came to me. That was the beginning of my special relationship with this handsome wolf, Sage, and those early years of wolf recovery in the Rocky Mountains.

In September 1979 I arrived at the Trail Creek Port of Entry to conduct my master's degree research with the University of Montana. The young border guard had his feet propped up on the log railing of the old log customs station as he read *The Monkey Wrench Gang* by Edward Abbey. Lime-green lichens edged the cedar roof shingles of the ancient log customs building which inspected the six cars per day that passed from British Columbia to Montana. This remote outpost was fifty miles from the three P's of civilization: pavement, power and phone, and there were less than one hundred full-time residents living within a fifty-mile radius of the border station. It was a wild valley with few humans, the perfect setting for wolf recovery to begin.

A quarter mile south of the customs station along the North Fork of the Flathead River lay a turn-of-the-century homestead ranch nicknamed Moose City: a haphazard collection of six timeworn cabins, three outhouses, a barn, ghosts of previous misanthropic inhabitants, and a spectacular view of Glacier National Park's majestic peaks. I became the official Moose City caretaker for the distant landowners that would occasionally come out for a visit. My arrival brought the permanent Moose City population to three: myself and my two dogs Stony and Max. However, if you count the mice, deer, elk, grizzly bears, coyotes and moose with whom I shared the place, the population would number in the thousands, a true wildlife mecca. Moose City would eventually become home to the Wolf Ecology Project crew consisting of myself, Mike Fairchild and a handful of volunteers, and the only wolf research project in the lower forty-eight states outside of the Midwest. I fell in love with the place and the lifestyle, and studying this recolonizing wolf population was my world for the next eighteen years.

My days were spent looking for wolf sign and trying to capture and radio collar every wolf in the area and as many coyotes as I could catch and radio collar for my graduate research project. I deduced their behavior by back tracking their trails in the snow, and avoided getting close enough to observe them to avoid altering their wild behavior.

My learning curve was steep, but I was aided by a little prior wolf trapping experience on Dave Mech's research project in northern Minnesota and a summer working for Steve Fritts as a wolf trapper in rural north-central Minnesota. At Moose City I had to learn how to heat my cabin with wood, maintain finicky propane lights, wade icy rivers with skis and field gear in my backpack, and learn the ways of the Rocky Mountain wildlife.

Wolves had been extirpated from the western US by the 1950's, even here in the remote northwestern corner of Montana that was also home to wolverine, grizzlies and lynx. Since the early 1970's Bob Ream led the University of Montana's Wolf Ecology Project and coordinated a handful of enthusiastic volunteers to search for wolves, follow up on wolf sightings, and try to simply find a wolf in Montana. It was monumental news when an adult female wolf wandered down from somewhere north of Banff National Park, Alberta, and left tantalizing sign in her new territory along the northern boundary of Glacier National Park. In April 1979 she was captured by Joe Smith who was hired by the Wolf Ecology Project. Joe fitted her with a radio collar in British Columbia, a stone's throw north of Glacier National Park, and named her Kishinena. Years of effort were validated by Kishinena's beeps as she wandered solitarily through the lodgepole pine and spruce of southeastern British Columbia and made an occasional foray south into Glacier National Park.

Kishinena was very shy of people and she was a survivor. One wintry day she killed a moose calf by herself, the tracks in the snow providing clues to her success. Kishinena's tracks mingled with the calf's tracks along the chase route, with occasional tufts of moose hair lying along the path. Then the wolf's tracks disappeared and only running moose tracks appeared for forty feet. When the wolf tracks reappeared mixed in with the calf's, the calf had slowed its pace, and lay dead at the end of the trail. I was puzzled by the disappearing wolf tracks until I skinned the calf and found the hemorrhages inflicted by the wolf's crushing canines along the calf's throat. Kishinena had leaped up and grabbed the calf by the neck and hung on as the moose ran, head held high, lifting the wolf off the ground until the calf succumbed to suffocation. As I investigated the dramatic scene I realized what a difficult life a single wolf has, and that simply scoring a meal could entail a life-threatening injury to predator as well as prey.

Kishinena was the only wolf in the North Fork for the next two years. Her radio collar failed after sixteen months of transmission, but we continued to see her sign in her usual haunts. When snow blanketed the landscape the Wolf Ecology Project field crew saw tracks of a three-toed, male wolf and a female wolf traveling together in Kishinena's territory.

In June 1982, the black, three-toed male wolf was accidentally captured in a grizzly bear researcher's foot snare, and despite efforts to help the wolf recover, the wolf was found dead the next day. A few days later a log truck driver saw the female wolf with seven pups, only five miles from where the male had died. I followed up on the report and I saw the pups, but not the mother. I was worried about the prospects of the female trying to raise seven hungry pups without her mate. The four black and three gray pups would require an enormous amount of fresh meat by the end of summer before hunting season could provide carrion to the growing wolf family.

But wolves are nothing if not tenacious and resourceful. That first winter the Wolf Ecology Project field crew saw tracks of all eight wolves along the frozen creeks and snowy game trails. We named them the Magic Pack because it was magical that they had survived. The wolves remained elusive and avoided being seen by people until one of those gray pups grew up into a handsome and curious yearling and paid me the "howdy howling" visit at my cabin that memorable November day. For the next month this wolf hung around my cabin, trying to get close to my two, large male dogs. I could tell from the wolf's urinations in the snow that it was a male, and I was afraid that he would make a quick meal of my dogs. One morning when the dogs were out I heard Stony barking and looked out to see that the wolf, Stony, and Max were only a few feet apart. The dogs were guardedly holding their ground while Sage stood playfully erect, slowly wagging his long sweeping tail, then dropping his chest into a play bow in the snow. I realized by his behavior that this naïve animal was very likely an adolescent wolf exploring life on his own. The wolf trotted across the meadow, looking invitingly over his shoulder, and when the dogs began to follow him I whistled them back and brought them inside. At this time no wolves were radio collared, a major detriment to our fledgling wolf research project. In August 1984, Dick Thiel set traps a few miles from Moose City that resulted in Mike radio collaring a one-hundred-ten pound, two-year-old, gray male wolf, and Mike named him Sage (#8401). He was almost certainly the same wolf that visited me at Moose City a few months earlier: right sex, right color, right age, in a land with only a handful of wolves. But Sage had itchy feet, and the two-year-old wolf began searching for his own territory of which Moose City was the epicenter.

Our research project expanded to follow the movements of the Magic

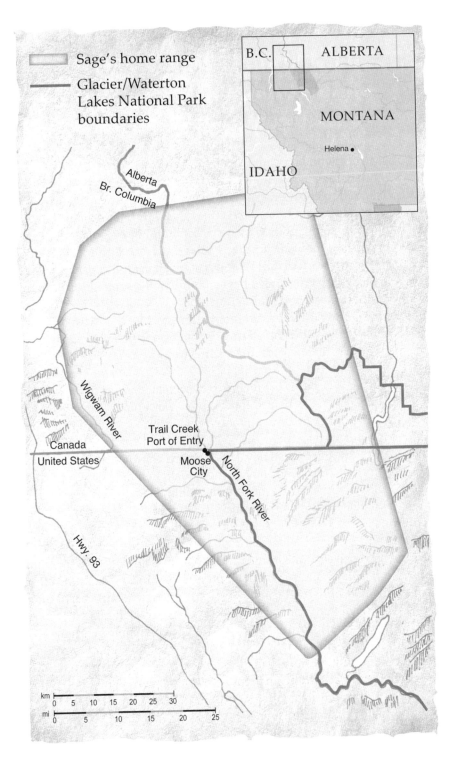

Sage's home range

Glacier/Waterton
Lakes National Park
boundaries

B.C.   ALBERTA

MONTANA

Helena •

IDAHO

Alberta
Br. Columbia

Wigwam River

Trail Creek
Port of Entry

Canada
United States

Moose
City

North Fork River

Hwy. 93

km
0   5   10   15   20   25   30
mi
0   5   10   15   20   25

Pack, Sage's long extraterritorial forays, and two more new packs that had sprung up. Between 1985 and 1987 I captured and radio collared ten wolves in three packs, and our research was on a roll. We hired one to four volunteers to help keep track of the wolves year-round. These dedicated wolf trackers were critical to the research efforts and we became a real team, sort of a pack of our own. Many evenings after writing up field notes, we would jam with Mike on mandolin and Andrea on guitar, the music and laughter mingling with the sounds of the rushing river.

On October 20, 1985 I found the skinned and decapitated carcass of a wolf two miles north of where Sage had been captured. I felt sick when I thought it was Sage, but a thorough search with the telemetry gear told me that Sage was alive and well in other parts of the North Fork. Five days later I had a date with Sage: I recaptured him on October 25 and fitted him with a new radio collar. Sage was the first wolf I trapped in the Rockies, and with his large size and massive head he was magnificent.

Sage wandered extensively within the North Fork, sometimes alone and sometimes paired with another wolf. As winter progressed Sage wandered widely over a huge area in northwest Montana, southwestern Alberta, and southeastern British Columbia. During this time of intensive exploratory forays we located him dozens of kilometers between successive locations. Sage taught us that neither raging rivers nor crossing the Continental Divide in the dead of winter could impede a wolf in search of space, food and a mate. On our telemetry tracking flights we saw Sage traveling with a smaller black wolf in November 1986, which we hoped was a female.

This newly formed pair dispersed to the Wigwam River area and set up a new territory. In the summer of 1987 while radio tracking in a Super Cub, I was delighted to observe Sage and his mate relaxing at their den with five pups. The pack fared well in the remote Wigwam drainage, with plenty of elk, deer, moose, and bighorn sheep to fill up their bellies. The other competing predators in the valley included mountain lions, grizzlies, and one determined hunting guide and outfitter, whom I will call Harry. In early October one of Harry's hunting clients shot one of the pups. We received a report from the British Columbia Wildlife Branch that a large gray wolf in the pack, undoubtedly Sage, had also been wounded by the hunter, but escaped. During our next telemetry tracking flight I observed Sage favoring his right front leg. A month later he seemed fully recovered from whatever his injury had been, and I breathed a sigh of relief.

The morning of the last day of the year in 1987 it was fifteen below zero Fahrenheit, clear and calm—perfect conditions to conduct a telemetry flight and track the four radio collared wolf packs. Our pilot, Dave Hoerner, and I located the three North Fork packs and headed over to the Wigwam. We observed Sage lying down on a snow-covered gravel bar along the Wigwam River. But something didn't look right—the snow was trampled and the willows were torn up. I asked Dave to make a low pass over Sage, and only then did Sage stand up and struggle to move away. His right rear leg was held fast in a leg hold trap, attached to a log by a three foot chain. To my horror, as we helplessly circled Sage, he headed for the partially frozen Wigwam River. He plunged into the water, swam across the river, hauled up on the other shore and headed into the willows, leaving a snowy furrow of the trap and drag log in his wake.

Sage was trapped a quarter mile north of Harry's backcountry camp. Harry had no love for the wolves that he viewed as competition with his livelihood of big game hunting. Dave swung the plane over the cabins, lodge, corrals, and outbuildings looking for evidence of life and a place to land the Super Cub on skis. The snowed-in tracks around the camp indicated that Harry hadn't been in to his camp for several days and we had no idea when he would return. Dave told me to hang on, he would try and land between the buildings and not slide into the river. As Dave dropped the plane down through the camp the wing tips missed the buildings by inches, and despite Dave's incredible bush pilot skills, he ran out of flat terrain and pulled up hard just before the looming trees along the river bank.

"Head for Polebridge," I directed over the crackling headset. It seemed like forever until the old Polebridge Mercantile and a handful of cabins came into our view. There is not a runway at Polebridge, but it did have the only telephone for twenty-five miles. Dave skillfully landed in a snowy field beside the Mercantile. I ran to the store to telephone Mike and then realized I didn't have any change in my pockets. I burst into the store and asked Betty if I could borrow a dime for the pay phone. She opened the till, handed me a dime, and didn't ask a single question, as if planes landed in her yard regularly to use the phone. I called Mike who was in Kalispell getting our truck and snowmobiles repaired, and he said he would have them ready to go by the time I got to Kalispell. Thank you Mike! Dave and I flew back to Moose City and I gathered up the gear, clothing, and capture equipment that we would need to free Sage. Then we flew to Kalispell where Mike picked me up and we drove north with the gear, mobile phone, and snowmobiles.

I hadn't thought about how difficult it would be to contact customs officials, veterinarians, and the appropriate Canadian wildlife officials on the afternoon of New Year's Eve. It was necessary to get permission from the Canadian officials to release Sage because he was trapped in British Columbia by a licensed outfitter and trapper. We had worked cooperatively with the Canadians for several years and we didn't want to create an international incident. If we botched this politically, we could jeopardize the future of our wolf research efforts in Canada. To further complicate things, there was no legal trapping season on wolves, so Harry broke the law when he trapped Sage behind his cabin. And Harry loved biologists as much as he loved wolves.

We called a veterinarian and received detailed instructions on how to best thaw a frozen foot and deal with the thermoregulatory problems of anesthetizing a wolf in subzero weather. Sage may have been in the trap for several days, and he surely suffered frostbite at best, and he could lose his foot or his life at worst. By now it was late afternoon, sunlight was fading, and we had been unable to contact wildlife officials in British Columbia to request permission to free Sage, presuming he would be alive by the time we made the long trip around to where I had last seen him. We just kept driving and dialing and we finally reached a biologist in Cranbrook who could not give us permission to free Sage. He said we needed to call the top wildlife administrator in Victoria, and we could not release the wolf without proper permission. I phoned the Director of the Wildlife Branch at his home at 9:00 p.m. I could hear in the background that he had a houseful of people partying and I apologized for the intrusion. I explained who we were, described our situation with Sage, and asked permission to release the wolf from the trap. The Director gave his permission, requested a write-up of our release efforts and wished us Happy New Year. I thanked him heartily and we headed for the Wigwam.

We drove from an icy highway, to a modest gravel road, to a nasty gravel road, to our turnoff into the Wigwam drainage where we could drive no further. It was 11:00 p.m. Then we saw the fresh tracks and realized that Harry had arrived and gone into his camp since my morning flight. We quickly unloaded the snowmobiles and began the long ride up the Wigwam drainage. The propane lights were on when we arrived at Harry's camp. We knocked on the door and we were greeted by Harry's wife with a raised glass and "Happy New Year, who are you?" We introduced ourselves, told her of our mission and peeked behind her, expecting to see Sage's carcass in the hallway. As it turned out, they had arrived after dark so Harry hadn't checked his traps. They had been liberally celebrating the New Year while warming up the subzero cabin. I asked to speak to Harry. The wife looked at me and said solemnly, "I don't think I'll wake him for this."

Mike and I left the cabin and organized our gear, sleeping bag, headlamps, and capture equipment. We opted to leave the snowshoes at the snowmobile, figuring they would be more nuisance than help. The temperature was seriously below zero as we headed to the river where I had last seen Sage. The full moon lit up the river bottom landscape so brightly that we didn't need to turn on our headlamps. The cold, dry snow squeaked beneath our pack boots; the air was dead still, but Sage was, hopefully, alive and waiting.

We walked to the spot on the gravel bar where Dave and I had first seen Sage. The drama was evident in the moonlight. The willows were flattened and chewed down as Sage tried to extricate himself from the cold steel clamped on his foot. We found the bait carcass at the capture site. "Looks like Harry used the back half of a moose for bait," I said as I gazed down at the black haunch in front of us. Mike looked a little more closely and said wryly, "Hmmm, looks like that moose was shod." Sure enough, Harry had shot one of his horses for bait, and the moonlight glinted off the steel shoes.

We followed the furrow of the struggling wolf to the river's edge where it disappeared into the water. Mike and I slipped into our chest waders and crossed the river, marveling at the slush floating past our legs. We changed back into our pack boots on the other side, and it was only a matter of minutes until the waders were frozen into a stiff, rubbery pile. We thought about Sage: no circulation in the foot clamped tightly in the trap, several days of subzero temperatures, his restricted mobility, and his waning strength. We continued along Sage's wide drag trail, leaving the river bottom, and we entered an enclosed, dark, spruce forest. Here we had to turn on our headlamps. Sage dragged the anchor log up a very steep slope for a couple of hundred yards. It was steep enough that Mike and I were pulling ourselves up the hill with the aid of brush and sapling trunks. My headlamp lit up the shine of a chain stretched tightly over a large deadfall laying across the ascending trail in front of us. All was silent as we stared at that chain. I slowly climbed uphill and peered over the top of the log: a massive, gray, frosty face raised up and stared at me, a much wiser face than the one I had seen howling at my cabin.

I slowly backed down to Mike and whispered "he's alive." We pulled out all of the equipment we would need to drug and take care of Sage, defrost his foot, keep him warm, and replace his radio collar. It was so cold that our liquid drugs had frozen in their vials, so we had to briefly thaw them in our armpits. A few minutes after we injected the exhausted wolf, his head dropped to the snow and we began our work. My watch read 1:30 a.m. as we worked together to remove the trap from Sage's frozen foot. From the ankle down, the paw was cold and hard as stone. For more than an hour, we took turns wrapping our mitten-warmed, bare hands around Sage's frozen paw, being careful not to rub it so as to minimize further tissue damage. We pressed our warm flesh against his wooden paw, awaiting signs of thawing. The paw eventually began to soften. When the toes were pliable, we gently worked our fingers between the wolf's toes while wrapping another warm hand around the paw. The foot eventually became flexible and warm. We wrapped him snuggly in my sleeping bag with only his affected foot and snout poking out. We replaced his old radio collar with a new one, kept tabs on his vital signs, injected antibiotics, and completed the processing.

We waited for Sage to wake up and walk away. Two hours had passed since we had drugged him and yet the big wolf did not move. We used a light dose of a fast acting drug (ketamine) and he should have been up and gone in less than an hour. Mike and I stood there in the moonlight, stomping our chilling feet and rubbing our arms and legs to keep warm. Another hour went by and still the wolf lay there, his massive muzzle sticking out of the sleeping bag, breathing deeply and slowly. As the hours passed without movement from Sage, bleak thoughts began to creep into our heads. Had he become so exhausted from his epic ordeal that he would die despite our efforts? Had he dislocated a hip dragging the heavy log? I thought to myself how terrible if we freed him and he died despite our good intentions.

At 4:00 a.m. I couldn't stand it anymore. I grabbed a stick and approached the form in the sleeping bag. I poked Sage and he jumped up, the sleeping bag sliding off into the snow. He looked even more surprised than us, shook himself off, stared at us for several seconds, and limped off into the shadows of the forest. Apparently he had been awake for quite some time, but he was comfortably tucked inside the warm cocoon and unaware that the trap that had held him tight for many days was gone. Mike and I looked at each other, shared a hug, and decided it was by far the best New Year that we had ever experienced.

We packed up our gear, retraced our steps across the wintry landscape, left the mangled wolf trap on Harry's doorstep, started our snowmobiles and headed back up the trail to our pickup. It was 6:00 a.m. by the time we reached our truck.

We watched Sage intently from the air during our next several tracking flights and saw that he limped on the damaged hind leg for several months. But eventually he regained his natural gait, the foot remained attached to the leg, and it seemed as if he had survived his ordeal in fair shape. He responded to Harry's trapping by denning a few miles from Harry's camp in the spring of 1988, leaving scats and tracks as a reminder that the big gray was alive and well. Sage and his mate produced a litter of six pups and Sage's tenacious genes were passed on once again.

But Harry may have written the final chapter in Sage's life—Sage's radio collar ceased transmitting during the fall hunting season. With no other radio collared wolves in the inaccessible Wigwam valley, it was difficult to monitor the pack. By the spring of 1989 evidence of the pack ceased with no sign of wolves at the traditional denning area or anywhere else in the Wigwam. The Wigwam Pack had disappeared as quietly as the melting snowpack. In August 1989, we captured and radio collared a handsome, young gray male (#8910) in the Wigwam who was joined by an uncollared female the following winter. We never knew whether or not these wolves were remnants of the Wigwam Pack, but the cycle began anew.

We don't get to really know the wild wolves we study, and we have to be content trying to comprehend the ecology of these complex creatures via brief glimpses into their lives. Sage may typify the fate of a wild wolf anywhere in the world: they are born, learn life's lessons, disperse, try to establish a territory, leave progeny if they are lucky, avoid humans, and then they die, most likely due to human causes. During the years of our research, wolves were a federally protected endangered species in Montana and a regulated trophy animal in British Columbia and Alberta, yet we found that eighty-five percent of the wolves in our study area died from human-caused mortality. Despite this trend, wolf recovery has been one of the most successful endangered species recovery stories since the Endangered Species Act was passed in 1973. The Rocky Mountain wolf population increased from one wolf in the western US in 1979 to more than 1,700 wolves in Montana, Idaho and Wyoming combined, plus several resident packs in Oregon and Washington in 2012. Similar wolf population expansions have occurred in the Midwest, and wolves have been delisted.

Sage's story unfolded through the help of telemetry, miles of snow tracking, and the passion of a handful of young wolf researchers. The challenges that we documented for this recovering wolf population were numerous: hunger, disease, mortal combat with other wolves, debilitating injuries, avalanches, and being killed by humans. But the most significant challenges that wolves faced then are no different than today: coexisting with humans on a human-dominated landscape. As a biologist, I relay Sage's story at the risk of appearing sentimental. But as the famed evolutionary biologist Stephen Jay Gould so eloquently put it, "We cannot win this battle to save species and environments without forging an emotional bond between ourselves and nature as well—for we will not fight to save what we do not love."

CHAPTER FIVE

Blow River Female 3410

Bob Hayes

 TODAY BIOLOGISTS RARELY OBSERVE wild wolves, even the ones they radio collar. As technologies change and more wolves are fixed with Global Positioning System (GPS) radio collars, wolf researchers may never actually observe their subjects in the wild. Instead, biologists infer wolf behavior and ecology from a matrix of habitat maps and satellite signals documenting GPS-tagged prey and wolf locations, all from the computers at their office desks. I was of an earlier era of airborne research with maps, notebooks, and pencils.

We named our study wolves by their radio transmitter frequency. In my early years as a wolf biologist I mistakenly named a few wolves after people I knew. Wild wolves rarely live more than a few years. Naming a wolf after a friend, or friend's son, seemed okay, until we found the wolf killed by other wolves, kicked to death by a moose, shot by a hunter, drowned, or smothered in an avalanche.

Each time we flew over a radioed wolf we scribbled onto a radio telemetry form its frequency, location, how many wolves were with it, whether they were walking, running, resting, sleeping, hunting, or feeding on a kill. The form also had places to record other collars present, and a place to record a kill site number.

We radio collared 3410 on April 17, 1987. It was our tenth day of fieldwork. The airport in Old Crow, Yukon Territory, registered minus ten degrees Centigrade at 9:00 a.m. The skies were clearing and there was a steady wind of twenty-eight kilometers per hour on the runway, gusting up to thirty-seven. A light snowfall the night before made for ideal conditions for snow-tracking wolves. Jammed into the narrow back seat, I left the airport in a PA-18 Super Cub, piloted by Hans Lammers. A few minutes later Tom Hudgin, one the finest snow-tracking pilots in the world, left in a Cessna 170. On board was Torrie Hunter, a conservation officer helping with the first study of Arctic wolves in the Yukon. Philip Merchant and Kevin Bowers, the darting crew, were loading the Bell 206B Jet Ranger Helicopter. They were getting ready to follow us 200 kilometers north to the Arctic coast with darts, drugs and radio collars.

Although it was late April and the Arctic sun was up until after midnight, the landscape below our Super Cub was still deep in winter.

The weather had been remarkably good with long days of clear skies, mixed with a few days of light snowfalls to help us track wolves. We had already flown eighty hours in each plane, and had surveyed much of the 40,000 square kilometer study area – from the Porcupine River north to the Yukon Arctic coast, east to the Mackenzie Delta, and west to the Alaska border. We had found eighteen packs and collared wolves in eleven of them.

The two planes flew north over the thousands of frozen lakes that formed the Old Crow Flats. After an hour the Flats disappeared behind us and so did the last of the tree line. Ahead of us were the creamy peaks of the Barn and British Mountains that filled the cockpit windscreen. Beyond the mountains lay the edge of the North American continent and the Arctic Ocean.

Hans called Tom on the radio to confirm their aircraft position. The Cessna 170 was over the Babbage River, looking to locate the Trout Lake Pack and add more collars. Norm Graham, the helicopter pilot, radioed that they were just behind Tom's plane heading over Muskeg Creek into the headwaters of the Babbage. As we passed into the broad treeless plateau of upper Blackfox Creek, caribou began to appear on the tundra. A large part of the Porcupine caribou herd had wintered in the north Yukon, and the cows were starting to head for the arctic slope of Alaska where they would give birth in about a month. In the maze of caribou trails and feeding craters, we cut a few old wolf trails, but nothing was fresh and worth following. As the sun rose higher in the sky, the winds began to blow, lightly at first, then the Super Cub began to yaw and twist to stay airborne in the mountains as the morning winds picked up. Slipping over the headwaters of the Babbage River, we heard radio chatter between the plane and helicopter. They had found the Trout Lake Pack, and Alan had already darted a black male.

We headed west, but found no fresh caribou or wolf trails on the twenty-kilometer-wide strip of lowlands that formed the Yukon coastal plain. The winds were blowing strong when we reached the Firth River Delta. The snow here was thin and hard as boilerplate, making it impossible to snow-track anything. As we turned to head upstream on the Firth River I could see a group of muskoxen huddled in the thick shrubs that lined the riverbank, long blankets of gray quiviut hair streaming from their sides in the wind.

When we reached the junction of Sheep Creek I looked out the right window, my eyes drawn to the spot where I had seen my first aircraft crash and fatalities ten years earlier. Judging by the short flight path, the plane was not airborne when it reached the steep bluff at the end of the Sheep Creek airstrip. We found it a few hundred meters away, its nose augured into the tundra. The blonde pilot was barely out of his teens, the son of the placer miner working the creek. He had somehow climbed out of the wrecked cockpit and was lying dead on the tundra, a useless tourniquet tied around his leg, his deeply sunburned face looking vacantly into the sky. The other man, his Inuit friend, didn't make it out of the plane. I recalled how my legs had shaken, and how I had suddenly felt sick to my stomach as I looked at the grisly scene. The camp, where there was a radio, was just a few hundred meters away. But it may as well have been 100 miles away.

Flying up the Firth we reached the junction of Glacier Creek where we saw a group of Dall's sheep ewes and lambs perched on the cliffs above the river canyon. Low on fuel, we headed directly for our cache 120 kilometers east at the Shingle Point DEW line site, near the mouth of the Blow River. As we refueled and ate our bag lunch, the helicopter arrived for fuel. They brought news that Tom and Torrie had tracked a new pack of four into the headwaters of the Blow River. Philip managed to dart a pup and yearling. He had attached radio collars around the thickly furred necks of the wolves and left them to recover.

The sleek gray-tan coated yearling, female Blow River Wolf 3410, was entering the prime of her life. She weighed 50 kilograms, 10 kilograms heavier than the average adult female wolf, and she was reproductively active. The black pup, weighing 40 kilograms, was also collared and became known to us as Wolf 153.450. That summer we did not hear from 3450, but 3410 was spotted twice near a den on the Fish River about 30 kilometers from Aklavik, Northwest Territories. We found both females together again in April 1988, traveling with two other wolves in the upper reaches of Cache Creek, indicating 3410 probably had pups, but had lost them sometime after denning in 1987. We managed to capture and radio collar a large five-year-old male with a luxuriant blue-gray coat. He was certainly a breeder, and he became Wolf 3660. That July the three radioed wolves were located close to the Fish River den. Various adults were seen, but no pups.

In early August wolf technician Alan Baer and I returned to the study area with plans to radio collar more wolves and visit den sites. Dr. Scott Smith, a noted soils expert, was along with us to study soil properties of wolf dens.

At about 4:00 p.m. on August 3, Fred Carmichael of Okanogan Helicopters flew his 206B Jet Ranger Helicopter from Inuvik, Northwest Territories, across the Mackenzie Delta with Alan and Scott on board, heading to Shingle Point on the Yukon Arctic Coast, our base of operations for the next week. At the same time I was meeting Fred Harms, my Super Cub pilot, at the Aklak Air hanger in Inuvik. Fred was 41, and a remarkably accomplished pilot. He had flown since he was sixteen, amassing over

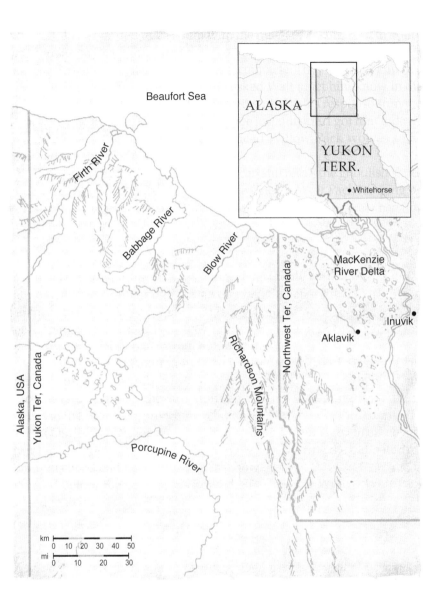

20,000 hours, mostly on Twin Otters around the world. As I climbed into the back of the Super Cub C-GRZY he told me he had only a few hours on a PA18 Super Cub. He also casually mentioned that he had never had a forced landing. That was about to change.

The helicopter departed the airport bound for our Shingle Point base camp. We taxied behind them on the runway. As we lifted off the temperature was a balmy seventeen degrees Centigrade, but the winds were increasing quickly, gusting to thirty-four kilometers per hour. We flew across the thousands of small taiga lakes that formed the Mackenzie Delta, and passed over Aklavik. The Northern Richardson Mountains in front of us were covered in a high thin overcast. I looked toward the coast and saw a heavy white fog bank amassing along the shore. I did not think much of it. The coast was often obscured in fog, but the worst weather rarely came far inland. We picked up 3410's radio signal within one of the coastal drainages of the Richardson Mountains and flew into Marten Creek, unaware that a huge storm was rolling onshore. Unknown to us, the helicopter crew had aborted their flight, retreating to Inuvik in a blinding summer snowstorm. As they flew back, they tried to contact us on the radio, but we were already in the mountain foothills and out of range. Alan had hoped we had heard the weather report and returned to Inuvik. Arriving at the airport and finding our Super Cub gone, he began to worry.

Marten Creek, like all treeless drainages in the Richardson Mountains, is deeply incised with narrow, black-walled canyons sinking 200-300 meters deep into the rock, topped with open tundra. As we flew above the canyon, I picked up a strong radio signal from one of the Blow River wolves, but soon realized I was listening to a ghost signal reflecting off the mountain slopes. The wolf was probably not in Marten Creek. Explaining this to Fred, I peered at the mountains, expecting to spot a ridge we could fly over to reach the next drainage.

We had failed to notice the high layer of clouds had dropped a few thousand feet. There was now no way to fly out over the mountain headwaters of Marten Creek. We would have to fly back down and out the creek bed. As Fred turned the Super Cub, a sudden wind caught the left wing and the plane shuddered. I looked down the creek to see a huge cloud racing towards us, filling the valley.

"There's no way out downstream," I said, trying to sound calm. I had been caught in a coastal fog years earlier, but luckily I was in a helicopter and we had simply landed and waited for the storm to pass. Now we were in a fixed-wing Super Cub. Within seconds of being engulfed by the approaching storm, we would be flying blindly in fog. No matter how good a pilot Fred was, he could quickly lose ground reference and lose his orientation, not knowing if the plane was flying level, going up, or spiraling down. The little plane could quickly spin out of control and we would crash hard. Fred turned the Cub around and headed back up the Marten Creek drainage, searching for an open ridge. The winds had strengthened. We looked back down the creek. The fog bank was gaining on us and would soon engulf the Super Cub. We needed to land.

Fred looked into the wall of white and said, "There's a bright spot.

Just to the right of the creek. We might be able to fly through."

I saw it too, and thought of the huge canyons that waited downstream. "It's a sucker hole. As soon as we pass into it, it'll disappear, and we're dead!" I said forcefully.

"Where do we land?" he asked me.

I looked down. The valley was treeless so lots of places looked good to me. Open tundra meadows scattered in the valley, separated by shallow ravines filled with low shrubs. "Anywhere. Pick a meadow. We have one more turn before we're into the fog bank."

Fred pushed the stick forward and pulled back on the throttle. The plane descended quickly. He nosed the plane into the coming wind and leveled it out just a few meters above the ground. I could see the high grassy tussocks and knew it was going to be a bumpy landing. The tires connected with the ground and we bounced hard along the meadow. It seemed like we would make it okay. Fred slowly applied brakes as we bumped toward the end of the meadow. Then we fell into a shallow depression.

The propeller drove into the soft tundra, sending the tail of the plane –and me–high into the air. The fuel line on the right wing tank popped off. Instantly aviation gas cascaded down the door of the Cub, covering the fuselage and blocking the only exit out of the cockpit. The plane swayed and teetered on the brink of going all the way over on its back. I hung suspended by my shoulder harness, unaware that Fred had switched off the engine as we landed.

"You okay back there?" he asked.

I looked down at him from my high perch. "It depends which way this thing goes," I said.

Somehow the plane fell back down on its wheels. And then the world turned white. The windscreen was pelted with thick wet snowflakes as the summer blizzard hit our plane and the sour smell of aviation gas filled the cockpit.

"The magnetos are off," Fred said calmly. "There is no spark to ignite the gas," he said, watching the last of the fuel drain down the window. If the magnetos were left on, the spark would have caused an inferno. Fred's extensive training and experience saved us from being trapped inside a burning plane. We sat quietly listening to the storm. The cockpit began to cool down. Fred looked up at the thermometer on the side of the windscreen.

"It's minus three," he said.

My mind raced. What if the magnetos were left on, and the plane was on fire? What if we could not get out of the burning door? What if we did get out, but were badly burned? There was no shelter anywhere. It would be a matter of minutes before we were soaked to the skin. In an hour we would be hypothermic, with no chance of getting a fire started.

Fred brought me back from the brink of my unpleasant daydream. "I'm turning on the Emergency Locator Transmitter. We're not far from Aklavik. It's six o'clock. Our flight note ends at 7:00 at Shingle Point. By 9:00 p.m. the search and rescue plane will come looking."

As the cockpit chilled, I remembered my survival pack stuffed behind my seat. From it I retrieved a down expedition parka and a small sleeping bag I flew with at all times.

I tapped his shoulder. "Down coat or sleeping bag? Your choice," I said.

"Thanks, I'll take the coat."

I reached into the pack again. "I have some food and tea."

We sat eating crackers, cheese and granola bars, sharing the thermos of tea between us, bundled in our down.

As the blizzard blew, Fred asked me about the wolves we were following. I told him the tundra wolves of the north Yukon were different than the wolves that lived in the forested mountains to the south. They did not hold territories and kill moose, but followed migratory Porcupine caribou year-round, sometimes for long distances. Packs congregated to hunt caribou, sometimes only a few kilometers apart. We had thirty-one wolves on the air, but sometimes the packs disappeared and we could not find them anywhere in the 40,000-square-kilometer study area. I told Fred we were locating the collars to find dens and radio collar any new wolves.

The snow stopped, but the winds continued to blow strong. We climbed out to inspect the damage. The cowling around the propeller was dented, but the rest of the plane was fine. I gave Fred my Leatherman pliers, and he bent the cowling back into shape so the propeller could freely turn.

"Let's turn this plane around and see if we can fly it off the meadow," he suggested. The gas had washed off the fuselage, so there was no danger of the plane catching fire. We picked up the tail and turned the Cub, managing to push it up onto the meadow. The engine started, but the small six-inch wheels sunk among the tussocks. I rocked the plane and pushed on the struts until it began moving forward, but we could not get enough speed to get airborne. We gave up after a few attempts.

We sat in the plane as evening approached, exchanging flying stories for a few hours before we fell asleep. I woke to the sound of a large plane flying overhead. Fred radioed immediately, contacting the rescue plane circling in the dark clouds above us. He told them we were okay. He gave them our coordinates, and at 4:00 a.m. Fred Carmichael landed his helicopter and picked us up.

Alan was waiting for us. The storm had been remarkably strong, and when they did not hear from us all evening, he was certain we had crashed somewhere in the mountains. He had already called my wife Caroline and told her we were missing, but probably okay. I called her immediately and confirmed that we were fine.

Fred Harms returned to Marten Creek in a helicopter on August 4, my birthday, while I slept late. The helicopter attached a lanyard to a round-eye bolt attached to the roof of the Cub and slung the plane onto a flat mountain ridge. Fred climbed in, flashed up the engine and flew the Super Cub back to Inuvik.

On August 5 the weather improved, and it was summer once again in Inuvik. Alan climbed into the Cub and headed for the mountains to locate radioed wolves and find den sites in the study area. Scott Smith and I followed behind in the helicopter. We stopped at eight wolf dens, collecting scats to determine summer food habits, and sample soils to describe the den sites.

The first den was 3410's, located on the Fish River close to the Mackenzie River Delta where there were thousands of lakes filled with muskrat, beaver and calving moose to feed wolf pups. The pack had moved off to a rendezvous site, so we landed. While Scott dug in the dirt and filled sample bags, I collected scats near the recently abandoned den. Judging from the small scat sizes, I knew 3410 had raised young here. Months later we dissected the scats and found forty-seven contained moose hair remains, and forty-nine contained muskrat or beaver. Wolf 3410 had found a good location to raise pups without relying on the unpredictable summer supply of migratory caribou. We continued west, stopping at more dens.

By the time we finished, Scott had figured out why the tundra wolves had selected their denning locations. He explained it to me as we headed back to Inuvik.

"All these tundra dens seem to evolve the same way. First, arctic ground squirrels establish breeding colonies, digging into the frozen permafrost, allowing the surface of the soils to thaw and dry out. Foxes arrive next, and dig down even deeper and have their kits in the mid-level dens, warming the permafrost soils further down. Finally, the wolves take over the site and excavate even deeper. These tundra wolves depend on foxes and ground squirrels to warm up and dry the ground, changing the soil conditions so they can later build their own dens. A sandy soil mixed with small gravel works best. The depth of the wolf den is obviously limited by the surrounding Arctic permafrost."

I thought about what shallow dens might mean. I had seen grizzly bears at North Slope wolf dens before. In 1976 and 1980 I watched a sow grizzly bear with cubs attempting to dig out wolf pups from the same den along the Babbage River. Scott's story of ground squirrel-fox-wolf den evolution began to make sense. These North Slope dens were shallow and largely unprotected from interested bears. Further south, in the forests, wolves typically denned under tree roots or near large boulders in unfrozen ground, making it harder for bears to get at wolf pups.

But an open Arctic meadow is another story. I summarized such an event in my 2010 book, *Wolves of the Yukon:*

> Alan was checking wolf activities in the north Yukon and found the Eagle River den completely demolished as if a backhoe had worked it over. The earth had been turned over and was deeply trenched. A grizzly bear had dug into the den and killed four pups. Alan found their tiny skulls neatly piled together in the trench. It was a small desert for such a great effort by the bear. The pups would have had no chance to escape once the bear tore the roof off the den.

The Blow River female 3410 chose a safe den in 1988. On September 18, Alan found her standing at the den entrance with eight pups around her. Between November and February 1989 as many as seventeen wolves were seen in the pack, meaning 3410 raised more than a dozen pups at the Fish River den in 1988, a remarkable feat of wolf productivity. It's also possible another Blow River female had pups nearby, and the two groups had joined together after September. However, in hundreds of wolf breeding events I documented over the years, I never confirmed more than a single female in a pack successfully breeding and raising young.

In March 1989 we began a detailed study of wolf predation on Porcupine caribou in the north Yukon. The Blow River Pack was the centerpiece of that research. We followed the daily hunting activities of seven different wolf packs for three to four weeks. The Blow River Pack was the largest group, traveling in two groups of twelve and five wolves. Radioed wolves were present in each group. Sometimes they came together for a few days before separating again. Wolf 3410 and the male 3660 always traveled in the group of twelve. Because the Blow River Pack was large, we located them twice daily, once in the morning and once in the evening, to see if we could have missed any kills by locating them only once a day.

In our work, locating study packs every day until April 17, representing 25 days of locations, we found 23 kills, all caribou. The Blow River Pack accounted for eleven. We visited 13 carcasses on the ground, including eight adult males and five adult females averaging the age of six years. None were calves.

From this we calculated an overall kill rate of twenty-nine caribou per wolf per year, based on the thirty wolves in the seven packs we had been monitoring. This meant the Blow River Pack would account for 131 caribou kills per year. We found that locating the Blow River Pack twice per day produced no more kills than we would have found with one flight per day, confirming that we had not missed kills and underestimated the predation rate.

Kill rates of our Porcupine study area wolves were similar to predation rates of other migratory caribou herds. Teaming up with Don Russell, a Canadian Wildlife Service biologist who specialized in studying the Porcupine caribou herd, we developed a kill rate model using seasonal location information from satellite collared caribou he had studied for decades. Our predation model estimated wolves took 7,600 animals from the herd in all seasons, about one-third of the annual adult caribou deaths. We concluded the wolves were not the most important cause of caribou mortality. Because they were committed to den sites each summer, the wolves could not follow the movements of the tightly aggregated caribou herds that travel widely through the north Yukon.

Shortly after the predation study ended on April 19, 1989 female Wolf 3410's radio signal disappeared. Her collar may have failed to transmit, or she may have dispersed from the pack; unlikely given her young age. Alan found her mate dead near the Fish River den site on July 15, 1990. Wolf 3450, collared as a pup along with female 3410 in 1987, was shot near Eagle Plains on October 30, 1992. She followed the Porcupine herd there, leaving the Blow River Pack 240 kilometers to the north.

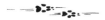

I have thought a lot about the hundreds of collared wolves I had the honor to study in my life. Female Wolf 3410 stood out, not because she was unique, but because she was an average wolf. In the end, I can hardly say I knew her.

We located this sleek, gray-colored wolf 63 times between April 17, 1987 and April 16, 1989 and saw her a grand total of maybe ten hours in the 17,500 hours her radio transmitted information to us. That represents 0.0006 percent of the time she was radioed. Most sightings were brief—often only a few seconds—circling in a plane for a few minutes to locate the radio signal before catching a fleeting glimpse of her on the tundra. But even this minuscule sliver of 3410's life told us some remarkable things about tundra wolves' dependence on caribou, and the difficulty of following their ever-moving prey.

She lived four years, a normal life span for an adult wolf in the Yukon. Her home range was 8,500 square kilometers, similar to other migratory tundra wolves in the far north of the Yukon. She successfully raised pups one of two years, the same fifty percent success rate observed among the twenty radioed breeding packs in the study area. Her pack's kill rate was similar to the other packs and not much different than barren-ground caribou wolves across the Mackenzie River to the east or further west into Arctic Alaska. Like most of the collared wolves I studied,

I glimpsed select, brief moments of her life, and tried to construct a history of her and her pack's lives from those collected moments. Adding similar histories from other packs, I did what I was trained to do, and developed population models that reveal ideas about how wolves interact with caribou and the people that live in the northern Yukon.

As it turned out the predation study involving Wolf 3410 and the other wolves influenced some important decisions. In 2009, the Porcupine Caribou Management Board, a group of government agencies responsible for managing the herd, was growing concerned. Unable to count the Porcupine herd for more than a decade, biologists thought it might be declining and was already below 100,000 animals. Some subsistence communities were discussing aerial wolf control to stop the decline. Invited before the Board, I described the work and the model Don and I published in 2000 showing that wolf predation did not cause high mortality in the herd. In the end the Board did not recommend killing wolves. That turned out to be a very good decision.

In 2011 the herd was finally counted. The Porcupine Herd had grown to 175,000 animals. The communities celebrated the news, but the biologists are still wondering how they could have figured the herd was declining when it was actually growing. Following the predation rates of radio collared wolves for twenty-five days in 1989 helped save wolves from being killed for the wrong reasons.

In the end, this gray-tan female wolf, 3410, was actually a pretty special wild wolf, and one I was glad to have briefly known.

CHAPTER SIX

Wolf 175–The White Female of the Step Mountain Pack

John Burch

 IN 1993 A WOLF ECOLOGY PROJECT began in the Yukon-Charley Rivers National Preserve (Yukon-Charley), a remote corner of interior Alaska where the Yukon River enters Alaska from Canada. This little 2.5 million acre Preserve is administered by the National Park Service and was created in 1980 for its rich Gold Rush history and its pristine example of interior Alaska's boreal forest, with its complement of animal and bird life. Sport hunting and trapping are allowed throughout preserve lands in Alaska but not on park lands. Subsistence hunting and trapping is allowed on all park lands in Alaska, authorized in 1980 under the Alaska National Interest Lands Conservation Act.

A fundamental question I often receive is, "why study wolves here?" Briefly, the project started purely as a research study focused on measuring predation rates of wolves on their prey. This area of Alaska has a low density of wolves and multiple prey species, primarily moose, caribou and a few Dahl sheep. The reason this project continues to this day centers around the State of Alaska's Department of Fish and Game (ADF&G) predator control program which has been in effect off and on for decades, as was a similar federal government program prior to statehood.

The Yukon-Charley Rivers National Preserve lies within a region known locally as the Fortymile Country for the Fortymile River that drains a large part of the area. It is home to the Fortymile Caribou Herd, the state's largest herd accessible by road. Most caribou hunting in Alaska is accessible only by airplane, unless you happen to be one of the few people that live in a village adjacent to a caribou herd. As a consequence, the State's overall wildlife management goal for this region is to create a larger harvestable surplus of moose and caribou for human harvest. It is the viewpoint of some state officials that caribou and moose numbers in the Fortymile country must improve in order to sustain and increase this harvest goal. The rationale is that by dropping predator numbers (mostly wolves, but also some bears) caribou calf survival would improve, even-tually increasing big game populations. In doing this work the State has focused on reducing wolf numbers up to the Yukon-Charley boundary because the hills forming that imaginary boundary are where the Fortymile Caribou Herd usually calves each spring. The National Park Service policies and mandates do not allow predator control activities within park lands except in extremely specific and limited circumstances. Producing harvestable surpluses for subsistence or recreational hunters is not among the list of justified exceptions. All of the wolves using Yukon-Charley routinely travel outside the Preserve boundary. In fact, half of several pack's territories extend beyond the Preserve's imaginary boundary.

Of course, the National Park Service would prefer that the Department of Fish and Game avoid killing a high percentage of wolves utilizing Yukon-Charley. Armed with ongoing information supplied by this wolf project, the National Park Service regularly negotiates with the State of Alaska about its predator control program in the area surrounding the Preserve. Information obtained to date would fill a whole book. That, in short, is why the National Park Service continues to monitor wolf numbers and pack home ranges within Yukon-Charley. It has been my job to keep that data stream flowing since my arrival on the project back in 1996.

In my seventeen years of work on this wolf project I have captured, collared, and followed many different wolves. Picking out a 'favorite wolf' was not easy. However, a particular wolf stands out in my mind, female Wolf 175 of the Step Mountain Pack. I first became aware of this female wolf about a year before she was finally captured on March 14, 2000. In 1997 I had darted and collared three other wolves in the Step Mountain Pack. They turned out to be her mother, female 136, a brother, Wolf 137, and a sister, Wolf 154. Wolf 175's mother was a white wolf, an uncommon pelage color in interior Alaska, including our Yukon-Charley study area. Wolf 175's mother was snared by a local trapper in mid-March 1998.

This event seemed to fragment the pack. The following month, April 1998, both wolves 137 and 154 dispersed independent of one another, moving north and northwest. They quickly disappeared, never to be heard from again. As a consequence I lost radio contact with the Step Mountain Pack. But I knew some wolves remained within their territory because I encountered tracks in the snow in the winter of 1998-99. I was even fortunate to see some pups near one of their old den sites the following autumn.

In addition to locating radioed wolf packs, we typically spent time in planes searching for uncollared packs each winter. This was done by flying routes in a Super Cub with the assurance that, given time and luck, we would encounter wolf tracks in the snow by keeping our eyes trained on the terrain sliding beneath us. By following the wolves' trails we sometimes caught up with the wolves, enabling us to count them and get locations

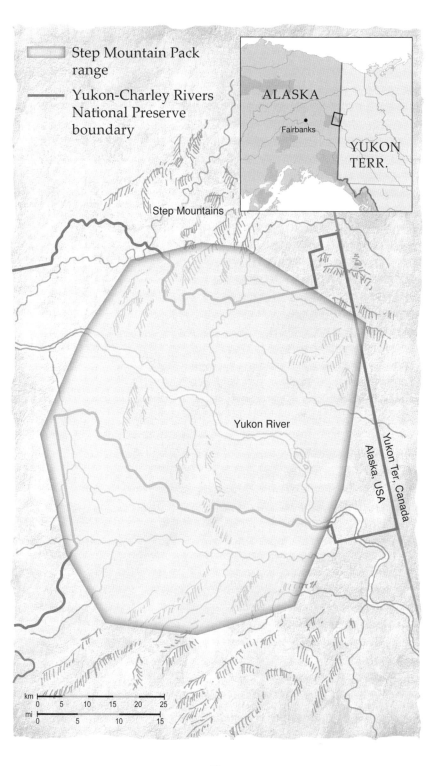

verifying that a particular space was, indeed, occupied by a pack. This task seems much easier said than it is in reality, especially since snow or weather conditions frequently confound searches.

Following the loss of radio contact, the area in which the Step Mountain Pack roamed was placed on the list of locales to be searched. In this manner I occasionally caught glimpses of this pack during the winters of 1998–1999 and 1999–2000. And I certainly recall a particular wolf that really stood out from the rest of its pack. It appeared nearly white.

On March 14, 2000 while net-gunning Dahl sheep within the Yukon-Charley Preserve, one of the flight crews encountered the Step Mountain Pack. Typically two or three aircraft are needed during these operations and their movements are coordinated via radio. Super Cub planes are used to "spot" sheep and guide the more expensive helicopter in for captures.

I had brought along a couple of wolf radio collars, a dart rifle, darts and drugs, just in case we ran across some wolves while conducting our sheep capture work. Our luck continued when Sandy Hamilton, one of the Super Cub pilots, radioed that they had found the Step Mountain wolves in heavy timber on the north side of the Yukon heading towards the river. However, upon our arrival at the site of the observation we found that the wolves had entered a thicket of tall spruce trees lining the banks of the Yukon River. Getting a shot at a wolf down through these tall spruces would be exceedingly difficult.

Helicopter pilot Rick Swisher and I decided to hang back to the north of the wolves and see if they would move out onto the frozen Yukon. Eventually Sandy radioed us that a white wolf followed by seven grays had dropped down the bank and were heading out onto the frozen river. Prudently we held back with the helicopter, letting them continue further out onto the ice and away from the heavily timbered shoreline.

Meanwhile Sandy Hamilton, who had found the wolves and was piloting the observation plane circling safely above us, was watching our traveling wolves. He radioed us as the wolves reached the middle of the frozen river. En route, we detached and cached the helicopter door. Rick deftly maneuvered the helicopter to some trees lining the river's edge. From this vantage point we got our first view of eight wolves, strung out, traveling single file along the expansive Yukon River. In the lead was a white wolf.

At this point, as we well knew, things happened fast. In reaction to our sudden arrival the wolves began to angle further out onto the river. Some fanned out and began running. I loaded a dart in the rifle. Rick dropped the helicopter down to just a few feet above the river ice and quickly caught up to the white wolf in the lead. I was able to hit the white wolf high on the rump with the first dart. This wolf, as I would later learn, would never make this mistake again.

The other wolves scattered, heading back for the river bank and the safety of the trees. Meanwhile the darted white wolf continued heading straight out across the Yukon. Fortunately, Sandy up in the Super Cub had it in sight. Rick and I decided to go after a second wolf. I reloaded. Rick picked out and began pursuing a second wolf, swiftly getting between it and the river bank. Following a momentary standoff when this wolf was deciding what it would do, it settled on paralleling the river bank while trying to get back to the trees. Rick wouldn't let it. The wolf ultimately made the wrong decision, bolting out across the river. Rick quickly closed the gap and we got a dart in that wolf as well.

The white wolf Sandy was watching started to go down in three or four minutes after reaching a long willow-covered island. Rick and I looked after the second one with Rick maneuvering the helicopter to keep the wolf out on the river until it finally collapsed from the effects of the drug. Once this second wolf was down, and with the aid of Sandy to guide us in, Rick flew the helicopter back to where the white wolf had gone down. It took us some time to locate its exact position within the thick brush fifteen to twenty yards from shore. Had Sandy not been watching this wolf and conveying information to us over the radio, it would have been very difficult to find.

Rick landed on the river about as close to the wolf as he could safely get the helicopter. Jumping out, I plowed through the drifted snow and brush to the drugged wolf and quickly removed the dart. It was breathing okay. It was a female. I managed to get her up on my shoulder and carry her back to the helicopter. Our intent was to fly her back to where the second wolf had gone down to process and radio collar them.

Rick dropped both me and the white wolf off, and then took off to retrieve the door. Sandy, meanwhile, was able to find a place nearby to land his Super Cub along the Yukon. Soon enough Rick returned, dropping his copter back down beside us. With tongue in cheek he yelled, "I'll bet I could get $500 to $600 for that jacket!" referring to the nice white pelage of what was thereafter known to us as female Wolf 175. This numbering system, used as a means to identify individual wolves, was simply assigned to captured individuals starting at 100 on a consecutive basis.

We worked together processing these newly captured wolves. The second wolf was a young, one-hundred-fifteen pound gray male that I guessed, based on tooth wear, was probably two-and-a-half years old. Our white female, Wolf 175, looked to be the same age as the male, exhibiting only light tooth wear and staining. They were likely siblings born in the same litter in 1997. Later genetic analyses confirmed my suspicions that their mother was the same Step Mountain female Wolf 136 that had been harvested back in 1998.

Wolf 175 was large for a female at one-hundred-five pounds. To those more familiar with wolves elsewhere these weights may seem high. Yet these two wolves' weights were only a little above the average for male and female wolves living within the Yukon-Charley study area.

A thought I distinctly recall going through my mind during the entire time it took to process her was what a beautiful white coat she had. Her light color, often a reflection of becoming grayish with advancing age, coupled with her behavior in leading the pack out onto the river when we were pursuing them in the helicopter, led me to guess she was the breeding female in this pack. However, when I rolled her over to inspect her nipples I was surprised to see they were very small and a light pink in color. Obviously she had not suckled pups.

Both wolves were in good shape and the process of radio collaring, measuring and drawing blood went smoothly. When the tasks of processing had been completed we transported both wolves to a nearby location just off the river. This, I felt was safer than leaving them out in the open where people in airplanes or on snow machines could possibly stumble upon and kill them before they recovered from the effects of the drugs. True, this was a very remote place and Rick thought I was kind-of nuts. But such an event actually happened to me while working on a wolf study just outside Denali back in the late 1980's. And it also happened to a colleague of mine long ago when he was collaring wolves in the Alaska Range. Not desiring to throw caution to the wind, I had long before decided that when it comes to capturing large mammals, Murphy's Law reigns supreme! I would take no chances.

While flying back to our field camp along Coal Creek later that day I was elated we had regained radio contact with the Step Mountain Pack. But I was also disappointed that we did not catch either one of the breeding pair and despaired that I was throwing those collars away on wolves that were likely to disperse, leaving me to repeat this whole process again next winter. I was mistaken.

About six months later in November 2000, during a routine surveillance flight, we picked up a mortality signal on her brother, Wolf 174's, radio. The white female's radio was signaling normally, but she was located about eight miles away. Staring out the plane windows we obtained a visual of her with two other wolves. They were feeding on a bull moose they had just killed.

We returned to inspect the site where Wolf 174's radio indicated he lay. My field notes described the scene and the evidence for cause of death:

> Necropsied male Wolf 174 in the field, only extremities frozen,
> chest and abdomen still slightly warm, must have been killed

yesterday or last night. Gored by a bull moose. One large hole to left side of sternum, punctured chest and lungs and severely bruised heart. Carcass found on moose and wolf trail in snow, in very contorted, unnatural position. When chest was opened about two liters of blood poured out. Carcass was skinned, no other wounds found, no debris found in chest, photos taken.

Was this the same moose the other wolves were seen eating from some eight miles away? Or was it a different moose? We didn't have time to trace moose and wolf trails between the two sites from the air to learn whether there was a connection. I've always guessed it's possible. It remains just one of many intangible sidebars to this business of studying wolves.

Due to the thickness of trees and brush near den sites we only begin to collect information on pups beginning in August or September. Because of this, given that pups are born by mid-May, we fail to notice early pup mortalities. This is the source of much frustration for wolf biologists who study wolves in forested country such as the Yukon-Charley area. The problem was so great that I suspended radio tracking during summer months altogether. As a result, all of our data on pup numbers are actually the number of pups that were counted alive in August or September. These counts should not be confused with estimates of litter sizes. The Step Mountain Pack denned in 2001. At least six pups were seen that September. And I learned that Wolf 175 was the mother. She had become the Step Mountain Pack's breeding female.

Over a seven-year period Wolf 175 was captured and radioed three times by helicopter darting. The first proved to be the easiest. Thereafter, she was notoriously difficult to dart from a helicopter, evading the helicopter by taking refuge beneath thick canopies of tall trees. Of course part of her luck (for her, at least) was that in each instance she just happened to be close to cover when she heard the helicopter approaching. The second capture was especially memorable.

We encountered the collared white female again on March 3, 2004 about ten miles south of the Yukon River near the west end of the pack home range, in heavily timbered, rolling hills. Right off the bat it wasn't looking good. However Sandy Hamilton up in the surveillance plane said he could see the wolves and they were near an opening in the trees. He thought we could do it. I, however, was not very confident. Sandy had the reputation of being extremely optimistic about my ability to dart a wolf in difficult conditions (I always visualized him with a big grin on his face laughingly telling me "no problem you can do it" over the radio).

Rick and I in the helicopter fell for the bait and headed over to Sandy's location to take a look. We could see Sandy circling above and a couple of miles south of us. Closing in, Rick started muttering something about not seeing much of an opening. I had to agree. When we got there we could see a small opening with a V-shaped peninsula of trees running into the middle of it. The wolves were toward the head of the peninsula.

Easily discerning the difference in sounds between the airplane and helicopter, the wolves scattered out at our approach. Sandy was doing all he could do to keep his eyes on 175 because she was the one I needed to catch. I wanted to replace her old radio collar with a new fancy GPS collar.

A white wolf against a white background in thick trees covered with snow is a real challenge to see. Adding in snow lofted by rotor wash and snow scattering off tree boughs, it was no wonder we quickly lost sight of her. Rick and Sandy both started circling the area with Sandy at a higher altitude. Rick picked up her track in the snow and followed it, contacting Sandy at the same moment via radio. Utilizing the advantage of height, Sandy peered ahead of us.

By now my helicopter door had been off for some time. Blasting in through the opening, a jet stream of minus twenty-five degree Fahrenheit air made it quite cold in the helicopter. I hadn't dropped the dart in the gun chamber yet because I was afraid the drugs contained within the dart might freeze before I was able to shoot.

Right at that moment Sandy yelled over the radio that he had her spotted, heading down through the peninsula of trees. We headed over and saw her, but she took off running across the small opening. Rick made a quick pass by her, but by the time the gun was loaded she had cleared the opening and was standing beneath some tall trees looking up at us.

Once again she received the prop wash treatment, again clouds of lofted snow blocked our view, and we, of course, lost her. Sandy saw her crossing back towards the peninsula moving so swiftly we couldn't reach her in time for a shot. Rick and I had her in sight once again, moving slowly in the trees toward the end of the peninsula. Ahead the trees gave out right in the middle of the opening. She was headed right where we wanted her to go.

Rick hung back. Our Wolf 175 trotted slowly, clinging just inside the edge of an opening among the trees, stopping now and then to gaze briefly up at us. She was in no hurry. She knew she was safe in the trees! But she didn't know she was about to run out of trees at the tip of the peninsula.

Rick and I were certain she would break for it across the opening once she reached the end of the trees. This time we were ready and waiting. I would get one very brief chance for a shot before she gained the other side. The pressure was really on. She finally arrived at the end of the trees and just stopped! There she stood, alternately looking at us, then across the opening, then back at us. Clearly she was sizing up the situation!

At this point Rick was behind her with the helicopter. Her options were limited. She could either go across the opening or pass beneath the noisy, snow-spitting helicopter to reach the safety of the trees. Of course, and to our great surprise, she turned and walked back under the helicopter to the security of the thick trees! Rick hollered to no one in particular, "Why you little bitch!"

In the past, under similar situations, I have had some success taking very long shots down through tall trees. We decided to give it a try as a last resort. Rick pulled up on top of her, keeping astride her as she was, by now, swiftly trotting through 90-foot spruce trees. I was trying to draw a slow and careful bead on her. With this type of shot, shooting almost straight down, the very limited range of the dart gun was not a big problem, but timing the shot to hit the wolf when it crossed the gap in the trees made it very difficult.

We would wait until she entered a small gap between two trees. I would have to lead her pretty far ahead because of the relatively slow dart velocity. Over the intercom Rick told me he saw a gap coming up and advised me to wait. I agreed but kept watching the wolf through the open sights of the dart gun, almost shooting at her several times. She finally reached the larger gap. I shot and the dart hit a branch and careened off into the carpet of snow. Uttering several expletives, I reloaded, ready to try the same thing once again.

I consoled myself that the dart just lost might have been frozen anyway so it was good to try again with a warm dart. I missed with that one as well and quickly reloaded. I missed two more times. Finally, on the fifth shot I hit her right in the hip. The entire time she never ran, trotting instead, looking quite carefree in the heavy timber, stopping for long periods under a very thick tree where I had no shot at all.

She went down in about four minutes. Rick was able to land the little R44 helicopter, and Sandy, still circling above, was able to talk me in to her over a hand-held radio. The processing equipment was contained within a day pack I preferred just for these occasions involving a long walk through deep snow to reach a drugged wolf.

Two years later we would go through a similar operation trying to dart the Step Mountain female a third time. It ended up being another long shot down through tall trees and a long hike in the woods to retrieve her, but it all worked out. By this time she surely was one of Rick's favorite wolves as well because she was so smart and cagy, not to mention her pretty white color.

The end of Wolf 175 came in the winter of 2007. On February 6 we found her carcass frozen, contorted in a moose/wolf trail. She had obviously gone down fighting because she had a large tuft of moose hair in her mouth, and her white fur had a spray of bright red frozen moose blood on it. The pack had succeeded in killing and eating the same adult cow moose that had managed to inflict lethal blows to Wolf 175 before losing her own struggle for life. The cow's remains were just 100 yards down the trail from Wolf 175's carcass.

The white wolf had been beaten up pretty badly, indicating there had been quite a battle. By wolf standards she was already an old girl. In the intervening years her teeth had become heavily worn. Ironically, her brother, Wolf 174, had also been killed by a moose, a most unusual cause of death—most collared Yukon-Charley study wolves die either in altercations with neighboring wolf packs or by people. Wolf 175 had certainly lived a long and productive life as leader of the Step Mountain Wolf Pack.

Wolf 174 was the breeding female of the Step Mountain Pack, holding that position for at least seven years. In that time she produced six litters of at least 25 pups that survived to autumn each year. This came out to about three or four pups surviving to fall, right about average for all the packs we monitored over the years. She was also a most dependable study wolf, always being where she was supposed to be somewhere within her home range. She was invariably in the lead and always gave the impression of being very serious and business like (we could actually discern this from an airplane window). Following her death the pack shifted its activity further to the south for reasons unknown to us. But during the years she reigned the Step Mountain Pack's territory remained fairly constant and most winters the pack consisted of six or seven wolves.

CHAPTER SEVEN

Challenge on the Tundra

H. Dean Cluff and Marco Musiani

IT WASN'T UNTIL THE SUMMER OF 1999 that we truly appreciated the skill and effort needed to capture wolves on the tundra. We needed many wolves radio collared for this wolf den ecology study, launched two years earlier, in order to monitor them through satellite technology over the huge, isolated expanse of the Northwest Territories, Canada.

In the previous two years fifty-nine wolves had been captured, but for that work we had enlisted the help of wildlife capture professionals, with their own helicopter, pilot and net-gunner. It made perfect sense to have them. But this year a professional capture team was not available. We needed to remove those aging satellite collars and replace them with other collars that would continue our monitoring for several more years. So how hard could that be? We had some capture experience ourselves and, having already collared wolves to track, it all suggested a routine effort. Okay, maybe not a walk in the park, but certainly a straightforward field exercise with no big surprises. In a nutshell, we were confident we could do the recapture collar replacement ourselves.

Contracting a helicopter locally would have been easy as the North answers a huge demand for helicopters for forest fire operations, mining and mineral exploration. We could also pick from a selection of pilots with thousands of hours of flying, including wildlife capture experience. We had contracted with these companies before for other wildlife projects including darting grizzly bears on the tundra or net-gunning barren-ground caribou. We even darted and collared some wolverines in 1996. Although no pilots had experience capturing wolves, we didn't consider that aspect a significant limitation. In hindsight, we may have been a bit too frivolous in that assessment.

In many studies researchers opt to capture wolves in winter, at least when captures are done from aircraft or helicopter. Capturing wolves in winter is easier because, after the leaves have fallen and snow covers the ground, wolves are more readily seen and tracked. If snow is deep, then that too restricts a wolf's speed and ability to escape. The key factor, though, is that the lakes and creeks are frozen and they become incorporated into the wolves' daily travels. Wolves are often spotted on frozen lakes, and their capture may soon follow. Darting wolves from the air is often the method of choice in winter because when wolf movement is restricted by snow depth, accurate dart placement can be more readily assured.

In our case, wolves had to be captured and collared in the spring or summer because we were interested in learning more about the ecology of wolves denning on the tundra. Diamonds had recently been discovered in the area. In fact, a map showing all of the mineral exploration leases for the region literally blotted out the landscape. Every parcel of land in what was called the "Corridor of Hope" was staked. A modern day gold rush indeed—except it was for diamonds!

Canada's first diamond mine, the Ekati™ mine, was under construction and more mines promised to follow. Mines and exploration camps need gravel for their roads, airstrips, and foundations for camps and buildings. Because there were no roads on the tundra, construction was needed. Gravel could be obtained from nearby eskers. These long, prominent land features are comprised of gravel and sand that formed when the glaciers melted from the last ice age.

We suspected eskers were important wildlife habitat, but how critical they were was unknown. We knew wolves dug their dens in and around eskers, so this was deemed a good place to start the study. While it was inevitable that some eskers would be required as a gravel source, perhaps we could identify some that were more sensitive than others. We could then make recommendations to industry about which eskers would be more suitable to meet their needs while keeping others unspoiled for wildlife.

We needed to collar wolves during the denning season to ensure we had the right wolves to monitor in the mining regions of our study area. Wolves collared in winter were more likely to disperse widely when they made their way back to the tundra, perhaps well outside our study area. In fact, tundra-denning wolves are migratory, that is, they follow barren-ground caribou from the tundra in summer to the winter ranges in the boreal forest then back again to the tundra. It was still possible for us to aerially capture wolves on the tundra in summer because of two key factors dealing with visibility. The treeless nature of the tundra and the extended daylight of the arctic summer helped us see wolves. Clearly, capturing wolves in winter was out and summer captures were in.

Although we had extensive experience darting grizzly and polar bears from a helicopter, we decided that wolves should be captured using a net-gun rather than darted. Wolves are obviously smaller than bears and, therefore, a smaller target. In addition wolves are quick and evasive, especially with no snow on the ground. Dart placement would therefore be critical. A dart that struck a wolf merely an inch or two off target could hit a vital area and result in its death or severe injury, the latter often a precursor to the former. A capture-related mortality was unacceptable to us—not

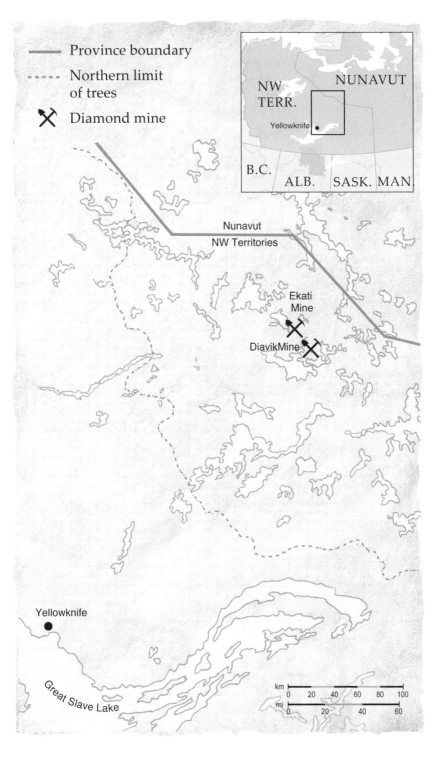

Province boundary

Northern limit of trees

Diamond mine

NUNAVUT

NW TERR.

Yellowknife

B.C.

ALB.   SASK. MAN.

Nunavut
NW Territories

Ekati Mine

DiavikMine

Yellowknife

Great Slave Lake

km   0   20   40   60   80   100
mi   0   20   40   60

even one. While there is never a good time for an animal to die in this way, it would be worse during denning when pups are present, because losing a parent would greatly reduce the pups' chances for survival. Breeding wolves also are very skinny at this time of year due to the nutritional demands of feeding pups. Even the shoulder or thigh of the wolf doesn't have much muscle or fat present to absorb the dart's impact and it could very easily hit bone. Alternatively, to capture wolves via net-gunning, restrain with a forked pole, and chemically immobilize them via hand injection seemed definitely safer for the animals at this time of year. We would still carry a CO_2 powered dart pistol and dart wolves in case the opportunity called for it. The dart pistol has a much softer impact than the powder-charged dart rifle; however, the pistol's range is very short and best suited when on the ground and only for close range.

We ventured out in June 1999 to re-capture our previously collared wolves and replace their collars with new ones. We based our activities out of a camp located at the Diavik™ Diamond Mine site. At that time it was still in the exploration and pre-feasibility stage. Diavik was a major funding partner of the West Kitikmeot Slave Study Society which sponsored a variety of baseline studies, including this wolf study, as a result of increased mining activity in the area and some concerns for their impact on wildlife. Diavik agreed to accommodate our capture crew on site while we captured and collared wolves for this study from 1997 to 1999. These contributions-in-kind greatly facilitated our efforts because they provided much needed logistical support.

We were only able to fly for two days that June and captured just five wolves. We had hoped for more, but strong winds prevented us from flying a couple of days, forcing us to re-schedule to later in the summer. Net-gunning was more difficult than anticipated, partly because the rental net-gun we had was more cumbersome than those we had seen used by others. Net-gunners we worked with previously had custom-made rifles with no stock. The lack of a stock is hard on the wrist because of the shot's recoil, but the increased range in motion is superior. This was enough of a difference that it really affected success rates. Our net-gun was heavy and slow to re-load, unlike other designs we have seen. Hopefully, we wouldn't need a second net for our captures.

We regrouped in late August to recapture the remaining wolves before their radio collars ceased to function. The satellite collars that we were using had break-away inserts, so the collars would drop off at a pre-set time once the collar's battery expired. However, while we could retrieve a collar once it fell to the ground by following its Very High Frequency (VHF) radio signal, we would not be able to monitor the wolf anymore. The wolves we collared were breeding females, and monitoring their movements and den site fidelity over several years was important. Therefore, we needed to replace each aging collar with a new one before it dropped off. Our window of time to do so was closing.

Work resumed on August 30, 1999. This time, no more rentals! We enlisted the help of an experienced net-gunner. We saw the utility of custom-made net-guns earlier, and this gunner had one. Although very experienced in wildlife capture, the gunner had not worked with our pilot before. The relationship between pilot and gunner is an important one, and it takes time to develop. We hoped this wouldn't be a big factor because we only had two to three days for this work to occur. Our concerns were mitigated by their personalities. Both were patient, understanding individuals. This was encouraging, because we didn't want people preoccupied in a blame game should a shot be missed or a wolf escape from a net.

We again based our capture operations at the Diavik site. Traveling from Yellowknife to the base camp took more than the usual two hours, because we needed to stop at a hunting camp along the edge of the tree line where a grizzly bear was in conflict with people. We were unable to locate the bear in a quick visit and search of the area. We needed to move on to do our wolf work, but we confidently predicted that the bear would likely return soon, probably by nightfall.

Nights were getting colder and longer now with the advancing fall season. Frost had long killed the mosquitoes and black flies. The tundra colors were rapidly changing to their glorious reds and purples. Soon snow would come. Indeed, later that afternoon, after checking out a den site for a collared wolf, we encountered an extensive snow squall. While we heard the radio signal of the collared wolf we targeted, visibility was so poor with the wet snow that we could not even see the wolf. Daylight was a concern now, and waiting out the snow storm might take too long. We decided to leave the area and try our luck at another site further west. We had success there and were able to replace one collar, but then we had to return to the Diavik camp for the night. Hopefully, the next day would be more productive.

Indeed, the next day was better. During the first part of the day, we captured four wolves at four different den sites and replaced their collars successfully. It was early evening now, but we still had a couple of hours of daylight left. We knew of another den site north of the Ekati Diamond Mine that was active with wolves. We had collared a male wolf there the year before, but the breeding female eluded us. We decided to revisit this site in the remaining daylight. The Ekati Environmental Department staff had referred to that den site as "Wolf Hotel" because six to eight wolves had been seen consistently there in the past. We had called it the Sable Lake Pack, after the small lake nearby with that name. In a mid-June 1999 fly-by, we saw four wolves in the area, but we could not revisit the site later that month with the capture helicopter because of the poor weather we had encountered then. Given that we had a radio collared male wolf at that site from the previous year, and he was known to be there this spring, we could home in on his VHF radio signal while navigating to the den site. Although not a candidate for capture and collar removal himself, locating this collared male wolf could lead us to the elusive breeding female.

We listened for the distinctive, intermittent pulse that his collar transmitted. The ultrasonic signal is beyond the hearing ability of wolves and people, which is good, because who wants to hear incessant beeping all day for years? Our electronic receiver, tuned to the collar's unique radio frequency, converts the signal into the "beep, beep, beep" sound streaming into our headphones. With the antenna attached to the front of the helicopter, we can direct the pilot to make small left and right turns, then use our ears to determine on which side the sound is strongest and navigate accordingly. We can quickly home in on the signal by winding our way toward it and making constant course corrections based on signal strength.

As we approached the den site, we checked the collared wolf's VHF signal. We could hear it okay and, as expected, it was getting stronger as we approached the site. Good news. That meant the wolf was likely at or near the den. Once we got within a mile of the den, and while still out of sight, we landed to drop the door for the net-gunner. This would allow him to reach out of the helicopter during the capture. We also dropped any unnecessary equipment to lighten our load to make the helicopter more agile. We wanted to be ready for a capture when going by the den in case we didn't get a second chance. Once in the air again, we checked the signal. Still there! After another half minute of flying, the den site came into view. We now heard variations in signal strength of the collar, suggesting the wolf was moving because it likely heard us too.

"There's a wolf," shouted the pilot. Sure enough, the motion of a running wolf caught all of our eyes. We saw the wolf in relation to where the den was, and we thought this could be a male. Often we've noticed the male was the first to get up and run, perhaps in an effort to lead us away from the den. All of a sudden this wolf stopped and assumed an awkward sitting position. We then realized he was defecating! We all laughed. We pursued this wolf for a few seconds, and then saw the collar. This was not the wolf we wanted. We confirmed the signal we heard came from that collared wolf, gave a nod and wave to the pilot, and we veered off to fly toward the den. Mere seconds after leaving that wolf, we saw another wolf running away from the den in a different direction. Just as we were assessing the second wolf, the net-gunner saw a third wolf very close to the den. This suggested to us that this third wolf was likely the female we were after, because of her proximity to the den. "There are two pups," came the voice breaking the silence over the helicopter headset. "No wait, there are four of them." We then gave our full attention to the third wolf. The third wolf became alarmed. Initially it didn't seem too concerned, probably because these wolves have seen helicopters before from mine exploration activities. However, the wolf realized that this was a different situation. This helicopter was coming straight for her. She ran. This was okay; she was doing what we wanted her to do. While we wanted to capture her quickly, a short chase for a minute or two was expected. As an animal tires somewhat, it does not zigzag as much when we move in to shoot the net over it.

We also wanted to have the capture occur away from the den to minimize our disturbance there. Pups invariably remain at the den during captures. Out of sight from the den, the capture process doesn't result in the wolves relocating their pups. It allows the pups to greet the newly collared wolf when it returns after its capture recovery.

In previous years we had watched collared wolves at other dens a month or more following their capture. We had pre-arranged for the pilot to fly near the den first, while maintaining constant radio contact with us as the helicopter came to pick us up at the end of the day. Wolves definitely heard the helicopter from far away, looking toward the sound, ears cocked. Typically many stay put or only stand up and look. However, some wolves are nervous and run, but return soon after. As an example of the behavioral plasticity of these wolves, one time the pilot mistook where the den was and flew right over it before our pickup. The helicopter got quite close and, presumably, when the wolves decided that the helicopter was going for them, they ran. However, as soon as the helicopter passed by and flew to our observation point about 800 meters away, they stopped running and returned to the den where they remained. These observations were very important to us. We did not want our capture procedure to warrant den relocations. To date this had not happened.

Not all places on the tundra are suitable capture sites. Sure, there are no trees, but there are shrubs and boulders and other obstacles that can easily hang a net shot over a wolf, which then doesn't land properly, creating an opening that allows the wolf to escape. Our targeted wolf now approached a pond. We thought that this would help us for the pursuit. We didn't want to capture her in the water, because she could drown; it is also not practical for us to handle an animal in the water. The water was not deep, and she didn't need to swim. We were pleased, though, that she took a quick drink, and the cold water likely cooled her down. While moving slowly in the water, as soon as she hit the shore she would pick up her speed again. We decided to zoom in as she approached the shore with the intention of firing the net over her. A loud boom signaled the net-gun was fired. With great dismay, we watched the net soar over her as she stopped suddenly, ducked her head and gave us the slip, all seemingly in slow motion.

The wolf now headed up a gradual rise toward a large boulder. Up above was a small plateau. Perfect. We'll get her there, we thought. We re-loaded the net-gun and were again in pursuit. "Where's the wolf?" someone asked. She vanished in the fraction of a second we took our eyes off her. Surely she should have been on the plateau. A quick check ruled that out. "Where could she go?" we asked. She could be by those boulders where we saw her last. We veered back and had a look. Nothing obvious, but we saw some crevices in the rocky hill. This was not a place for a net-gun.

We had the pilot land nearby, took our dart pistol, and raced to the crevices. We needed to prepare for a sudden burst by a wolf from its hiding spot and perhaps get a shot away. Peering down the cracks of the rocks and boulders we saw some white fur and ears. Our wolf was hunkered down there. We could see her left front paw and leg, her neck, and parts of her thigh and flank. There didn't seem to be any forward escape, and the only way out seemed to be where she went in.

We thought we could reach down and drug her in the front leg by hand injection. For this purpose, we would use a syringe and then pull her out from behind. However, it wasn't that simple. Below her neck area, we could see some ice, and it was likely there was some water pooled there too. That made it difficult, because when the immobilizing drug would take effect she would lose control of her neck muscles, her head would drop and her nose could dip in the pooled water. As a result, she could drown. All considered, for this capture to work we would have to hold her head up by the back of the neck while we pulled her out. We had the space to do this, but the timing of immobilization was the key, because who wants to hold a wolf's neck with bare hands if the wolf is not yet immobilized?

The immobilizing drug we use on wolves is very safe, with wide safety margins, and once injected, the progress of anaesthesia is very predictable. The hind end of the wolf typically goes down first, then the front, and finally the head. Recovery occurs in the opposite direction. We therefore decided to proceed. One of us tunneled in behind the wolf, while the other readied the syringe for the hand injection. The first attempt bent the needle, probably from a nervous jab, and some of the drug sprayed. The wolf didn't react. We waited, one of us behind near the tail and the other near the front, ready to grab the neck at a second's notice.

A couple of minutes passed with no effect. One of us grabbed the tail and could feel resistance. We would need to administer another dose. Because we were uncertain how much of the drug the wolf received the first time when some of it sprayed out, we gave it only a half-dose. This second effort proved successful. After another couple of minutes, we could see the drug taking effect. At this point, we needed to act swiftly. One of us grabbed the neck and held. No resistance; the drug had taken effect. Now came the chore of inching the wolf backward by the person behind by the tail, while the other held up the head. It took a few minutes, but we cleared the wolf from the crevice.

Once free of the crevice, it was awkward to lift the wolf up and out of the boulders. We used a belt and looped it around the wolf's chest to lift it out of the small cavity. We gave a big cheer, but also felt a sense of awe from the pilot and net gunner at what just happened. With the wolf safely immobilized, we proceeded to assess its condition and take its weight and a few other measurements.

The wolf, now known as W356F, was clearly an adult female, about four or five years old, showing moderate tooth wear. The collar, while only a VHF radio collar, would last four or five years, allowing a multi-year assessment of her denning locations and behavior. As we suspected, she showed signs of lactating that year. No doubt those pups back at the den were hers. We were elated, for we had finally collared the Sable Lake Pack's breeding female and could now track her movements. It was important to do so, because this wolf den was close to the Ekati mine site. Learning how this pack's pups fared with this industrial activity nearby would be of interest to many. It was 9:00 p.m. now, and we hurriedly completed our efforts, retrieved the net by the pond and safely returned to camp by dusk.

Indeed, W356F continued her use of that den site for the remainder of the year and subsequent years. Some years she also used a den site about a quarter mile away. We recaptured her again in late June 2003 at the same Sable Lake den site and replaced her collar. She was lactating again that year, but had heavily worn and missing teeth. It was clear our wolf was old.

Our last contact with Wolf W356F occurred the following year on June 2, 2004. She died sometime after that at an estimated age of eight to ten years. We recovered her collar near her favorite den site on June 1, 2005.

This was a wolf that challenged us every step of the way during her capture and stood out as a hardy wolf, coping with the hardships of the tundra, raising pups, and living to a ripe old age. While we always grapple with the need to collar these majestic animals, there's no doubt the information we obtained from W356F and others like her contributed to our better understanding of wolf ecology on the tundra and our continued management of them.

CHAPTER EIGHT

Ole Gimpy–
Last of the Buffalo Wolves

Lu Carbyn

 I SAT AT THE EDGE OF A CLEARING near the Sweet-grass meadows watching ravens feeding on the remains of a wolf kill. It was very cold, minus 30°C, but already the rays of the February sun began to take the sting of coldness out of my body. The air was dry, so what could be unpleasant coldness elsewhere was not uncomfortable in this setting. Water was boiling next to me in my billie can, a primitive container essential to my basic needs.

In this northern landscape the trappings of civilization are replaced by more basic, fundamental needs: warm clothing, dry feet, food and a good cup of tea. I was in Wood Buffalo National Park's wilderness setting because, from early times in my childhood, I always enjoyed the challenge of being in wild, remote places. As a seasoned twenty-four year veteran biologist with the Canadian Wildlife Service, I took opportunities to be in the field when official projects in the park had been cancelled because of changing Canadian government and sets of priorities.

I had first visited the Park, which I affectionately identified as "Wood Buffalo," back in 1964 during field studies for my Master's degree through the University of Alberta. Situated in the northeast corner of Alberta and adjacent Northwest Territories, the park encompasses a huge watery environment where two great interior river systems, the Peace and the Athabaska, merge. Great swaths of wet meadows lay interspersed with aspen parkland forests in this enormous Delta ecosystem. Years later, as an employee of the Canadian Wildlife Service, my relationship with the Park deepened. I had been assigned to a project studying wolves and their relationship to bison numbers in this very unique setting. Parks Canada and my agency, The Canadian Wildlife Service, were working together in partnership, but this was not to last. These two federal agencies parted company with the election of a conservative government in 1984. The official wolf / bison project was terminated. My interest, however, did not. Thereafter I continued an informal connection with the park's wolves in the wilds of the Delta as a private citizen.

In each of the twelve years between 1985 and 1997 my travels took me there on foot and by canoe. During every visit I found buffalo herds wandering across mud flats and through forests surrounding Lake Claire. The bison's only natural adversary in Wood Buffalo was wolves. It was a unique experience, and one that extended my natural inclinations of discovery and exploration in my formative years.

I glanced across the sedge meadows and noticed movements. A grayish body, with little definition as to size, progressed forward slowly and haltingly at the edge of the willows bordering a ridge. I strained through the binoculars, trying for a better view, and a strange apparition gradually materialized. At intervals its forward motion was hampered by an awkward hop, like a worn down street person slowly ambulating on crutches through a city slum area. Gradually I obtained a better view; first I was able to discern its outline, then, as it stopped and moved its head, I could clearly see that this was a very large, long-legged wolf. It had motley fur, not as thick and uniform as that of most wolves I observed at this time of year. No doubt its ragged condition was brought on by poor health and malnourishment.

Color variation among wolves has also interested me. In earlier studies I conducted on wolves in Jasper National Park I noted that many wolves there were of the black color phase. Here in Wood Buffalo National Park many were white. When wolves are seen from a distance, I would frequently categorize their color patterns as gray, white and black. The relative percentages worked out to 58 percent gray, 26 percent white and 16 percent black. However, when handling wolves, I saw great variations in color, remarkable because not many other mammals have such a wide range in color patterns. From our capture we formed some descriptions: black, gray-black, white, yellow-white, blonde, brownish-gray, gray-grizzled, blue-black, brownish-black, and gray-brown with black streaks. I never saw a blue-black in the Delta, a very unusual color phase that I noted in Jasper National Park. In reality, it is a younger black wolf that over time turns grizzled in color and may even end up being completely white.

I moved in closer. The wolf took little notice of my presence, allowing me to approach slowly to within 150 meters, which afforded me a much better view. At first glance his coat color appeared grayish, but studying him more carefully with the binoculars he looked to have once possessed that classical white coat underlain by a solid coating of black guard hair. Having been subjected to the rigors of winter and hot summer days prior to that, and with the loss of guard hairs obvious to me at this close range, this old timer's coat appeared dirty gray with a brownish base. I was impressed with the creature's size and how gaunt and long-legged it was. This wolf was limping and its head was tilted. Likely blind, I thought, or possibly it had only limited vision in one eye.

He had to be an old animal. Out here, though, age is a relative thing. Captive wolves and dogs can live up to 15 years or more. Here, in the wilds of Wood Buffalo National Park, a five or six-year-old wolf is already old. In an earlier day this gimpy old wolf making its way in front of me had made its living preying on bison here in Wood Buffalo National Park. Now, as a lone wolf, no longer associated with a pack, it could no longer kill bison and had to depend on other sources for sustenance. It might be slim pickings in this environment. Some biologists have suggested that wolves can go on very little food for long periods of time, possibly months, before dying of starvation. A lone wolf such as this one could make it by garnering bits and pieces, scraps from bones, the odd leftover from a goshawk-killed ptarmigan, a piece of bison skin, the occasional mouse—anything. This animal likely would do well if it ingested ten ounces of food a day!

When the opportunity presents itself at fresh kills, wolves can devour up to ten kilograms of meat at one sitting. Historical records refer to wolves eating ravenously on bison flesh, becoming "meat drunk" to the point of stupefaction, so much so that, according to legend, a hunter could approach the wolf and kill it with the butt of a rifle or a club. As so often with exaggeration, grains of truth may be at the center of such stories. I once came upon bloated wolves that had just fed on three bison calf carcasses. I approached within a reasonable distance while the predators moved away slowly in considerable discomfort. What a difference from the gaunt skeleton of a wolf in front of me on this cold winter's day.

Bison are the largest prey for wolves, so naturally one would expect these wolves to be the largest on the continent. Europeans who first encountered wolves on the Great Plains of North America noticed they seemed to prey exclusively on bison. In those early days systematics, the study of species and how they are naturally organized was in its infancy, limited to scholars in the great learning centers of distant Europe. The fur traders, explorers and pioneers were largely unschooled in, and cared not at all for such matters. Reports that managed to reach such institutions as the British Museum, the Muséum National d' Histoire Naturelle and the like, were flush with varying names for wolves. Wolves roaming timbered lands and heavy forests were commonly called timber wolves; gray wolves were so named because in some regions the only color noted among wolves was gray. And so when Europeans first watched wolves pursuing bison they naturally named these buffalo wolves. Here among the Athabaska country First Nations people the Cree refer to them as Maheegan and the Chippewayan name them Segolia.

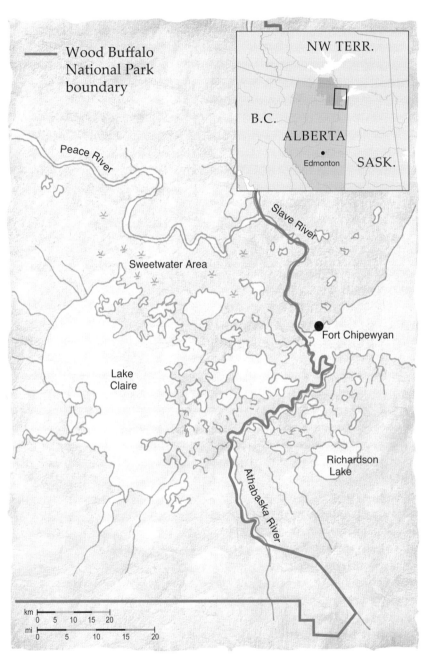

As it came to be, Great Plains wolves specializing in bison were wiped out long before science had a chance to study them. Only a handful, taken between the 1890's and 1920's, survive as specimens within the great learning institutions on the east coast of America. Were they larger than other wolves on the continent? Ron Nowak, a biologist who studied wolf taxonomy worldwide, has suggested that the wolves historically roaming the Great Plains, the "buffalo wolves" of the olden days, were actually a smaller version of the wolves roaming throughout the boreal forest areas further north on the continent. He concludes that these are all related to wolves inhabiting forests and prairies further east in mid-continent America and south down into Mexico.

Saddled by my own bias, I had the impression that no wolves, worldwide, could be heavier than these Wood Buffalo National Park bison hunters. How heavy are Wood Buffalo National Park wolves? Gathering dust in my office many hundreds of kilometers south are records on the subject that graduate student Sebastian Oosenbrug, warden Duane West and I kept on the subject. Upon my return to the laboratory following my encounter with Ole Gimpy, I sought out that information. Eagerly I leafed through yellowing capture sheets that listed males, females, and young of the year in columns. Sometimes it pays to be a "pack rat" and not discard files!

The heaviest Wood Buffalo wolf captured during our formal 1978 to 1981 study was a 58 kilogram male. The heaviest female weighed 41 kilograms. The average male weighed 47 kilograms and the average female 39 kilograms. Pups, captured in mid-winter, weighed an average 33 kilograms. Considering his size and emaciated condition, I would have pegged Ole Gimpy's weight at about 40 kilograms.

By comparison, the heaviest wolves captured near Canada's Jasper National Park and transferred to Yellowstone National Park weighed 56 kilograms. The average male weighed 52 kilograms and the average female weighed 43 kilograms. An exceptionally heavy male from the Yukon Territory tipped the scales at 77 kilograms. So it appears the Rocky Mountain wolves used in the Yellowstone transfer were, on average, somewhat heavier than Wood Buffalo National Park's buffalo wolves. In tongue-in-cheek humor, I have suggested to my American colleagues that their weigh scales were all manufactured in Texas, and I wonder if possibly the springs have been weakened by the southern sun.

In his historical book, *The Wolves of North America*, author Stanley Young provided a description from a nineteenth-century buffalo hunter who remarked, "The great buffalo wolves are the very incarnation of destruction…with (his) powerful jaws of shark-teeth, (his) wonderful muscular strength, the tireless endurance of a compact body, the speed of a gray hound, and the cunning of man." This was an apt description, for bison hunting wolves had to be so equipped.

Bison have the strength, size and sheer weight to defend themselves, but wolves have dagger-like canines that are designed to rip through the tough hides of bison, inflicting lacerations that cause extensive bleeding. Holding on to prey at top speeds can be a hazardous activity. Teeth locked into prey creates a tremendous strain when the predator is being dragged for considerable distances or tossed into the air only to be trampled by the attacking defender.

Ole Gimpy was undoubtedly a worthy adversary a few years earlier when in the prime of his life. He had likely been a dominant male, possessing the fierceness of a tough warrior following his biological calling to kill, eat and reproduce in order to keep the predator/prey system functional and viable as part of the Delta ecosystem. But here wolves suffer incredible bone injuries from battling with prey. It is likely that Ole Gimpy had accumulated his share of injuries over his brief life, including perhaps more recent ones that now accounted for his awkward movements. Lagging behind the pack meant certain isolation and premature death.

Here, on foot and by canoe, in the midst of the great Delta environment, all I could hope for was to glean snippets of information and try, as best I could, to piece some parts of the wolf/bison puzzle together. With 365 days in a year and possibly 200 wolves in Wood Buffalo, there could be as many as 73,000 wolf/bison days and 73,000 wolf/bison nights a year for a wolf to encounter a bison. I despaired to think that my observations would add up to only a fraction of those interplays. Moreover, each wolf has a personality and character of its own. Each affects and alters the innumerable interactions between predator and prey.

The best I could hope for was to obtain brief glimpses, and mere glimpses would never be enough to piece together the entire puzzle. I clung to the happier thought that whatever I could learn would be new and would add to the very little known at the time about the relationship between wolves and bison. And so, over the years I had, on numerous occasions, witnessed intensive struggles between predator and prey.

On a particular chilly October morning a slight breeze stirring the naked aspen branches woke me from my contemplation. This morning I would indeed observe a snippet in the epic struggle between predator and prey. I cannot recall having had a premonition that something important was going to happen, but I do recall being particularly sensitized to the pulse of the moment.

The night before, I had heard two wolf packs howling nearby surprisingly close to each other. Studies elsewhere have shown that wolves are normally territorial. Perhaps here it appears that other rules apply. Maybe the Wood Buffalo wolves are territorial, but they have a different way of defending their territories. Maybe they are territorial only at certain seasons and not at others. Maybe members of neighboring packs are interrelated. Only the occasional wind, the willows, and the ravens are witness to much of what takes place in the world of wolves, bison, and the other elements that complete the fabric of this boreal ecosystem.

As I pushed open the flaps of my tent, a wall of dense, cold fog obscured my view. The warmth in my tent tempted me to linger longer, but it was time to explore the outside world. Early morning is the best time to see wolves and bison. I reached for my pants that had served as my pillow, slipped them on, and crawled out into the fog. Wanting to get an early start, I had prepared breakfast and lunch the night before and now placed them into my day-pack. It was stashed in a corner of the tent inside a bear-proof container. I reached for it and made a quick exit.

Fog obliterated the landscape as if there was nothing but air. This nothingness was so thick that the willow bushes, only meters away, looked like dendrites on a frosted window pane. But I knew exactly where I was, recognizing the turns in the bison trail rutted by decades of trampling. Bison use this trail to move from one meadow to another. Wolves use the same trail, following the herds. Slowly and silently I walked along, treading lightly on the soft, moist ground. Not a whisper of a breeze stirred the air.

As I walked along, I smelled fox in a way you can only smell in the wilderness, far from exhaust fumes or the purification of air conditioners. If the sun had breached the horizon, I could not yet see it. I fully expected that once the fog lifted I would find bison out in the meadows, having spotted them there the day before. And where there are bison, wolves are not far off.

The bison herds put on magnificent displays of their presence in the landscape as an empty arena comes alive with a mass of black bodies. Flying overhead were the opportunistic, ever-present ravens. The wolves had large litters that spring. Several evenings before I had watched a pack of twenty-eight animals at one of their activity sites near my camp. Conditions seemed ideal for observing the interaction between predator and prey.

The trail I was following led to my favorite lookout. In time, the sun's rays began to warm the earth and penetrate the mist, gradually lifting the blanket from the meadow. In front of me I began to make out a small herd of bison—thirty of them, mostly lying down. A few were grazing. I watched as the air continued to clear. It was a peaceful scene, a good place to relax and eat my breakfast. I un-shouldered my pack and pulled out a thermos of tea.

Two ravens landed near the small herd. As they did so, I glanced off to the side. There, in the distance, I saw a faint long line of black and recognized the familiar sight of a larger herd of bison joining the ones lying down nearby. The mist still dominated the scene, but its grip on the land was loosening. The larger herd was coming my way, possibly two-hundred head. I watched as they slowly moved to the south in a straight line. Then I noticed a shorter, white line moving briskly toward the herd—wolves!

The bison began to run, and as they did the wolves picked up their pace. The wolves closed in, pulling alongside the bison, and shortly I saw the black line split into two. Calves, the prime targets for wolves in summer, usually move to the center of the herd when the wolves are in pursuit. The wolves had succeeded in splitting the herd, exposing the calves. Well aware of the opportunity, the wolves pulled past the straggling herd and caught up with the back end of the leading herd, where the calves were. I saw the black and white streaks intermingling. Meanwhile the herd in front of me appeared oblivious to the drama unfolding in the background. A few minutes later they, too, became embroiled in the melee. One very large wolf stood out. Could it have been Ole Gimpy in his prime? Possibly, but I could not verify this as the event took place two years prior to my winter encounter with the old cripple.

With wolves pressing hard, the large herd suddenly wheeled around and stampeded westward, directly toward the small herd and me. First came the lead cow, thundering in my direction at full speed, with the rest of the herd following. Then, dashing in and out, came the wolves. There were too many bison to count, although I tried. Except for the muffled rumble of hooves, both predator and prey were so eerily silent that it all seemed surrealistically mechanical. I saw wolves attempting to tear at the hindquarters of bison. I saw bison wheeling about to face the wolves and then running again in panic, leaving their hind parts exposed. I could feel my heart pounding in my throat. The closer the action, the more engrossed I became with the drama. It was primeval, cruel, and very real. There was no escape for me, no cover if I were to be surrounded by prey and predator. Nothing to do but wait and see!

The wolves isolated a large calf, almost the size of a yearling. Within minutes they were slashing and tearing at its hind end. In their frenzy they also attacked its front and middle. Most of the adult bison moved on, but three cows made a vain rescue attempt. Soon they left the calf as well. It seemed that the victim's fate was sealed. The wolves and the calf formed a single, moving mass of bodies. As the calf's stomach was ripped open, warm air from the body cavity mingled with the cold air around it, forming a halo of condensation around the wolves and the calf. That image was burned into my mind—both the beauty and the cruelty of the sight. The calf got up and lunged forward. This time a large wolf (Ole Gimpy?) braced its hind legs firmly on the ground and clawed itself up onto the calf, gripping the calf's back with its teeth. The wolf repositioned itself, and once more I could see the teeth sink into the calf's rump. If the calf was in pain or in shock, I could not tell. I could not hear any vocalization, no bleating, and no cries of pain. Why? I am told that in captivity distressed calves vocalize a great deal.

Suddenly the action stopped. Inexplicably, the wolves slunk off, abandoning the injured calf, which now lay half hunched in a crouched position. It was bleeding from the back and head, and part of its abdomen hung open. Mortally wounded, I thought. I was perplexed. What had prompted the wolves to relinquish their meal, now so imminent? Was it my presence? I didn't think so. To this point the pack had ignored me altogether, so why would it suddenly interrupt its actions? Why this change in behavior?

Faintly at first, then louder, came the answer—motorboats—two of them. Duck hunters on Lousy Creek. During part of every fall and spring, native hunters from Fort Chipewyan travel along rivers and creeks shooting ducks and geese. Although wolves have little to fear from duck hunters, they are terrified of anything motorized, probably a result of trappers on snowmobiles chasing them in open terrain during winter. The wolves dispersed over the meadow, some lying down, others moving about restlessly, but unwilling to finish off the wounded calf. One wolf was licking blood from its front paw, the white fur around its muzzle smeared red.

At this stage I could count the wolves: seventeen, all light colored. In the fall the packs are large like this, but in the ensuing winter pup wolves suffer high mortality. Thus few of this year's pups are likely to see the next spring, and the pack will shrink.

After some time, four wolves returned to the injured calf. The calf had remained at the same location, exhausted, abandoned by the herd. These four wolves were evidently the boldest of the lot, perhaps dominant wolves or ones driven by a greater hunger. The other wolves held back, likely to recover their energy, trusting that the mortally wounded prey would soon lie still and be easy pickings. The foursome grabbed at the victim, which, once more, stood up in an attempt to defend itself. As they toyed with their quarry, much as a cat would do with a mouse, the bison herd returned, attracted by the injured calf. I thought it possible the calf had uttered a distress call, one the bison had heard, but I had not.

The mist had dissipated by this time and sunshine was warming the landscape. The four attackers seemed to lose interest in the dying calf. The drone of the still-approaching motorboat became too threatening for them. A single cow deliberately and rapidly advanced, then sniffed the calf. In response the youngster managed to rise to its feet. The cow was almost certainly its mother. Then the most heartrending sight unfolded before my eyes. The calf, injured as it was, began to follow the cow. It could manage to move only very slowly, head leaning forward and bent down to the ground. A few remaining wolves watched from a distance. Ravens were winging about, apparently confident that it would be only a matter of time before they would gorge themselves on this moving carcass. The cow and calf moved off into the aspen forest along Lousy Creek.

I sat in a daze. How tough and stoic the calf was. Although it suffered numerous wounds, bleeding all over the body, a large rip in the flank that almost disemboweled it, bites on the head, nose, rump, neck, and back, it had made no sound. I tried to master my feelings of pity for the animal. At this point I would have been happy to help end its misery, but in a National Park nature must be allowed to run its course unimpeded.

The calf had suffered the vicissitudes of nature on that October morning years earlier. And now, on this cold February morning, it was Ole Gimpy's turn to suffer. This once healthy alpha male had been reduced to scavenging as a cripple, a welfare bum, trying his best to survive one more harsh northern winter, likely his last. I watched him maneuver through the deep snow and disappear from view as, in the far distance, I could hear a pack howling.

His kind will survive, and so, in the cycle of life and death, wolf predation can be part of one of the world's most remarkable boreal ecosystems.

At that same period in time I was realizing how rapidly areas in the north were changing. That was particularly the case for the wilderness character around Wood Buffalo National Park. The world's attention had been drawn to that region because of the oil sands, yet few have written about how the mining activities could be impacting park values. Environmental focus has primarily centered on strip-mining, on dirty oil, climate change and on downstream pollution impacts along the Athabasca River. Wilderness buffer zones around the park are rapidly melting away and it will be difficult to maintain the pristine qualities of the Delta ecosystem as modern civilization keeps extending northward. Governments and human interventions will be needed to protect some of the inherent values of this highly unique region.

CHAPTER NINE

A Tail of a Wolf

Maggie Dwire

THE SMALL OBSERVATION BLIND at the Sevilleta Wolf Management Facility is perched atop a cliff over-looking six pre-release enclosures, each about an acre in size. Built by a Boy Scout in the mid 1990's, it is surprising to me how well this structure has endured the extremes of the New Mexico climate. During the winter the cold air constantly blows in through the observation window making the small building function like a refrigerator. I suspect someone thought better of placing the blind on the other side of the canyon, facing the sun and protected from the wind, fearing winds would carry the scent of eavesdropping biologists to the alert noses of dozens of captive Mexican wolves below. I huddle within, tasked with selecting the best wolves for release, observing breeding behavior late January through March. Bundled up like the kids in the old Charmin commercials, I sit motionless in the freezing cold temperatures watching wolves, ahem, well, breed.

I began working for the U.S. Fish and Wildlife Service as an intern on the Mexican Wolf Reintroduction Project in Alpine, Arizona in 2000. As interns we primarily drove around all day (or flew around in a small plane) listening to the clicks and pops of static on our receivers that every biologist comes to know well. In 2001 I helped move a new pack from the Sevilleta pre-release facility to an acclimation pen in the Blue Range Wolf Recovery Area. For the wolves it was a move from one chain-link pen to another. For the people involved, pro or con, those wolves were taking another step toward freedom. One of my fondest memories of wolves came when the decision was made to let the new pack go. I opened a ten-by-ten foot section of the pen and hid in nearby trees watching as the six wolves cautiously stepped out from the safety of the chain-link world they had known.

With each subsequent step the Saddle Pack, as it was named, gained confidence, eventually loping off out of sight. I'd love to say that as they passed over the hill, one of them paused slightly looking back over its shoulder as if to say thank you. But that vision lives only in my imagination. They moved off, the beeps of their radio collars growing more faint until the only sound remaining was the familiar static from the receiver.

Preparing wolves in captivity for release is still a necessary component of Mexican wolf recovery. To help accomplish that I spent my first winter in the Sevilleta observation blind in 2002. A female wolf was placed with two males, brothers, and allowed to choose a mate. The lucky male would earn his ticket to freedom. The other male would put back in line and continue to wait his turn for release. The darker and more reddish male followed the female wolf everywhere, his nose so close to her rear that each time she stopped he crumpled like an accordion into her backside. The other male wolf was equally attracted, but was always put in his place when he approached the female.

That spring the female disappeared into a den box for several hours and a few days later I poked my head into the den box and counted five Mexican wolf pups. At ten weeks of age we captured the pups to administer their first round of vaccines. For the wolves this process must be akin to an alien abduction. A dozen or so humans entered the pen and formed a "human wall." Taking advantage of the wolf's fear of humans, the capture crew slowly moved through the enclosure, pushing the wolves towards the strategically placed den boxes. The pups, used to the comfort and protection of the den box, quickly hid inside. Unfortunately for the pups the den box converts to a capture box; the crew closed the door and lifted its lid, easily extracting the pups from within.

All five pups were male; two more grayish in color and three more reddish in color like their father. Curiously, one of the latter was missing its tail tip and a second reddish pup had only a blunted tail like that of a bobcat. Veterinarians indicated the tail abnormalities were natural, due to some sort of trauma. We guessed one of the pups may have suckled the tail of its brother and its own tail, causing the deformities.

Studbook numbers were duly entered: 728, 729, 730, 731, and 732. No names in this project. I've come to learn that some numbers mean more to me than any name ever could. Mile marker signs, addresses, phone numbers, etc. all remind me of wolves I have known. I'd be lying if I didn't admit that some wolves inevitably earn nicknames for their story or certain characteristics they exude. The pup with the blunted tail, male 732, was one such wolf... although perhaps our creative juices were lacking for he was nicknamed Bob.

Bob and his brothers spent their first year of life at Sevilleta. His blunted tail was hardly long enough to wag during play or excitement. I grew fond of Bob; he was one of the more dominant pups, but silly looking at best, marching around the pen holding his little stub of a tail in the air and his chin high.

In June 2003, Bob, his brother, male 729, and their parents were given the name the Red Rock Pack and released to the wild. Immediately things went awry. Bob's dad was struck and killed by an 18-wheeler on highway

60. His mom suffered a serious foot injury and had to be recaptured for treatment. His brother quickly dispersed from the area and managed to locate a female wolf that had dispersed from another pack, and the two established a territory of their own. Alone and with almost no experience in the wild, Bob wandered outside the recovery area boundary to a waste facility on the Fort Apache Indian Reservation. With little hope that he would contribute toward recovery and after only ten weeks of freedom, Bob was recaptured and returned to Sevilleta to await another chance at freedom.

Boundaries on a recovery area can be problematic; especially given wolves can't read maps. Similar to Bob, the Saddle Pack also eventually moved outside of the recovery area. They had taken up residency on the San Carlos Apache Reservation (Tribal lands that did not support wolf recovery), and were depredating cattle. This trifecta of strikes resulted in the U.S. Fish and Wildlife Service committing to removing the pack from the reservation.

The adult female, suspected to be pregnant, was spared lethal removal, and instead captured and taken to Sevilleta where, shortly thereafter, she gave birth to five pups. The Saddle Pack male eluded capture for months, and following additional depredations was one of the first Mexican wolves to be lethally removed from the wild.

An enormous investment of staff time and energy is required in bringing captive wolves to the point of release. The general public also invests through interest or literally through things like adopt-a-wolf programs that help fund the activities of the captive facilities. Understandably, when a wolf is selected for release it may have quite a following from the caring people who have invested so much in the particular wolf's journey. They share a sense of excitement and guarded anticipation when "their" wolf is given the opportunity to experience freedom. But life in the wild is inherently dangerous, and it has fallen on my shoulders to notify these people of the fate of their wolf.

The first time I had to make one of these untimely phone calls was when the Saddle Pack male was lethally removed. I telephoned the Rio Grande Zoo in Albuquerque, New Mexico, to let them know that not only had their wolf died, he died because we had chosen that fate for him.

The Saddle Pack female 797, was a wild-born wolf, and government authorities had taken her from the wild and killed her mate. She and her pups were now surrounded by inescapable chain-link. The meals were easy and free, but I doubt that was of any consolation. The U.S. Fish and Wildlife Service wanted her removal to be temporary but translocation of a female with five young pups without the help of a mate wasn't ideal. Plans were made to introduce a male into the group. Bob was pacing in

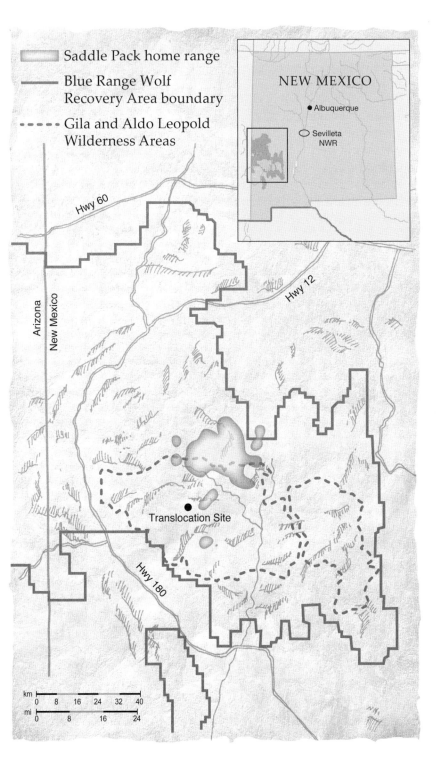

Saddle Pack home range

Blue Range Wolf
Recovery Area boundary

Gila and Aldo Leopold
Wilderness Areas

NEW MEXICO

● Albuquerque

○ Sevilleta
NWR

Hwy 60

Arizona

New Mexico

Hwy 12

● Translocation Site

Hwy 180

km
0   8   16   24   32   40
mi
0   8   16   24

a neighboring pen when the capture crew came to collect him. He would be given a second chance at freedom, and much like his father, this ticket was contingent upon winning over the hearts of the, now captive, Saddle Pack female and her pups.

The pups were almost six weeks old when Bob was released into their enclosure. I sat in the familiar blind observing as female 797 ran along the far fence line and Bob paced close to the gate area. This went on for some time and wasn't interrupted until two or three of the pups emerged from under a group of trees. Spotting them, Bob stopped suddenly in his tracks, and my worst fear seemed realized. He ran full speed at the pups. The closer he got the tenser I became, until I had the distinct impression of time slowing down just as it does when you witness a tragic accident.

Helpless to interfere, I focused only on Bob as he ran. Just when I expected to see him grab one of the pups, something blurred into view and knocked him several feet sideways. Peering over the scope I realized that female 797 had clobbered him. Hackles up with teeth bared, she stood over her pups that by now had all emerged from under the tree. Bob circled around the pen trying to come at the pups from the other side. Swiftly charging him, she pinned him to the ground.

From what I could tell, she wasn't backing down, and Bob was not giving up. I watched female 797 pin Bob time after time, wondering all the while if Bob would kill the pups. I felt awful knowing there was no way I could stop him if he did. However, as time passed I saw that female 797 was not injuring Bob, and he wasn't actually aggressive in his charges at the pups. In fact, he eventually appeared playfully stupid and his resistance to being pinned was non-existent.

Not having much luck, Bob retreated back to the other side of the enclosure leaving the female to her pups by the tree. After a long separation he approached again. This time he moved very slowly, only a few steps at a time. The closer he got, the more submissive he became until, finally, when nose to nose with female 797 he was army-crawling with his head low, ears back, and what tail he had, tucked. Female 797 seemingly accepted this behavior and offered a half-attempted play bow. Perhaps anticipating being pinned once again, Bob flopped onto his back as the female darted off in play. He quickly righted himself and took off in chase.

They disappeared in and out of view, their interactions playful. The female would stop abruptly and place her chin on the Bob's shoulders or rest her front paws on his back. With each test Bob dutifully submitted, allowing her to display whatever dominance she wanted. This went on for several hours before Bob tried, or was allowed, to approach the pups again.

Bob was lying down as the pups moved out from under the tree. He rolled onto his side, allowing all five pups to inspect him, absolutely still save for the heaving of his chest. The pups excitingly crawled all over him, biting at his face and neck, yet Bob remained stoic. By the time the sun went down that day the pups had retreated into the trees, and when I left the observation blind Bob was obediently following female 797 around the pen as if attached to her with Velcro.

Three months later we prepared to release them back into the wild, fitting Bob with a GPS collar, while female 797 and her pups received standard radio collars appropriate for their size. Bob and the pups were easily captured from a den box. The female, on the other hand, put up a good fight and was surprisingly difficult to handle for such a small wolf.

The newly reconstituted Saddle Pack was translocated by mule into the heart of the Gila Wilderness in western New Mexico. Placed within a nylon mesh pen designed for self-release, they chewed out that night. A year after he was removed for dumpster diving, Bob was free once again; this time with his very own pack.

Within days the Saddle Pack moved several miles from the release site, but radio fixes indicated that one pup had not. While discussions ensued deciding whether to leave the pup alone or capture and try to move it near the pack, the pup and pack reunited on their own. I assumed the pup had managed to find its way to the pack, but a closer look at location data downloaded from Bob's GPS collar suggested he had traveled to the release pen and the pup, and then returned to the pack.

Bob's GPS collar fell off sixty days later due to a programming error. However, over the next two years we continued to get observations of the Saddle Pack, and due to his distinctive bobbed tail and reddish coloration it was easy to confirm Bob was still alive. In addition, female 797 denned both of those years and genetic tests confirmed Bob as the sire of both litters.

Finally, Bob was recaptured and fitted with a GPS radio collar once again. That same summer another adult male wolf joined the Saddle Pack. An unrelated male wolf joining a pack that already has a breeding male is fairly rare. We thought he might be their offspring but genetic tests confirmed he was from a neighboring pack.

The Saddle Pack's territory lay within the Gila National Forest. Also located within their territory, and throughout a large portion of the entire Blue Range Wolf Recovery Area, are local livestock producers and their cattle. In 2007 several wolf packs were getting into depredation trouble resulting in the U.S. Fish and Wildlife Service removing a record number of Mexican wolves.

The Saddle Pack was not guiltless of livestock killings. A dead cow in March, 2006, a second in November 2006, and, finally, a third in February

2007 brought them to the knees of an old protocol that scripted removal after three depredations in a year. However, instead of removing the entire pack, the U.S. Fish and Wildlife Service opted to lethally remove the new and unrelated male, hoping his exit would stop the depredating behavior and keep the breeding members of the pack in the wild. Unfortunately, two months after the unrelated male was taken the Saddle Pack depredated again. A removal order was issued for both Bob and female 797 on April 2, 2007.

The situation became eerily reminiscent of 2004 when female 797 was spared lethal removal because she was pregnant. Now, in 2007, she was again pregnant and would soon have pups. Therefore, according to the removal order, Bob could be taken lethally, but female 797 would be spared for the second time in her life.

An agent from United States Department of Agriculture, Wildlife Services was brought in from out of state to do the job. At the same time, a trap-line was established, primarily to capture the female, but if Bob was caught prior to being shot his life would be spared as well. It became a race between aerial gunning and ground trapping. One day, using a small plane, the agent located the pack and honed in on the tail-less wolf. Shots were fired and they radioed they had shot and killed him. Searching the area to retrieve his carcass, field crews discovered from Bob's radio signals that he was moving off quickly as they approached. Obviously Bob was not dead.

The plane was brought in a second time. Again they located the pack and honed in on Bob. Shots were fired and they confirmed Bob had been killed. Scouring the area for his body resulted in the same find: the collar was functioning properly and Bob moved off quickly as crews approached. He still was not dead.

The plane was brought in a third time. Listening to the plane in the distance must have been excruciating for personnel continuing to run traps. The agent fired at Bob and this time a biologist in a spotter plane confirmed seeing Bob hit, flip and roll on the ground as he disappeared into the trees. A check later indicated the collar was in mortality mode, signaling that Bob had not moved in more than four hours. Finally, at day's end on May 16, 2007, it was confirmed: Bob was finally dead.

Biologists hiked in to retrieve his carcass the next day. I snickered that it might be funny to find Bob's collar moving off as they approached, but there was no such luck. The collar remained in mortality mode. They moved closer and closer until they found the collar—and only the collar. The gunfire had hit the break-away detonation device on the GPS collar, causing it to release off the wolf. Based on the amount of blood and damage to the collar, and what the agent and our biologist observed from the planes, Bob could not have survived. Without a collar, finding his carcass would be difficult unless, perhaps, ravens and other scavengers moved in.

For a second time, government officials had shot and killed female 797's mate while she was pregnant or, this time, tending to pups. We continued our attempts to capture her, all the while supplementally feeding her near the den so she could better provide for her young pups. We used trail cameras to monitor her condition.

The one-or-so inch screen on the cameras themselves enabled us to confirm female 797 was using the food cache. The images were downloaded on the office computer in order to better determine her condition. Female 797 was obviously nursing, a very good sign. In some frames, though, she looked a bit odd. Her belly was unusually large for a female that had just recently given birth, and she didn't appear to be missing much belly hair—as most female wolves are when nursing. Then one photo showed the same wolf in the previous images, but it had turned away from the camera giving a clear view of its hind end. It had no tail!

News of Bob's survival traveled fast. Up in the chain of command, discussion quickly focused on lethally removing Bob from the ground, perhaps by stationing an agent to shoot him at the den. Miraculously, before a decision could be made on Bob's fate, and after several emotionally draining weeks of trying, he was caught in one of our traps on May 26, 2007.

In the wee hours of the night,—with only minor injuries from the errant buckshot that was fired at him—Bob was put in a crate, taken from his family and from the wild, and driven, once again, back to Sevilleta. I crossed my fingers as I headed out to run traps that we could quickly catch female 797 and safely reunite her and the pups with Bob.

Most livestock producers were adamantly opposed to wolf reintroduction, but that doesn't make them innately difficult to deal with. In fact, after getting chewed on for a few minutes about wolves and the government, most are pleasant people to interact with. I've had some of my most interesting conversations with these so-called difficult ranchers over a pleasant cup of coffee or a bite to eat.

Unfortunately, the producer permitted to graze cattle in this area was not included among them. In fact this particular gentleman would later twice punch the truck mirror as he yelled at one of my coworkers. I saw him only once while running traps for the Saddle Pack. His truck approached our camp while I sat under a tree entering information into my field journal. I stood and waved to intercept him, but instead of stopping he drove by slowly, glaring at me with his window rolling up as he passed.

This particular assignment was bittersweet for me. I was relieved that

Bob was out of the government's cross-hairs. But I also had reservations about female 797's removal, and mostly the innocent pups, from the wild. The den-bound pups' only crime was having been born to parents that, through regurgitation and teaching their young how to kill prey, might train them to depredate cattle. They would remain candidates for re-release, but a sibling group raised in captivity was unlikely to ever be released together en masse. Thus, they would await their chance at freedom, one by one, paired with other wolves just as their parents had.

Jen, my trapping partner and an intern at the time, woke me up around 2 a.m. because a trap monitor had been triggered. Gathering our gear, we investigated the site and found the trap had been taken from its hole. Presumably it was attached to the unsuspecting animal that had stepped in it. I hoped, as I always do when I catch anything, it wasn't a bear cub or a mountain lion. Drag marks led us a short distance and in the dark we could hear an animal struggling to be freed. Eventually our headlamps illuminated the reflection of two eyes. As we moved in closer, the body of a wolf materialized around them.

At first I worried the wolf was injured because her body seemed oddly contorted. Her trapped foot was stretched over and behind her head, her body twisted somewhat in the chain to the drag. I worked quickly to remove her from the trap while Jen prepared to administer subcutaneous fluids and other treatments. Female 797 appeared well, in good health and lactating, and though the trapped foot was swollen, it was not abnormally so. We easily slid her into the crate and without adjusting her position she awkwardly rested her head on the crate floor. I remember thinking how difficult she was to handle at Sevilleta. Now, if ever a wolf looked defeated, this was it.

We hiked up the drainage to the den—an old bear's den—a couple hundred yards away from where we left the crated female. The den was big enough for me to turn completely around in, although only tall enough to do so lying down. The pups weren't immediately noticeable, but the den had several carved out cubby areas along the sides where they could easily be hiding. After a cursory swipe of these areas on one side of the den without finding any pups I started to worry. This was the den. We'd seen the female coming and going. The pups had to be in there. Jen and I took turns excavating the cubbies and continued to come out empty handed.

The clock was ticking. The pups could not go too long without their mother's milk. We used the satellite phone and called the field office to set in motion at least fifteen people heading to the remote location to help in the search.

In the back of the den a dirt lip gave way to a hole that, because of the angle and the narrowness of that part of the den, could not been viewed. I dug almost unconsciously at that hole, convinced the pups must be there.

It was nearing mid-morning when the others arrived, and I was in the den moving dirt methodically but without purpose. I'm not sure what it was exactly that triggered it, but I curled on my side as tears streaked the dirt on my cheeks. I was in a den, but no longer *the* den, and somewhere out on the landscape was another hole in the ground containing pups, only three weeks old, likely wondering where their mother was.

Was I anthropomorphizing this? Exhaustion certainly played a pivotal role in the release of these emotions. I'd been up handling wolves and digging in a den since 2 a.m. Their father was taken away, we had locked their mother up in a crate, and now we couldn't find the pups I presumed to be very hungry. Since the day I first released them, the Saddle Pack had seen its ups and downs. Now, in that den, I sunk into wondering whether there would ever be an up to this down.

Finding a den hole, quickly, in the middle of a forest when you're relatively unsure where it might be, isn't easy. As the day progressed we had no luck. It turned into afternoon and we began discussing our options. Female 797 wasn't doing very well in the crate. She was fairly motionless and non-responsive despite being overseen by our veterinarian. The pups had been without her for at least twelve hours now. The veterinarian chimed in recommending that female 797 would need to be let out of the crate at nightfall. We decided to search until sundown and if we didn't find the pups female 797 would be released with a GPS collar.

What little hope I had disappeared as the sun sunk beneath the tops of the trees. At that point I was leaning against one of our trucks taking my first break since two in the morning when people started yelling from one of the neighboring drainages. Suddenly everyone was running to meet a couple of our biologists coming down over the hill. The needle in a haystack had been found. Distributed between two of their backpacks were seven three-week-old pups.

We gave the pups subcutaneous fluids and Karo syrup orally to boost their sugars. Female 797's crate was put into the back of a covered pick-up. The pups, placed in a plastic storage bin, were set on the tailgate while we quickly packed. For the first time since she was trapped, the mother wolf lifted her head and peered at the plastic tub. Seeing, or more likely smelling the pups, she shifted her weight in the crate, her ears perked up. The sun was almost down now and the tub of pups were put in the cab of the truck so they could be kept warm and tended to on the long drive to Sevilleta. If female 797 could hang on a few more hours the whole pack would be reunited.

We arrived at Sevilleta around midnight. As we entered the pen we could hear Bob jumping at the chain link, no doubt trying to escape yet another abduction by his human captors. We put the pups in one of the den boxes and placed the female's crate next to the den box. After giving her time to sense that the pups were present, we opened the crate and left the facility. I made my way to the observation blind above the pens. Yes, I was exhausted and emotionally drained, but I felt I had to observe the pack the following morning to assure myself that everything was alright.

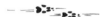

Sunrise at Sevilleta is one of the most beautiful and peaceful things to experience. The cool crisp night gives way to the blinding New Mexico sun ever so slowly, and in the summer you can almost hear the ground crackle as it warms. The sunrise that morning was no different, and the bill snapping and caws of the ravens hoping for a free meal broke the night silence.

As it became light enough to see, Bob was lying on the ground awake, perpendicular to a sleeping female 797 under a tree. I could only see her head and her front feet, and for about an hour they remained in that right angle formation. Despite using binoculars and a scope I could not see if any pups were with them.

I dozed off for a bit and when I awoke it was warming quickly and, in the same positions, Bob was snapping at the flies gathering around the female's face and ears. My heart plummeted into my stomach. The female remained motionless. She'd hardly moved in her crate and now, slumped in the dirt under a tree with Bob loyally by her side snapping at the gathering flies, I knew she was dead. It had been too much for her. Reuniting them had taken too long, and I sat in the blind in shock watching Bob clean her motionless face. I dug in my bag looking for my phone. Before the U.S. Fish and Wildlife Service put out any news releases saying the pack was successfully reunited at Sevilleta I needed to report that female 797 didn't survive.

As my phone turned on I watched a wolf through the blur of my forming tears trot across the pen to one of the water tubs. I felt angry that Bob could trot across the pen so spryly after all that he'd been through. As I considered this I saw the wolf had a tail just before she submerged herself in the water tub.

I couldn't believe it—and at the same time I cursed these wolves for the years of life I was losing because of the stress they were putting me through! This is why biologists are supposed to remain emotionally unattached. Female 797 emerged from the tub sopping wet and trotted back to the spot I had presumed was her deathbed. As she approached, Bob wagged his stump of a tail and one by one six pups stumbled out from under the tree. The mother wolf lay down and the pups began nursing. A wolf in an adjacent pen huffed, and Bob ran towards the fence line growling, ears forward and coat puffed out in aggression (of course his tail was also raised but I'd be surprised if any of the wolves noticed). Female 797 also got up and moved a bit from the tree to see what the fuss was about. I counted the pups again, stumbling along trying to dangle from her teats. Only six. Bob came back to where the female stood, his coat slowly lying back in place, and the seventh pup—quite a bit darker, and redder like his father and his father's father—came stumbling out and joined its siblings in nursing.

While Bob and female 797 were never re-released, their adventure didn't stop in that pen at Sevilleta. They would have one more litter despite female 797 being contracepted at the time. Apparently the technique of forcing ovulation in a female prior to when males produce sperm, and thus throwing off the synchrony required for breeding, failed to consider the male was the seemingly immortal Bob! Eventually we moved the Saddle Pack to the Endangered Wolf Center in Missouri to make room for additional wolves at Sevilleta. Sadly, a large inoperable tumor was discovered on Bob's neck and he was euthanized on August 5, 2011. I was in the field surveying the damages from the largest wild fire in Arizona's history when I got the phone call. Despite having given the news so many times, I now know that nothing prepares you to receive the news that "your" wolf has died.

Stories
of Conflict

CHAPTER TEN

Whatever Happened to the Durango Pack?

Ellen Heilhecker

I MADE IT TO MY NEW HOME in Catron County, New Mexico, on Monday morning January 15, 2007 after twenty-six hours of driving, eight of which were in blowing snow with white-out conditions in Nebraska. I arrived in Apache Creek, an unincorporated community, only to find my rental bunkhouse locked. I was told the place would be left open, and just as important, the place would be cleaned. My landlord had forgotten my arrival plans and was not at home. At the Apache Creek store I asked if they knew were he might be.

The woman behind the counter was nice enough to make several phone calls trying to locate him. While she was on the phone, I kept myself busy reading the "No Wolves" and "Wolves are Government Terrorists" bumper stickers displayed in the store, all the while hoping she wasn't going to ask why a single girl from Wisconsin was moving here. The landlord wasn't to be found, so the clerk told me where she thought a key was hidden for the bunkhouse. She was right, I easily located the key and let myself in, uncomfortable with the realization that anyone probably knew where to find the "hidden" key for the place I was living.

My bunkhouse was the middle of three. The neighboring woman warned me to be prepared for people coming and going from her place at all times of the day and night, mostly due to her ranching and fencing business. However, she warned, sometimes the "not so desirable" types show up. She reassured me not to worry; if they don't go away she kept a loaded .357 magnum close at hand. I never heard any shots. I wondered what it took for her to decide what was "undesirable," because after a week's time I had seen enough to know I would have had a standing delivery order for ammunition.

Tuesday was my first day of work as a wolf biologist for the New Mexico Department of Game and Fish. I was part of the Interagency Field Team assigned to the Mexican Wolf Recovery Program that consisted of six agencies including the New Mexico Department of Game and Fish, Arizona Game and Fish Department, U.S. Fish and Wildlife Service, U.S. Forest Service, Wildlife Services and White Mountain Apache Tribe.

I had to get a New Mexico driver's license in order to drive my state-owned work truck. For this I needed two proofs of residency. Since I didn't have a formal lease agreement at the Apache Creek bunkhouse, I had to register to vote in Catron County, the largest county in New Mexico with almost 7,000 square miles of land, less than twenty percent of it privately owned. The county boasted the third smallest population at one person for every two square miles. Reserve is the county seat with a population of 340 people.

Two women were working in the county clerk's office. One was helping me register; the other was working on a county ordinance that had just passed that week. The voters had approved killing wolves by their own wolf depredation "expert," the Catron County Wolf Investigator. The county ordinance provided the Interagency Field Team a grace period of 24 hours to take care of any depredating wolves. After that the locals believed the matter fell to the authority of the county's Wolf Investigator. Catron County had declared a state of emergency due to economic, cultural, and social hardships caused by the approximately twenty-two wolves in the county, an area close in size to Connecticut and Rhode Island combined. Seeing this woman working on the ordinance, I discretely flipped over the letter of residency the Department of Game and Fish had given me to validate my employment. I didn't really care to get into any discussions should she see the big bear-head, game and fish logo on the letterhead.

I found myself living in a county where all heads of households are required to carry firearms and environmentalists are required to register upon moving into the county. Yes, just like sex offenders, we environmentalists must register. I never did. When I registered to vote, I saw the Democrat and Republican check-off boxes, but noted nothing for environmentalist, so I thought it best not to ask. I was probably the first and only Democrat anyway, and I felt safe in assuming everyone in the county already knew I was an environmentalist. But I stayed, not only because it made for good stories to send back home, but mainly because I had realized my goal to be a wolf biologist.

Mexican Wolf Project policy prevented us from referencing a wolf as a "he" or a "she" in written documentation. We were to refer to a wolf by its studbook number or call the wolf an "it." I am going to break the rule in telling the story of alpha male 973 and alpha female 924, as I never agreed with "it" anyway.

On April 12, 2007, alpha male 973 and alpha female 924 of the Durango Pack were mule-packed to the Miller Springs translocation site in the middle of the Gila Wilderness Area and placed in a soft-release pen. The pen was approximately 525 square meters in size, built of nylon mesh, with electric fencing interwoven into the structure. These pens weren't overly secure, and occasionally some wolves had managed to escape.

Wolves can only be translocated into New Mexico if they have previous wild experience. The definition of "wild" experience is a little odd. For example, in May 2007, we removed the Saddle Pack for cattle depredations. The pack consisted of the two alphas and their seven, approximately three-week old pups. Born in the wild, those pups had "wild experience" even though they were completely dependent at the time of their removal. The two Saddle alphas were given a life sentence in captivity without the eligibility for parole. The pups, however, were not involved in the depredations and, to this day, remain eligible for release into Arizona or New Mexico.

The Interagency Field Team had planned to call the pair the Granny Mountain Pack after the name of a mountain close to the release site. But the Adaptive Management Oversight Committee, which administers and guides the project and the overall operation of the Interagency Field Team, deemed the name was too reminiscent of "Little Red Riding Hood."

The male wolf was formerly a member of the Aspen Pack. He had been removed from the wild in October 2006 and placed in captivity for non-injurious dog interactions, and for "nuisance behavior," being in close proximity to residences in Greer, Arizona. The female wolf, a former Francisco Pack member, was also removed in 2006. She had two "strikes" against her for confirmed cattle depredations. According to the Blue Range Mexican Wolf Reintroduction Project Adaptive Management Oversight Committee Standard Operating Procedure 13 titled "Control of Mexican Wolves," a wolf "known or likely to have committed three depredation incidents within a period of 365 days shall be permanently removed (i.e. three strikes and out) from the wild as expeditiously as possible." Both wolves remained eligible for future translocations. Hence their mule trip to the Gila Wilderness in April 2007.

I was not there when the wolves were stuffed into individual metal panniers, placed on the back of a mule and taken down the bumpy trail-ride in. I can only imagine what the mules were thinking. I took the second shift, eight days of pen sitting duty, and was there for their release. On April 17, I entered into the Gila Wilderness Area to backcountry camp for the first time. The Gila Wilderness Area within the 2.7 million acre Gila National Forest was established in 1924 as the first designated wilderness area made famous by the renowned wildlife ecologist, Aldo Leopold. Leopold, who had his own experiences with Mexican wolves, started the wildlife management program at my alma mater the University of Wisconsin, and now here I was in the Gila releasing Mexican wolves.

The Gila offers a diversity of habitats from mountains reaching over 9,000 feet to deep canyons. For someone who grew up a few hundred feet

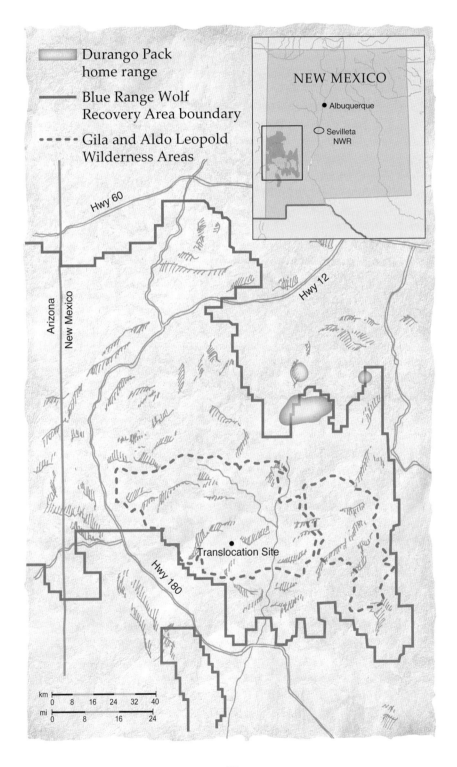

above sea level, the lack of oxygen is very noticeable when hiking. There are arid grasslands and mixed conifer forests of spruce, fir and aspen, but pinion-juniper woodlands and ponderosa pine dominate most of the area. Unlike the Midwestern forests, there is very little undergrowth, making walking through the forest relatively easy as long as one avoids running into an occasional cactus.

Nick Smith, a retired New Mexico Department of Game and Fish employee and ex-Interagency Field Team member, packed U.S. Fish and Wildlife Service volunteer, Jen Timmer, and me in on his mules. I was a novice rider, and this was my first time meeting Nick. He gave me the gentlest mule, but, unfortunately, he did not know how short I am and wasn't prepared with a small saddle. I rode with my legs sticking out at an odd angle, my feet pretty much dangling for the entire five-hour, thirteen-mile ride. It took three days for my inner thigh muscles to recover.

Nick camped with us that night, leaving us two novices on our own the following morning. Each morning Jen and I hiked a mile up the dirt trail to check radio signals to verify the wolves were still in the soft release pen. The rest of the time we read, did crossword puzzles, sat by the fire, hiked, collected firewood, filtered water to drink and got paid for it. The water actually tasted okay, but it smelled like we were drinking Wisconsin lake water. Every other day we were to observe the wolves for five minutes to make sure they were okay and still had water. For these observations we hid behind a tree and watched the wolves run laps in the pen. Jen and I did just as were told; like they could not smell or hear us coming?

Female 924 was pregnant, and the best estimates suggested she would whelp around April 27. At the time, it was the U.S. Fish and Wildlife Service solicitor's opinion that the wolf could not be allowed to give birth in the pen. If that happened, it would have been a captive birth and her pups would have had no wild experience. Hence, they would not be allowed to reside in New Mexico. We had a plan; release the wolves two days before she was scheduled to whelp. So close to whelping, she would dig a den in the Gila Wilderness, give birth and stay anchored in the Gila Wilderness, establishing their territory. Male 973 and female 924 had a different plan.

On April 24 Nick returned to pack Jen and me out. The wolves were still in the pen. We tied up one side of the pen to create an opening for them. This was my first time releasing Mexican wolves into the wild, a thrilling, goose-bump forming moment. Later that night, sitting at the campfire, we heard coyotes howl and yip way off in the distance behind us. Then we heard a howl in front of us. I didn't even think to get out the telemetry equipment to see if it was one of our Durango wolves. In retrospect I am sure it was one of them.

The next morning, while Jen and Nick packed up the mules, I hiked up the trail to check the wolves' radio signals. Not more than fifty feet down the trail from camp I encountered wolf tracks. I followed these tracks from the camp back to the area where we checked for their daily radio signals. The release pen was empty. I would like to think they stopped by camp the previous night to thank us for their freedom after enduring several months of incarceration at the captive facility, the mule ride, and all the other terrifying things they had endured. On May 1 the weekly telemetry flight located the pair over thirty miles northeast of the release site where female 924 had previously been removed in 2006. She had gone home.

It didn't take long for the citizens of Catron County to become angry with us, yet again, for our deception. The Catron County paper reported: "Although the Catron County Commission had been informed that the female wolf was to be released on April 25 along with the male wolf, *in fact* the two wolves were released April 24, according to an Arizona Game and Fish news release." I admit that I released the wolves a day early, but I have yet to figure out any importance to what amounted to be a seven-hour difference. The locals saw it as another in a litany of examples of how the government is operating covertly and withholding information from them in regard to the wolf project. The pen was opened around 5 p.m. on April 24, not April 25. I feel better now that everything is out in the open.

The next day, Catron County demanded that female 924 be removed as an "imminent danger," stating in a letter sent to the U.S. Fish and Wildlife Service that if the female was not removed within 24 hours the county would take matters into their own hands. The letter referenced the county ordinance I saw back when registering to vote.

Not only was female 924 a depredating wolf, the county alleged that she had bitten a member of the Interagency Field Team and should have been euthanized. The person was actually scratched while handling the wolf. County officials said that they wanted to prevent problems "as opposed to waiting for one of these wolves to kill a child, and then what?" The County Manager went on to say, "We're derelict in our duties," in an Associated Press release. The Catron County Wolf Investigator and Catron County began posting their own signs: "Dangerous Wolf in Area—Use Caution."

The two wolves didn't show much fear of people, but neither did they approach people or let people approach them. The wolves were simply indifferent. They didn't see humans as a threat and would either watch people or just walk right on by.

One day I was out tracking the pair when I pulled over to wait out a lightning storm. Upon disconnecting the vehicle-mounted antenna from the receiver I noticed male 973's signal still coming in loud and clear on the receiver. I looked out the driver's side truck window and there, on the hillside amongst the pinion-juniper trees, was 973 watching me! He was lying on his stomach with his front legs stretched out.

The female wasn't much different. Shortly after their release I was searching for the den hoping to get a pup count. While I had no successful count that day, I managed to view the female as she moved from tree to tree, keeping an eye on me as I searched the area. These wolves weren't stalking or approaching me; they weren't growling or barking; their hackles weren't raised. They were literally just sitting there, watching me, with what appeared to be curiosity and a little leeriness, ready to run, just in case. I never felt threatened by either one and don't quite understand why other people do.

I am aware of wild-born Wisconsin gray wolves behaving similarly. A member of that state's Bear Bluff Pack was seen peeing on truck tires at the shop of a cranberry farm. Another wolf, a female named "Flint," raised a litter of pups along a state highway. When a car approached, the pups would get up, move off to the side, and move back as soon as it passed. Like these wild-born wolves, the Durango pair appeared to be lackadaisical, but I don't believe they terrorized a family, causing posttraumatic stress disorder, as Catron County residents claimed.

Unfortunately, the Durango pair established a den about a half mile from private property, and about five miles from a house. This forty-acre parcel of private property was within the Gila National Forest and completely surrounded by federal land. It didn't take long before we got the first reports of wolf tracks near the private property. The people living on this section of private property were given several different options for hazing the wolves, including fladry, flagging hung from an electrical wire. The flagging hangs down and blows in the wind. If the wolves try to walk under it, they get a small shock. But the people didn't want it.

Most people in the county don't prefer this technique of hazing wolves. Admittedly, it takes maintenance to unwind the tangled flags after a high wind, and elk will consistently knock it down. It is also inconvenient to have it dangling across driveways, necessitating one to get out and open up a makeshift gate every time one enters or exits. It can also make a yard look like a used car sales lot. Cracker shells fired from a shotgun are also available, but most rejected these devices for fear of starting a fire. Shot in the general direction of a wolf, the shells explode with a loud bang much like a huge firecracker. If aimed correctly, the shells go off and fall harmlessly to the ground, but in this arid environment the landowners' concerns had merit.

Not surprisingly, the complainants weren't always the most reasonable or cooperative. Just as unreasonable, an interagency field team member suggested I park a camper trailer and stay out there, "so you can be available to the people." No way was I going to sit in a camper trailer twenty-four hours a day, waiting for these residents to knock on the door to say "we need you." This was a prime example of the ends to which wolf project personnel were willing to appease the demands of some area residents.

The ranching family wasn't seeing the wolves, just their tracks, but the Durango Pack was labeled a "nuisance" by the Adaptive Management Oversight Committee and the field team was required to haze them. Since they claimed the wolves were coming at night, we worked at night.

One Monday night in early June, temporary summer employee, Angela Dassow, and I arrived at the site at 7:00 p.m. and stayed out until 7:00 a.m. By that time I had been up for twenty-two hours. We found the wolves around 9:30 p.m. and parked on a forest service road across from the private property. Every half hour we checked the wolves' signals. This approach, I thought, was more reasonable. If we were to follow the wolves all night, we would always be behind them. By the time we would catch up to the pair, they would have already walked through the yard. Sitting out all night long wasn't as bad as I thought, considering I had the brilliant idea of bringing our laptops. We sat in the truck and watched DVDs to stay awake and pass the time. It was like our own private drive-in movie theatre in the middle of a national forest.

Eventually, we were spending so much time monitoring the Durango Pack that we started working nights alone. We couldn't afford to allocate all the staff time on just one pack. The first night Angela was alone she didn't hear the wolves. But the dogs at the residence barked a couple of times, causing the cowboy to come out of his house and walk around the yard.

The second night, the dogs barked again. This time Angela, with night vision binoculars, saw a mountain lion walk through the yard. She told the people about it the next day. The lady of the house thought it was pretty cool, and the cowboy commented how that hadn't happened since the previous autumn. We weren't following their logic: mountain lions—good, wolves—bad.

On the third evening, the people approached Angela. They had talked to our field team leader, complaining that we should not be parking across from their property at night. It caused the dogs to bark, preventing them from getting a good night's sleep. In checking with our field team leader I learned the cowboy had told him no such thing. To be cooperative, over the next two nights Angela parked a half mile or so away from the house. The wolves never approached the area while Angela was there.

I took watch the last night, and to be especially cooperative, I parked one and a half miles away from the house on the road adjoining the south side of their property. The dog kennel was attached to the house's north side. I could not see the house from where I was parked.

At 2:30 a.m. two vehicles drove up to my truck. The cowboy got out of the first truck and sauntered over to me. He told me how I should not be sitting up here, but instead with the wolves. I tried to explain to him that I was here to watch his yard and keep the wolves off the property. He switched the subject to how we were keeping him up at night by causing his dogs to bark. I was a little confused considering it was 2:30 a.m. and he hadn't even been home since I got there at 7:00 p.m. I told him I was aware of his concern, which is why I parked such a distance from his house, out of sight of his dog kennel and his house. He offered no rebuttals to anything I said.

He then told me I was wasting my time tonight, the wolves wouldn't be at his house and I should just leave, so I did. Over the seven-night vigil maintained by Angela and me the wolves did not walk near their property. Several days later I was told by a federal agent that the cowboy was complaining we were keeping him up at night, shooting off the shotgun outside his house, because the wolves were on his property.

Amazingly, the day after we concluded the seven-night stint at this property, the wolves reportedly started showing up every night. Several project members, including some on the Adaptive Management Oversight Committee, thought this was an odd coincidence and wondered whether the people were lying or doing something to entice them onto the property. At this point, Catron County got involved because, of course, we weren't doing anything. The County claimed the 13-year-old daughter was suffering from posttraumatic stress disorder after seeing wolves in her yard. I was told this is the reason this young lady carries a handgun.

Catron County served the U.S. Fish and Wildlife Service with a notice that if female Wolf 924 were not removed within 24 hours they would take action. In response, the Service requested a restraining order for the County. Given it was a Friday, the restraining order wouldn't be ready until the following week. The only thing we could do was monitor the Catron County Wolf Investigator and his activities until the restraining order could be served. Once served, if he did not comply with the order, federal marshals would arrest him and all the Catron County Commissioners.

I went out to monitor the Durango wolves the next day and, more importantly, keep an eye out for the Catron County Wolf Investigator. I didn't see him until I left the area late that afternoon, passing him on the road. He was carrying a cage trap in the back of his truck. He pulled over and wanted to chat. Normally I do. He is actually a very nice person; he just has a personal agenda that doesn't match mine. I didn't stop this day because I was forewarned he sometimes secretly tape-recorded conversations, editing portions to his advantage. I wanted no part in this. I left a message with a federal agent informing them I had seen the Catron County Wolf Investigator transporting a cage trap in his pickup. On Sunday morning I talked with the federal agents. They knew nothing of the trap, but they got him to admit to having the trap. It was on private land and he wouldn't say where.

The Catron County Wolf Investigator's camp was located on private land in a different section than where we had conducted the nighttime nuisance monitoring. This camp, however, was less than a half mile from the den. Cowhands had just completed castrating calves and notching the ears at this particular location, a normal practice in the ranching business. I could see the remains as I sat in my truck parked along the public road.

The Catron County Wolf Investigator can legally shoot a wolf in the act of killing a cow on private property. While monitoring this site he claimed to have taken twenty-nine photos of the wolves near his camp, proving the wolves were a danger to humans. I have witnessed male 973 walk through this particular spot. It was a common path to and from the den.

The federal agents informed me that the Wolf Investigator wanted all the wolf tracks in the yard back at the ranch house documented, but he made stipulations. The Wolf Investigator did not want me on the private property unless I was escorted by him. I was also told to stay away from the barn. This led the federal agents and me to believe that the trap was in the barn. For obvious reasons, I did not go.

On June 29, while I was away vacationing, a United States Department of Agriculture, Wildlife Services agent confirmed a cattle depredation in the area. This was female Wolf 924's third strike in 365 days. According to Standard Operating Procedure 13 she "was out." Her previous depredations on August 25 and November 13, 2006 were still held against her. On July 5 female Wolf 924 was lethally removed by Wildlife Services, leaving male 973 to raise the pups on his own.

Shortly after the female's death, while scouting locations to set trail cameras and a food cache to help the pups, I stumbled upon a rendezvous site. Four pups bounced up out of the grass and took off in the direction of the male wolf's signal. As the summer passed, trail camera photos confirmed the presence of only two pups. By the end of October only one pup was left. In mid-October a dispersing female from the Luna Pack, number 1047, found male Wolf 973 and his pup. She had traveled approximately 25 straight-line miles from her old territory before joining the Durango Pack.

Throughout September and October wolves were once again reported near the house. Though not seen on the private property, we did pick up some telemetry signals and mostly tracks in the area surrounding the property. Interagency Field Team members continued to pull overnight monitoring/hazing shifts. I went back to parking on the forest service road directly across from the house to watch for wolf activity. On October 25, I received a call from the field team leader. He relayed a message that the cowboy reported the wolves had come to his yard after I left my overnight shift. The cowboy stated there were wolf tracks on top of his truck tracks that very morning.

I had documented the cowboy leaving his house at 8:00 a.m. Since I had not picked up the wolves' radio signals near the house all night long, I had wanted to locate them before leaving the area for the day. As I left at 8:50 a.m., I saw two hounds at the end of his driveway walking up and down the road. When I drove by, the hounds ran up the driveway and back into the yard. Of course, I cursed and kicked myself for not having a camera to document this.

I came out again at midnight, sat all night, and waited for the wolves. They did not appear. The next morning, the lady of the house drove over to where I was sitting and asked me if I would come down to their property to "legally document" the "wolf" tracks that were made the previous morning. They showed me all the tracks. All were the tracks I watched the hounds make the previous morning. They insisted they hadn't let their dogs out since May. I don't know if all the previous reports of tracks made on that forty-acre private parcel belonged to the dogs, but I am certain that those tracks on that particular day were made by dogs. Given the established territory of the wolves where this particular piece of private property was situated, surely wolf tracks would be expected at times.

Meanwhile the Durango male and the pup were causing legitimate problems at a neighboring ranch house. Wolf 973, with his pup, frequented that ranch to eat dog food which was stored in the open barn. They walked around the house, defecated in the yard, scent marked the ATV, and lay about in the sun. This is not appropriate wolf behavior. The neighboring rancher did not report the problems immediately, but had waited several days to videotape the wolves, documenting the evidence. The Interagency Field Team was denied access on this private property to try to remedy the situation.

Male Wolf 973's signal was heard for the last time on November 1, 2007, 190 days after his release. The signal of the newly arrived female Wolf, 1047, coincidentally disappeared that same day. The pup never carried a radio collar. The Durango Pack was officially listed as "fate unknown." Genetic testing of wolves captured since their disappearance has failed to confirm the existence of any surviving offspring from the Durango Pack.

Thanks to the Durango Pack, I was assigned my first and only backcountry camping trip into the Gila Wilderness. I set my first pair of wolves free and observed my first litter of Mexican wolf pups running in the wild. It was also my introduction into what would be several years of working with the local anti-wolf sentiment and the uphill battles of the Mexican wolf recovery program.

Most residents of Catron County were usually very cordial and polite, and all are certainly entitled to their opinions. It was very frustrating when their opinions were based not on fact, but on misconceptions and distortions, and, sadly, some downright untruths. Some county residents didn't mind the wolves. While they likely didn't support wolf reintroduction, they could be described as indifferent or impartial. Some residents knew the outspoken anti-wolf people were irrational, but as neighbors they felt it inappropriate to speak out against them.

Locals don't express the same outrage when black bears, coyotes, or mountain lions depredate on livestock. Since these animals never disappeared from New Mexico, ranchers have learned to coexist with them. Coyotes can be killed year round and hunting seasons exist for bears and lions. A Catron County local once asked me what I thought it would take for the wolf hatred to fade. I told him only when sufficient time had passed, when there had been a couple of generations who have lived with wolves on the landscape, and when residents could no longer sense the experience of government "forcing" wolves upon them.

The Adaptive Management Oversight Committee approved the removal of 18 wolves from New Mexico for livestock depredations in 2007. At year's end a minimum population count totaled 23 wolves in New Mexico. A reintroduced wolf population can't grow with such heavy-handed removals so early in the recovery stage. Residents never should have been told that "bad" livestock killing wolves would be removed and only "good" wolves would be allowed to remain. Most wolves in the Gila have killed a cow, whether or not we catch them. It is also unrealistic to expect that wolves can be manipulated to stay off isolated private parcels located within a national forest, just as is it unreasonable to insist wolves stay where placed. I still believe in the possibility of success, but the project is dominated by decisions based on politics, not sound science and impartiality.

CHAPTER ELEVEN

Wolf 475 of the
Dog Killer Pack in Wisconsin

Adrian P. Wydeven

ADULT FEMALE WOLF 475 was not a particularly remarkable wolf. Missing were her lower canines and some outer incisors from a previous accident. This told me she wouldn't be around for long. Putting a collar on her would just be a way to figure out when she would die. Little did we know this wolf was destined to set a new record for the length of time a radio collared wolf remained on the air in Wisconsin; and her Shanagolden Pack became the most infamous dog killing pack in Wisconsin.

Wolves began recolonizing Wisconsin in the mid-1970's. By 2004 the wolf population had grown to 373 wolves. Wolf 475 and the Shanagolden Pack roamed the Great Divide District in the Chequamegon National Forest in northwestern Wisconsin. By 2004 the forest was almost solidly occupied by wolf pack territories.

Here upland forests consist of sugar maple, basswood, yellow birch, hemlock, white ash, white pine, red pine and northern red oak, with quaking and large-leaf aspen, white birch and balsam fir dominating younger forests. Lowlands consist of white cedar, black ash, balsam fir, white spruce, black spruce, tamarack and alders. The topography is gently rolling. Hardwood ridges align in a diagonal southwest to northeast direction following the flow of the retreating Chippewa lobe of the Wisconsin glacier as it receded about 10,000 years ago. Sedge meadow, bogs and open lakes occur in low areas throughout the region; lakes are more abundant in the western parts of the district. Upland forests are interspersed with small openings of bracken fern grasslands. I lived in the Lake Namakagon area, northwest of the Shanagolden Pack. My office in Park Falls was to the southwest, and, thus, several times a week my forty-three mile commute to the office took me through the northern portions of her territory.

State Highway 77, the only major highway in the district, cuts through the Great Divide District. Another road, County GG, extends north to south along the eastern side intersecting with Highway 77 at the small unincorporated town of Clam Lake. It boasts three bars, one gas station, and a cluster of houses. Seasonal and year-round homes dot surrounding lakes.

The pack's name derives from Shanagolden Township. Eighty percent of the township occurs on National Forest lands. The remainder, mostly on the eastern margin, is where most of its one-hundred and fifty residents live. White-tailed deer are the Shanagolden Pack's most important prey. An elk herd, reintroduced to the area in 1995, roams mainly west of the Shanagolden Pack's territory, but occasionally these elk and the Shanagolden Pack meet up.

The Shanagolden Pack got its start back in the winter of 1999-2000 when a pair of wolves was picked up in the area on one of our winter track surveys. Two to three wolves occupied the area through the winter of 2002-2003. Either they produced no pups, or few survived. I was, therefore, surprised to encounter the tracks of nine to eleven wolves in this area during the winter of 2003-2004. This could only mean some six to eight pups were produced and managed to survive. It was time to capture and collar a wolf so we could monitor the Shanagolden Pack more carefully.

On the morning of June 24, I met up with Forest Service biologist Dan Eklund and his supervisor Geoff Chandler in Clam Lake. They were joining me on the trap line. It had been a cool night and was still in the low 40's as we headed east toward the trap line. Driving south off Highway 77, we passed our first trap. No activity. As we approached the second trap we knew we were in luck. A wolf had stepped into the trap, pulled it out of the ground, and wrapped the trap chain around a good sized paper birch tree just off the road. I prepared a Ketamine/Xylazine mix for the syringe; Dan grabbed the noose pole. I approached the wolf from the right of the birch tree. Dan moved in on the wolf's left, allowing me to swiftly inject the syringe needle into her rump. Upon impact she swung her head my way in dismay.

The wolf was tranquilized within five minutes. We spent the next hour processing the wolf, which included placing a collar on her. She became female Wolf 475F. We collected blood for disease testing, implanted an identification microchip, took various measurements, examined her carefully for any injuries, and treated minor injuries related to trapping her.

Her enlarged nipples revealed that she had recently nursed. She weighed 60 pounds, about ten pounds less than the average adult female and had lost her lower canines and outer incisors from a previous injury, possibly a kick from a deer or elk. Wear on her teeth suggested she was at least three or four years old. She may have even been one of the original pair that settled the area four winters earlier. If so, she was five years old. At 9:36 a.m. I injected Yohimbine into the wolf, and within about three minutes she was stumbling off into the forest.

The same day we also caught a lactating female, 477F, from the adjacent Hungry Run Pack about ten miles to the southwest. Although in excellent condition and weighing 75 pounds, she died from complications associated with Sarcoptic mange three-and-a-half years later.

The following month I escorted a group of people on a tour and howl survey of wolf packs in the Clam Lake area. Sponsored through the Wisconsin Natural Resources Foundation, the tour was an opportunity to teach about wolves, show participants where wolves lived, and, hopefully, hear some wolves howl at night. We loaded up a locally rented school bus and spent the afternoon touring the forest. In the early evening we sampled some good food at a local restaurant. I hoped that perhaps local merchants connecting with people from across the state could serve as a form of ecotourism, alerting these local businesses that travelers were willing to pay for opportunities to encounter wolves and other wildlife in their area.

For our wolf-howl tour we focused on the neighboring Hungry Run Pack area. We stopped at one mile intervals along the various fire lanes. Getting people to quietly exit a bus, walk about 150 feet away, and gather along a forest road in the dark, is somewhat challenging. Our first three stops were unsuccessful, but people were starting to get the hang of the routine, and were enjoying the beautiful night view of the summer sky poking through the dark forest canopy.

At our fourth stop, a bout of howling performed by my wife, Sarah Boles, and I elicited a full chorus howl about a half mile off. The night air filled with vocalizations of wolf pups and their high pitched voices trying to compete and join in with the low howls of the adults. There were at least three adults and three pups. The wolf response location was close to where we caught Wolf 477 the previous month. We attempted to get the Shanagolden Pack to howl on our return. This night though, Wolf 475 and her pack remained silent.

A few weeks later, in early August, a couple of bear hunters from central Wisconsin were training hounds within the Shanagolden territory when they ran into trouble. Shortly after treeing a bear, three hounds were attacked by wolves. By the time the hunters arrived two were dead and a third was seriously injured and died soon thereafter.

The tradition of black bear hunting began in Wisconsin before the wolves returned. Hunters may use baits to condition bears to their presence beginning in mid-April. From July 1 to August 31 bear hound hunters are allowed to train hounds on bears throughout wild lands in northern Wisconsin; at the same time wolves occupy rendezvous sites where the packs' pups are located. The hunting season starts between the first and second week in September and lasts four weeks ending in early to mid-October. The long baiting season provides opportunities for wolves to also acclimate to them. In addition to being protective of their pups at summer home sites, wolves are also defensive of their food. Sometimes the same hounds are used to hunt coyotes, so some might naively follow wolves until

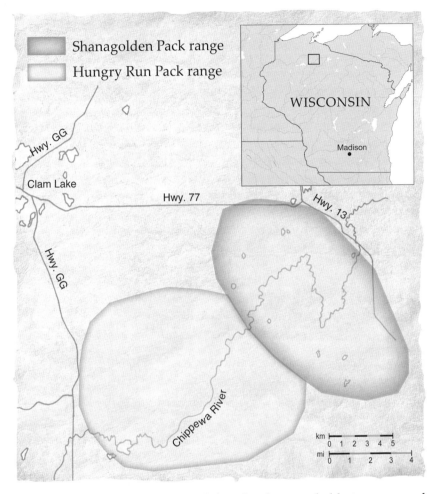

Shanagolden Pack range

Hungry Run Pack range

WISCONSIN

Madison

Hwy. GG

Clam Lake

Hwy. 77

Hwy. 13

Hwy. GG

Chippewa River

km
0 1 2 3 4 5

mi
0 1 2 3 4

they actually encounter them, and then the chase probably turns around. For these reasons hounds are especially vulnerable to wolf depredation.

In 2004 wolves were down-listed as a threatened species by the U.S. Fish and Wildlife Service in Wisconsin, allowing U.S. Department of Agriculture, Wildlife Services and the Wisconsin Department of Natural Resources to euthanize wolves at depredation sites if necessary. Lethal removal of wolves was only used in situations involving depredation of livestock on private land or pet dogs near residential areas. The state agency reimbursed pet owners for domestic dogs, including hunting hounds killed by wolves, for values up to $2500. Because of this all incidents had to be investigated and confirmed.

This was my fourteenth year leading wolf recovery and management programs for the Wisconsin Department of Natural Resources. By this time certain patterns of wolf pack depredation on hunting hounds were evident. Packs were likely to continue hound depredations during the same year and in the following year. In addition to paying for losses, the agency put out a news release alerting hunters about a hound depredation.

Bear hunters are probably as territorial as their canid competitors. Most groups traditionally had used the same training and hunting area year after year, and, in being displaced, they were liable to move into an area already in use by another bear hunting party. We did not expect hunters to totally avoid these areas. Our hope was that hunters would modify their behavior by avoiding areas near the immediate depredation site, stay closer to their hounds, and check more carefully for wolf tracks before releasing hounds at bait sites.

The day following the attack I received a call from Dave Ruid at Wildlife Services. He had been in charge of the follow-up investigation on these hounds. I prepared a news release of the new wolf attack that included "caution areas" outlining roads that approximated the extent of the Shanagolden Pack's territory. On my way home that evening I dropped off some of the news releases in several taverns and the restaurant where a month earlier I had dined with people for our wolf howl and tour.

I left town about 9:00 p.m.—late enough to start howling for wolves. I found Wolf 475, with four or more other adults and at least three pups, right in the area where the depredation had occurred the day before. Attacks seemed to occur at or near pack rendezvous sites, the home sites where pups were left. Adult wolves vigorously protect the pups from threats such as other wolves, other predators, and hounds. It was no coincidence that hound depredations occurred shortly after the start of the bear hound training period in early July.

The attack on August 5 by the Shanagolden Pack was the first such attack on hounds in 2004. The news release had little effect. On August 7 another attack occurred. Three hounds had been chasing a bear. When they crossed a road only two hounds were following. Aided by tracking collars typically worn by hounds, the hunters picked up a signal from the third hound, and they heard wolves howling in that direction. They soon found its skull, part of its vertebrae, and bones of one hind leg. Ruid inspected the site the next day. Wolf 475's locations that week placed her a half mile from the August 4 depredation and a little over two miles from the August 7 depredation sites.

On August 20 two more hounds were killed within a mile of the first depredation site. Wolf 475 had been only two miles north of the new depredation site when located by a Department of Natural Resources pilot two days earlier.

Following each depredation new news releases were put out. On August 23 one hound from a group of five was attacked, but the hunter was able to disrupt the attack before it was killed—it died later at a veterinary clinic. He saw at least two adult wolves and three pups chasing his other hounds. All seven hounds had been killed within about two miles of the Shanagolden Pack's rendezvous site.

The bear hound training period ended on August 31. I had hoped with the bear hunting season in September, when wolf use of rendezvous sites declines, we would not have any additional depredations. But on September 26 it happened again! Two hounds were killed five miles north of the pack's territorial core where all the previous depredations had occurred. The wolves may have been traveling near the northern edge of their territory when the unfortunate dogs just happened to stumble into them. Then again, Wolf 475's most recent locations were documented in the week prior to this most recent attack and close to the site. Maybe the pack had a late season rendezvous site near the northern edge of the territory.

The end of the bear hunting season came in mid-October. By then nearly all wolf packs become more nomadic within their respective territories, reducing risks of hound attacks. Some hound hunting for coyotes and bobcats continued into fall and winter, but to a much lesser degree than for bear hunting.

The spate of news releases generated some unnecessary concerns about wolves. That fall I handled several calls from grouse hunters worried about hunting with their dogs in the Clam Lake area, and I reassured them that risks were mostly to hounds. Although ruffed grouse and woodcock hunters course over the same forests beginning in late September, only one attack on bird hunting dogs had occurred in Wisconsin up to that time. Later that winter, as I prepared for another wolf howl tour for the next summer, I called the same restaurant where the group had dined the previous summer. The owner was not interested in serving a group associated with wolves. He had apparently read about the Shanagolden Pack. His bar-restaurant was a favorite hangout for bear hunters, and our $900 of business in one hour was not worth it. So much for trying to promote wolf ecotourism!

The agency's advice that hunters use bells on their hounds and the news releases perhaps had some effect. No hound depredations occurred within Wolf 475's territory between 2005 and 2007, despite high numbers counted within the pack. Nine were observed in the winter of 2005, ten in 2006, and four to eight in 2007, a time when mid-winter pack size in the state averaged four wolves. This indicated good pup survival each year. Wolf 475 was likely the pack's breeding female and, apparently, was good at providing for her pups.

After a several year hiatus 2008 came along. On July 27, 2008 a hound, separated from the rest of a group of hounds, was killed by wolves. The same hunter had also lost a hound back in 2004. Wolf 475 was four miles southeast of the depredation site a few days earlier. While she may not have been involved in the attack, the depredation was well within her territory.

The Shanagolden Pack wasn't finished. Three depredations occurred in August and one each in September and October. The depredations were distributed broadly across the Shanagolden territory, but all were confined to six miles of each other in the core area south of Highway 77. At least three of the hounds had bells. One hound was attacked by wolves as it was leaving a legal bait site set for bears.

Bear hunters seem to accept occasional losses of hounds to bears as part of the risks of the chase, but tend to be very resentful when wolves kill hounds. Loss of hounds to bears is possibly much higher than those killed by wolves, but there is no formal reporting system and no payments for those losses. Wolf kills on hounds are usually more gruesome because, unlike omnivorous black bears, wolves often eat the hounds and disarticulate the bodies.

In 2009 the Shanagolden Pack attacked hounds on three occasions during bear hunting season. The attacks followed a pattern similar to previous years. All occurred within the core of the pack territory.

On April 6, 2010 Wolf 475 was located in the central portion of the pack territory near the pack's traditional den site. But over the next month and a half she moved northeast about five miles near residential areas in the Town of Shanagolden. Was she attending a den on her own? In the past, deposed alpha females have attempted to raise pups by themselves or perhaps with a helper from the pack. We have had cases where such pups have become nuisance animals because they have learned to rely on food sources near people. Generally, these second litters on the edge of pack territory are unsuccessful.

On May 16 a black lab dog was attacked at a nearby residence and dragged fifty yards into nearby forest cover along the Chippewa River. Previous to this attack the Shanagolden Pack had only attacked bear hounds. Pet dog attacks often seemed to occur early in the morning or in the evening when dogs are let out to void. This coincides with daily peaks in activity levels of wolves. Wolf 475 was only a mile from the dog kill site the following day. Whether she attacked it herself or other wolves aided in the attack, we do not know.

This type of depredation would normally have precipitated a lethal control action. But by this time wolves were once again listed as a federally endangered species in Wisconsin as a result of a 2009 lawsuit settlement. The couple who had lost the dog also had two small children and felt this was a human safety situation. After discussion, it was decided to wait to see if additional incidents occurred. As it turned out this was not necessary.

Wolf 475F again traveled extensively through her territory in the summer of 2010. In June she concentrated in an area near the eastern edge of the national forest, possibly a rendezvous site. Later that same summer her movements expanded in a fairly broad portion on the east side of the Shanagolden Pack's territory.

On October 5, 2010 pilot Phil Miller was unable to pick up 475's signal. We were not surprised. The radio collar she wore had been functioning for six years, a new record for a radio worn by a Wisconsin wolf. But during his next flight her signal was heard, this time on mortality mode. The area was heavily forested private lands with scattered homes and old farm fields located on the east side of the township.

I tried approaching from several directions in late afternoon, but I was unable to get a radio signal at sites that seemed to be within a half mile. With darkness approaching and the need to have a conservation warden join me to access private land, I decided to return the following day.

The next afternoon I returned with Ashland warden supervisor Dave Oginski. It was cloudy with temperatures in the mid-50's. We drove down a rough gravel road into forested areas near the east side of the Chippewa River, parking the truck near the end of the road in a dense forest close to a gated driveway that led to a hunting cabin. Following an old railroad grade along the river, we walked about a half mile south toward the pilot's plotted location of Wolf 475. As we approached I turned the receiver on and we listened for the radio signal. A fairly strong signal came from nearby. Soon enough I found her.

She was lying on her left side. The sun had since come out, and I could hear the sound of flies buzzing about her. Her fur had bleached to near white since her capture six years earlier when she appeared gray. Maggots on her face and beneath her and the splashing of white wash on her side where ravens had scavenged from the carcass told us she had been dead for a week or more. Nothing at the carcass site hinted at any illegal activity. It appeared likely Wolf 475 arrived at this site on her own power.

We double bagged the remains into two plastic bags. I threw her onto my shoulders and began the half mile walk back to the vehicle. Dave offered to help carry her. I figured at this point there was no need for both of us to get smelly. Thankfully, it was a cool day.

A month later Wisconsin Department of Natural Resources pathologist, Nancy Businga, informed me that the advanced decomposition prevented a necropsy. A radiograph of the carcass was telling. It revealed 25 shotgun pellets about 3mm in size toward the hip and leg region. Still yet, her cause of death could not be fixed because of the lack of an official necropsy.

Paula Holahan, Curator of Mammals and Birds at the University of Wisconsin Zoology Museum, received 475's carcass and cleaned it. She then deposited it into the dermestid beetle colony to clean up the bones. The following April Holahan called with some interesting results. Wolf 475 had nine placental scars, indicating she had pups in the spring of 2010. Because of the advanced stage of decomposition, it was not possible to age the scars, so not all placental scars may have represented live births or have come from a single, relatively large litter.

Holahan also detected shotgun pellets. These represented at least three different events where Wolf 475 had been shot. At the time of her death 475 had lost all her lower incisors, and just a stub remained of the lower right canine, deterioration from the injuries we had recorded at the time of her capture. But that injury had not been caused by a kick from an ungulate as we had surmised. Instead it was caused by a shotgun blast that hit her in the lower jaw, probably before the wolf was two years old. Shotgun pellets from other events were embedded within her skull, scapula, upper portions of the front leg (humerus), and portions of the hind leg (tibia). A recent shot to the side of the skull may have contributed to her death. Based on this excellent assessment, I changed Wolf 475's mortality classification to illegally killed.

Wolf 475F was on the air exactly six years, three months, and twenty-one days. The size of her Shanagolden Pack territory varied yearly from 54 to 86 square miles. During this interval the Shanagolden Pack injured one and killed eighteen domestic canids. Of the 108 to 181 packs in the state at that time, seven to twenty-one packs were involved in attacks on hounds yearly. The Shanagolden Pack accounted for thirteen percent of 141 hounds killed and 56 injured by Wisconsin wolf packs between 2004 and 2010.

Wolf depredations on hounds peaked in Wisconsin in 2006 with twenty-five hounds killed, declining to only eight in 2012. Our news release system may have helped reduce the number of hounds killed, but probably escalated overall concerns about wolves. In 2010 the Department of Natural Resources developed a direct email notification system to inform hunters of hound attacks. This approach focuses on contacting people with an immediate need to know, while not exacerbating wolf concerns by the general public.

Wolf 475 was probably over ten years old at the time of her death. She produced pups in at least seven years, despite a major disabling injury at an early age causing the loss of her lower canines and, eventually, all her lower incisors. Whether this altered her behavior and made her more aggressive toward dogs is speculative, but obviously the defense of litters of pups factors into this. That she survived and was productive indicates the toughness of some of these wolves. Her survival reflects, as well, the benefits of group living. Without her pack she would have died a long time ago. She was indeed an amazing wolf.

CHAPTER TWELVE

Elvis and Chewy

Donald Lonsway, Dean Beyer, and Brian Roell

 IT WAS THE SPRING OF 1999, mid-May, and the temperatures were finally staying above freezing every night, all night. That meant it was time to begin capturing and radio collaring wolves. Radio collars are one of the tools of the trade. They allow us to glimpse the life and doings of the animals we find so interesting. In this case, we were interested in collaring a wolf from a pack that lived on the west side of Lake Gogebic. Creatively, we had named this group the West Lake Gogebic Pack. What can I say, we are an imaginative bunch.

Lake Gogebic is a large lake, covering almost twenty-one square miles. It is a great landmark when locating wolves from the air. On a clear day it can be seen from thirty miles away. It is nestled in the Ottawa National Forest, a picturesque forest setting. The area sounds wonderful and peaceful. It should be, except a lot of weird things seem to happen around Lake Gogebic. So many in fact, we have learned to expect the unexpected when working in that area.

Our overall goal was to radio collar one wolf in as many packs as possible. The wolf population was recovering nicely in Michigan, but both state and federal governments still listed them as an endangered species. To remove them from the federal list, we needed to demonstrate that over 100 or more wolves existed in Wisconsin and Michigan combined for a minimum of five years. Removal from the state list required 200 or more wolves for five years. Thus, the most important piece of information was an annual estimate of population size.

How do radio collared wolves help us estimate wolf abundance? We primarily base our estimates of wolf numbers on a winter track count. Radio collared wolves help us identify the boundaries of wolf territories. Once territory boundaries are known, we assume wolf tracks found within these areas differ from the tracks of those we find outside a particular wolf territory. Is it a perfect system? Hell no! As scientists, we realize every measurement has some error associated with it. Wolves do not always stay within their territories. Sometimes they trespass into other pack territories. Fortunately for us biologists, through the aid of an airplane, collared wolves provide counts of packs of which they are members. These can then be compared with track counts of the same pack, and over the years these comparisons verified that track counts work pretty well.

I, Don Lonsway, had just started working for the U.S. Department of Agriculture, Wildlife Services after working on wolves seasonally for the Department of Natural Resources (DNR) for almost ten years. The focus of our work was different from Wildlife Services staff in neighboring states. In addition to the normal work on wildlife damage control, we were heavily involved in wolf research and monitoring.

I had strung a line of traps along a series of two-track tote trails west of Lake Gogebic on May 20. I had located a wolf den nearby the year before and, based on the tracks and scat I was finding, I felt confident that I would catch a wolf soon. It turned out I was right.

The next day I caught a male wolf weighing 77 pounds. It was a perfect day for catching and handling a wolf. The temperature was 55 degrees Fahrenheit with heavy cloud cover; conditions that help keep the wolf from overheating. Immobilization drugs often interfere with the animal's pant reflex and their ability to regulate body temperature. Therefore, we monitor body temperatures closely. A wolf's normal body temperature is about 101 degrees Fahrenheit. This male wolf maintained a temperature around 100 degrees during the handling process.

While in the trap the wolf had chewed on nearby sticks and brush stems. As part of the handling process, we always check the roof of the mouth, having found sticks occasionally wedged across their palate between the teeth. Sure enough, I found and removed two pencil-sized sticks. I fitted the wolf with a radio collar and put tags 108 and 109 in the ears. His left front foot had been the one caught in the trap. It looked okay, with only one small cut on the top of the foot. I treated the wound and administered a shot of penicillin.

Our collared wolves are identified by a four-digit number. The first two digits identify the county in which we captured the wolf. In this case, 27 is the numeric code for Gogebic County. The last two digits simply record the sequence of wolves captured in each county. In this case 03 indicated he was the third wolf captured in Gogebic County. A subsequent report from the DNR lab showing Wolf 2703 to be five years old, based on a count of growth rings in a section of the root of a premolar tooth extracted for that purpose. Almost exactly an hour after the drugs immobilized the wolf, I gave him an injection of a reversal drug. About fifteen minutes later Wolf 2703 got up and walked away.

The wolf was very calm in the trap and the entire handling process went smoothly. This worried me. It has been my experience that when something goes well, something bad will happen in short order. This is such a common occurrence that I have given it a moniker: "hero to zero." One minute you are a hero, and the next minute you're a zero. In this case,

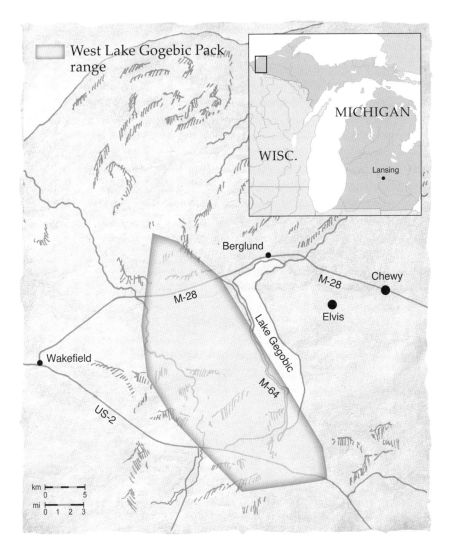

West Lake Gogebic Pack range

MICHIGAN

WISC.

Lansing

Berglund

M-28

M-28

Chewy

Elvis

Lake Gogebic

Wakefield

M-64

US-2

km
0   5
mi
0 1 2 3

the zero took a while to catch up with me.

After the wolf moved off, I jumped in my truck to finish checking my trap line. Along the way, I called Dean Beyer, wildlife research biologist for the Michigan DNR and coordinator of the state's wolf research work. I wanted to let him know we had another wolf on the air so he could tell the pilot to begin locating 2703 along with the other collared wolves. Dean's response was predictable, "Great, now tighten up and catch a few more!"

We monitored Wolf 2703 for about three years and two months. In that time, we located him 222 times. He stayed within the West Lake Gogebic territory which encompassed about 140 square miles and stretched about 18 miles from north to south and about eight miles east to west. Often wolves use roads, especially major roads, as part of their territory boundary. Wolf 2703 apparently did not read the manual. His territory crossed two primary highways, M-28 on the north end and US 2 on the south end. His habit of crossing these highways put him at risk.

On July 27, 2000 the phone rang at 6:00 a.m. Fortunately, I was up drinking coffee. The caller was Bob Evans, a wildlife biologist with the United States Forest Service. He had taken a call reporting a wolf/car accident on M-28 near Wapato Creek. The driver reported the wolf was wearing a radio collar and that the wolf was limping before he hit it. The wolf had been feeding on a road-killed deer and spooked as the car approached, causing him to run the wrong way and hit the car. I quickly gathered my telemetry gear and drove to the area.

I found the dead deer and determined that Wolf 2703 was very close. Collars such as his have a mortality switch. If the collar remains motionless for more than four hours, the pulse rate or number of beeps per minute speeds up and we can tell whether a wolf is alive or dead. The collar was still in active mode. Not knowing when the accident had occurred, I didn't know if sufficient time had elapsed for the mortality mode to switch on. I decided to return later in the day to check. Returning that afternoon, I noticed that wolves had dragged the deer carcass deep into the woods. The wolf's collar was still in active mode.

Almost two years later, July 7, 2002 I received a call from the Gogebic County Sheriff reporting that a collared wolf had been hit by a car on US 2 about one-half mile east of the M 64 intersection. I was sure Wolf 2703 had been struck a second time. Over the past two weeks, I had received several reports of a limping, gray-faced collared wolf, hanging out in that area. Grabbing the receiver and antenna, I headed out. By the time I arrived Wolf 2703 had already moved off about a mile. His collar was active. It appeared he had survived his second encounter with a vehicle.

About that same time I discovered that Lake Gogebic had its very own Wolf Theater, and the gray-faced male, Wolf 2703, was one of the actors. In mid-July I received reports of adult and pup wolves acting boldly around roads and homes on the west shore of the lake. I had hoped the wolves were just moving the pups to a new rendezvous site. In that case the sightings would stop. But the reports kept coming in. The last day of July a woman who lived on the lake called and reported seeing thirteen wolves, including six pups, on M-64 near Marshal Creek. I decided to spend some time in the area and figure out what these wolves were up to.

Poking around the area a couple of days later I drove into a gravel pit close to where the woman sighted the wolves and was surprised to find six pups and two collared adult wolves standing before me. One of the collared animals was a lactating female, but I could not detect a signal from her collar. The other collared wolf was a large gray-faced, limping wolf. Male 2703 was alive and as well-as-could-be following two vehicle collisions.

Surveying the gravel pit I shuddered when I saw the dog food, smoked and raw fish, hamburger, and table scraps that people had been leaving for the wolves. I called Jim Hammill, DNR Wildlife Supervisor, to relate my findings. Jim told me to "move those animals out of there."

That evening I returned to the pit and parked my truck out of sight. I not only wanted to see what the wolves were doing, I wanted to see what the people were doing. About a half hour before dark, cars and trucks started pulling into the pit. The people stayed in their vehicles. Then the wolves showed up. The pups began to feed on the food placed in the bottom of the pit, while the adults spaced themselves out along the rim and began howling. It was quite the show. I needed to close down this outdoor theatre, and fast, before something bad happened.

The next day I located the owner of the pit, and after I explained the activities at the "theatre," he agreed to lock the gate to the pit. I then posted signs warning the public to keep out. Desiring to collar some of the pups, I set five small traps for the pups in the bottom of the pit. Returning that evening I found fresh wolf sign but the traps remained undisturbed. The next morning two traps were sprung. Two adult wolves had stepped in them and pulled out. Once again, that hero to zero feeling returned.

The next morning I caught two male pups, padding the collars with foam before placing them on the pups to ensure the collars would be large enough when the animals were full grown. Two days later, I recaptured the collared pups plus another. I fitted this new pup with a padded collar and released it, then pulled the traps, deciding to give the pups a few days to recover from the stress of handling before I tried to chase them from the area.

The next few days I monitored the collared animals, learning their travel routes. The wolves were consistently crossing M-64 and using an old logging road to travel west; it looked like a good location to implement my plan. I gathered some gear: cracker shells, rubber buckshot and a signal/ flashing light device used to scare wolves. With these devices I intended to harass them, hoping they would vacate the area.

On the evening of August 13, I waited near the old logging road the wolves had been using. About an hour before dark, two adults and six pups appeared and started down the logging road. I let them get out of sight and then moved in quickly behind, firing several cracker shells over them. The wolves bolted, and I followed with the telemetry gear. I was able to fire cracker shells at them as I caught glimpses of them moving through open hardwoods, pushing them until, at dark, I was about a mile from the truck. Marking this location with my GPS I planned on returning the next morning.

The next morning I found them resting by a fallen tree at the base of a hill. Another adult wolf had joined them. Stalking in close I fired first a rubber buckshot shell at an adult and then more shell crackers over the wolves as they fled. The three adults and pups ran west, and again I followed them for about a mile until they ended up at a log landing site. Returning to the truck, I retrieved the siren and placed it at the log landing.

The next morning the signal of only one collared pup was picked up. It was on mortality mode. I collected the siren and followed the signal back toward the highway. There, at the wolves' resting site of the previous day, I found the collar. It had been chewed until it fell off the pup. Over the next five days I checked to see if the wolves had returned. They stayed away, and I did not receive any more wolf complaints from this area for the rest of the year.

During the Wolf Theatre episode we obtained our last aerial location of Wolf 2703. Despite searching a wide area, our pilot could not locate his signal. In the commotion over the last few days I did not know if he had been one of the wolves I chased. My daily notes revealed nothing on the whereabouts of the gray-faced male during this time. He had disappeared.

We always notify our Wisconsin colleagues when we lose a collared wolf. Most wolves disperse when they are younger, but wolves can disperse at any age, and collared wolves regularly move between the two states. In late September a Wisconsin pilot picked up Wolf 2703's collar signal south of Suring, a distance of about 123 miles from his former territory. We had solved the mystery of Wolf 2703's disappearance. We were wrong. On October 17, Wisconsin biologists investigated a mortality signal from one of their collared wolves, identified as male Wolf 453, in the general area where Wolf 2703's signal had been discovered. After recovering the dead wolf and turning off its collar, the pilots were unable to locate our wolf. The frequencies of both radioed wolves were nearly identical! Thus, the mystery of Wolf 2703's disappearance remained unsolved.

In August of 2004, nearly two years after losing radio contact with Wolf 2703, a depredation was reported five miles east of Gogebic Lake. I was surprised when the farmer led me to the barn, expecting the dead calf to be in a pasture. The calf had been chained in a stanchion alongside three others. The calf, named Elvis, was a registered purebred Holstein. The farmer had aspirations of it becoming a champion stud. Instead in was dead with large rips in its hindquarters, severe hemorrhaging under the hide of the neck and back, and a severed spine. The attacker had ripped open Elvis's body cavity, consuming its heart and lungs. The size and

The distinctive track of Old Two Toes.

Photo: Daniel Q. Thompson

The white male Wolf 192 and other members of Yellowstone National Park's Bechler Pack on an elk kill.

Photo: Dan Stahler, National Park Service

The famous Superior National Forest, Minnesota female Wolf 2407, following one of her many recaptures over an eleven-year period.

Photo: Tim Pierzina.

A sedated Sage with Diane Boyd when recaptured on October 25, 1985.

Photo: Diane Boyd

Close-quarters helicopter pursuit of
a wolf in full stride during attempt to
place a sedative dart safely in its rump.
Note the gunner perched outside the
copter, and the wolf seemingly levitating
as it attempts to evade its pursuer!

Photo: Tom Meier, National Park Service

Alaska's Step Mountain Pack's
white female 175 following a
successful recapture being held
by helicopter pilot, Rick Swisher.

Photo: John Burch, National Park Service

Typical conifer-covered low mountainous terrain of west-central Alaska, home to the Step Mountain Pack.

Photo: John Burch, National Park Service

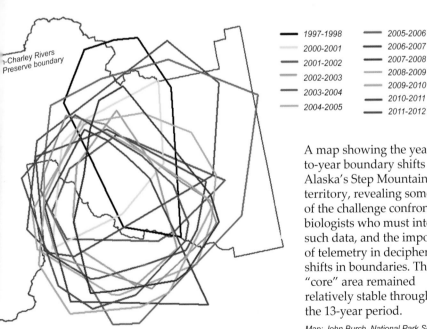

—Charley Rivers Preserve boundary

— 1997-1998	— 2005-2006
— 2000-2001	— 2006-2007
— 2001-2002	— 2007-2008
— 2002-2003	— 2008-2009
— 2003-2004	— 2009-2010
— 2004-2005	— 2010-2011
	— 2011-2012

A map showing the year-to-year boundary shifts of Alaska's Step Mountain Pack territory, revealing something of the challenge confronting biologists who must interpret such data, and the importance of telemetry in deciphering shifts in boundaries. The "core" area remained relatively stable throughout the 13-year period.

Map: John Burch, National Park Service

Wolf pups at a monitored densite in the Northwest Territories. *Photo: Paul Frame*

Tundra wolves from the MacKay Lake Pack following helicopter darting in the Northwest Territories.

Photo: H. Dean Cluff, Environment and Natural Resources, Northwest Territories

A wolf in treeless tundra habitat, Northwest Territories.

Photo: H. Dean Cluff, Environment and Natural Resources, Northwest Territories

A tundra wolf sauntering by near a Northwest Territories densite.

Photo: Paul Frame

A ragged and worn out wolf from Wood Buffalo National Park.

Photo: Lu Carbyn

"Bob", the nearly tail-less Mexican wolf, on the prowl.

Photo: Maggie Dwire,
US Fish and Wildlife Service

The Mexican wolf, Bob, on an elk kill.

Photo: Maggie Dwire,
US Fish and Wildlife Service

Bob and two Saddle Pack members in the Gila National Forest, New Mexico.

Photo: Maggie Dwire, US Fish and Wildlife Service

One of the Saddle Pack pups after being removed from its den.

Photo: Maggie Dwire, US Fish and Wildlife Service

The seven Saddle Pack pups shortly following retrieval after their den was finally found.

Photo: Maggie Dwire, US Fish and Wildlife Service

Authors Ellen Heilhecker and Maggie Dwire handling the Saddle Pack's pups following the harrowing search for their den after their mother female 797 was captured and removed from the wild.

Photo: Maggie Dwire, US Fish and Wildlife Service

Mexican wolf male 973, calmly watching as Ellen Heilhecker pulled her vehicle over to scan her telemetry receiver in search of him!

Photo: Ellen Heilhecker

Lower elevational habitat within Mexican wolf range, and signs placed out by the mistrustful Catron County Commission.

Photo: Ellen Heilhecker

DANGEROUS WOLF IN AREA USE CAUTION

Female Wolf 475 of Wisconsin's dog-killing Shanagolden Pack.

Photo: Adrian Wydeven

Inside view from a helicopter darting a Scandinavian wolf.

Photo: Marianne Linder Olsen

The Scandinavian wolf, Ulrik, awakening from the effects of drugs used to handle him during re-collaring, January 2006.

Photo: Ulf Risberg

The large male Wolf 760, of the Delta Pack atop Yellowstone National Park's Trident Mountain shortly after being darted in 2010.

Photo: Doug Smith, National Park Service

The Delta Pack male 760 in January of 2011 being processed by Dan Stahler.

Photo: Doug Smith, National Park Service

Canid 49-09, the Axe Lake Pack's eastern wolf X coyote hybrid of Ontario calmly poised to defy attempts at her removal to extract her pups.

Photo: John Benson

Red Wolf 344 following
capture and placement
of a telemetry collar.

Photo: Mike Phillips,
US Fish and Wildlife Service

Fifteen pound Big Al, The Little Gal, of Wisconsin's
Bootjack Pack, being held during processing by
Technician, Ron Schultz, July 1982.

Photo: Richard P. Thiel, Wisconsin DNR photo

The "Old Gray Guy" of Isle Royale National Park with pack-mates in February, 2006.

Photo: John Vucetich

Yolanda Cortés and J.C. Blanco in their telemetry vehicle's cramped interior during a night-time surveillance run monitoring the movements of the Spanish wolf, Ernesto.

Photo: Franciso Márquez

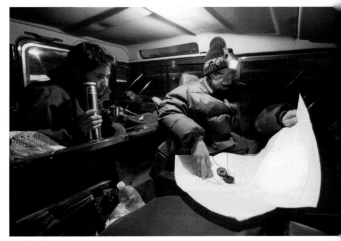

A sedated Ernesto from the agricultural plains along the Duero River being carried to a shaded spot to place a radio collar on him.

Photo: Franciso Márquez

The standard approach to obtaining a radio fix of—in this case—the Spanish wolf, Ernesto, by stopping at intervals, sweeping the receiver antenna in a 360° arc, and plotting the direction of the loudest signal on a map.

Photo: Franciso Márquez

Aerial view of the agricultural region in which the Spanish wolf, Ernesto, roamed.

Photo: Juan Carlos Blanco

A kill-site within the grain field habitat of the Spanish wolves of the Duero River region where the only cover was an occasional drainage ditch or cluster of trees and shrubs.

Photo: Juan Carlos Blanco

spacing of the holes in its hide were consistent with wolf. Inspecting the surrounding area, I found the track of one adult wolf inside the barn and wolf tracks and scat outside the barn. Clearly a wolf had killed this calf.

The tools I used to address wolf depredations varied depending on the federal classification of wolves. Non-lethal control measures such as guard dogs, fladry (flagging on a rope used to scare wolves), lights, and a number of forms of harassment were always available. By 2004 wolves had been delisted to federally threatened status, and use of lethal control to resolve a problem could be employed. Dean Beyers and I discussed the situation, and we decided since the wolf had entered a barn it should be removed. Brian Roell, newly hired DNR wolf coordinator, agreed and received the final approval from his supervisor.

I set six traps before nightfall, including two inside the barn. Setting traps within the barn was unusual; but a wolf entering a barn and killing a calf was also unusual. Two wolf pups were caught in the barnyard the next morning. The traps in the barn were undisturbed. I was sure the pups had not killed Elvis, so Dean and I decided to fit the pups with radio collars and let them go. The next morning three of the traps held wolf pups, including one trap set inside the barn. The pup had been feeding on the dead calf. We did not want barn visiting to become a learned behavior, so we decided to ear tag the two pups captured in the pasture and euthanize the pup in the barn.

I returned that evening in an attempt to locate the wolves by howling. Their response was immediate and loud, just east of the barn. Using the radio collared pups I was able to determine the pack's rendezvous site was only about 100 yards from the barn in a narrow brushy draw between the pasture and a cornfield. It was a great spot with plenty of cover, and the pups had readily available water because the draw had a ditch line with a flowing stream.

Inspecting it I found lots of pup tracks, but only tracks of one adult. "What if we catch the breeding female?" I thought to myself. Dean and I talked it over, deciding it was not a good idea to remove the breeding female, especially if there was not another adult in the pack. This was a new situation and no instruction manual could guide us in our decision. Over the next eleven days I checked traps and searched for sign of a second adult wolf. Nothing further was caught in the traps and tracking conditions in grass were poor. It had also rained more or less continuously, putting the traps out of commission.

Several mornings and evenings I sat watching the area with a rifle, hoping to see two or more adults. I managed to see the pups quite often and, based on those observations, figured there were seven. Then one morning the adult female came into the pasture, not knowing I was there. I had her in the crosshairs, thought about the pups and lowered the rifle, letting her walk away.

On the fifteenth day "zero" finally caught me. I had checked the traps and was sitting in my truck on the road in front of the pasture. Predictably, I was talking with Dean when I looked up in time to see an old gray-faced wolf with a radio collar limp across the road about fifty yards in front of the truck. The wolf was heading in the direction of the barn. "I've got to go," I yelled into the phone, and throwing it down, I grabbed my rifle from the case and jumped out of the truck. I could see the wolf was limping badly on its front right foot and it was suffering from mange. "Damn it." I could not shoot. A county grader and dump truck were working further down the road and I could not get a safe shot. The old wolf ran into some tall grass and disappeared. I missed my chance.

When I got back in the truck, I discovered Dean was still on the line. I told him what had just happened. We were not tracking any other collared wolves in the area. It was either a Wisconsin wolf or one we had lost contact with. I pulled out my receiver and tried the frequencies of all missing wolves, including Wolf 2703. I did not hear a beep.

In my view the old limping wolf was a good candidate for the animal that went into the barn and killed Elvis. With renewed hope, I reset some of the traps ruined by the rain, hoping the old limping wolf would be waiting for me the next morning in one of my traps. Sure enough, the next day an adult stepped on a trap, but it did not fire because of the mud. Apparently the "hero and zero" did not balance out the day before. There was no way to tell if it was the adult female or the old gray-faced limper.

The following day, a Sunday, wildlife biologist Doug Wagner received a call from the Sheriff's Department reporting that a wolf was hiding under a house trailer about four miles from where I was working. The complainant reportedly heard a loud noise about 6:00 a.m. and thought a vehicle had hit their dog and the dog had crawled under the trailer. When they looked through a hole in the skirting they saw a large collared wolf, and they assumed the vehicle had hit the wolf which then crawled under the trailer. Not surprisingly, they wanted someone to come and remove the wolf as soon as possible.

Arriving at the scene, Doug found the gray-faced collared wolf under the trailer just as the home owners described. Unfortunately, Doug also found the family's dog, Chewy, a ten-year-old German Shepherd mix; he was partially eaten. As one might expect, Chewy's owners were distraught, describing their dog as friendly and protective of their grandchildren, who enjoyed playing with him.

Doug decided to drug the wolf. He removed some of the skirting from the bottom of the trailer to access the crawl space, realizing that scrambling under a trailer with a wolf therein was not the safest idea. His sole drug delivery device was a jab stick, and with it he would have to get close. Both Doug and wolf jockeyed for position. This cat and mouse game continued for quite some time before Doug was finally able to administer the drugs and pull the wolf from under the trailer. He then retrieved Chewy, inspecting the dog to determine the cause of death. Doug was sure the wolf had killed it.

The old, collared wolf was taken back to Crystal Falls and held overnight. There was no doubt; Doug noted the wolf's ear tag numbers, 108 and 109, and the collar's frequency which was not working; it was our very own wolf, male 2703. After a series of phone calls we determined that the old, gray-faced male wolf was almost certainly the collared wolf I saw crossing the road at the farm three days earlier. Everything matched. He was missing two toes on his right front foot that probably caused him to limp, and he had mange. With the depredation of the dog and strong likelihood that he had also killed the calf, we decided to euthanize the old-timer. Nobody had desired this outcome for him. In accordance with standard procedure, we sent 2703 to the DNR diagnostic lab for a complete necropsy.

Even though the killer of the calf, Elvis, had been dispatched, we still had a wolf rendezvous site within one-hundred yards from a barn containing calves. My work was not yet finished. I wanted to make sure the adult female was with the pups when I started to harass them. Fortunately, when I returned the adult female was lying in the pasture next to a hay bale. I loaded my shotgun with shell crackers and stuffed a bunch more of the shells into my pockets. Using the telemetry gear and moving like smoke, I got as close to the pups as I could, undetected. At the sound of the first shell crackers exploding, the adult female and her pups began running. I followed, hoping they would all stay together. Each time the pups slowed I closed the distance and fired more cracker shells. This continued until the pups were about two miles south of the farm. Would they return to the farm?

For three days the pups stayed away from the farm, but on the fourth day I saw the pups and the adult in the pasture. They again received the harassment treatment. This time the wolves headed southeast when the shell crackers started exploding. Over the next three weeks I periodically checked the location of the collared pups and, fortunately, they stayed away from the farm. After more than a month of work, the depredation issue seemed resolved.

In early December the diagnostic lab returned Wolf 2703's necropsy report. He weighed 67 pounds, had no fat deposits, and was just over ten years old. An old fracture and arthritis were found in the femoral-tibial-fibular joint (knee joint) of his right rear leg, likely the result of one of his vehicle collisions. Toes two and three were missing on his right front foot, most likely the result of an old trap-related injury after stepping in a coyote trap sometime after I had originally caught him. His upper incisors were missing, and there was severe wear on all other teeth. He was also recovering from a bout of mange.

Ten years is a long time for a wolf to survive; most do not live half that long. Wolf 2703 survived a lot of adversity. Vehicles hit him at least twice, he escaped from a coyote trap, and he survived mange. We will never know when or why he left his original territory. At the end, his teeth were worn or missing; he had lost thirteen percent of his body weight, and he had no fat reserves. All of these factors suggested he was struggling to get enough to eat. Likely his declining condition contributed to his depredation of Chewy and, possibly, Elvis.

CHAPTER THIRTEEN

The 06 Female

Rick McIntyre

ON DECEMBER 6, 2012 an iconic and famous wolf was legally shot in Wyoming's wolf hunting Zone 2, adjacent to the eastern border of Yellowstone National Park. She was the alpha female of Yellowstone's Lamar Canyon Pack and had been seen by tens of thousands of park visitors over the years. Her death was reported in the *New York Times* and many other papers and news outlets throughout the world.

I had known that female wolf well, for nearly all of her life, and also knew many of her ancestors. Informally called the 06 Female because she was born in 2006, she was later radio collared and given the identification number 832.

Her great-grandparents had been captured in Alberta in January of 1995 as part of Yellowstone's Wolf Reintroduction Program and were released in the park two months later. Her great-grandmother, Wolf 9, had eight pups that spring and one of her sons, legendary Wolf 21, became the alpha male of the Druid Peak Pack. One of his daughters was destined to become the alpha female of the Agate Creek Pack and gave birth to the 06 Female in 2006.

The 06 Female left her family as a young adult and lived a colorful and independent life for the next few years. She became a master elk hunter, one of the best in Yellowstone, and was famous for killing elk by herself. In addition, she had scores of suitors over the years. During one mating season she set what might be a world record by breeding with five different males. However, she left each of those males and continued to live independently, sometimes in temporary association with a few other wolves, sometimes as a lone wolf.

In early 2010, when nearly four years old, 06 Female finally settled down. She ran into two yearling brothers, who were later collared and given the numbers 754 and 755, who had just dispersed from their pack. These brothers had just inaugurated a partnership with seven sisters who controlled a high quality territory. That pack's alpha male, father to the sister wolves, had recently left the group. Despite such favorable circumstances, 06 Female managed to lure the two away from the other females, and in joining her they established a new pack, the Lamar Canyon Pack. Evidently the brothers judged 06 Female to be a better bargain than seven

123

females. Male 755 took on the role of the new pack's alpha male. But, perhaps due to the significant difference in their ages and experience levels, the brothers willingly yielded to 06 Female as the undisputed leader of the new group.

As yearlings these brothers knew nothing about breeding, whereas 06 Female had already been around the block quite a few times. Both brothers bred her a month later. She discovered an old wolf den near Slough Creek and prepared it for her pups. The site was centrally located in an area with enough prey to support her family. But it had one disadvantage—grizzlies were very common in the region. In mid-April, 06 Female had four gray pups in that den, two males and two females. Since the opening to the den was visible from the road corridor, we often saw her nursing the pups or carrying them back into the den when they strayed too far away.

Fiercely protective of her pups, 06 Female frequently had to deal with grizzlies that approached her den. Each time she would run at the intruder, get behind it, bite its rear end, and then run off in the direction opposite her pups. The hapless grizzly would chase her, unable to match her speed or agility. Each time the bear stopped, 06 Female would run back, bite it again on its hind quarters, and thus draw it further off. In one case she spent twelve hours decoying a grizzly away from her pups before she felt it was lured safely away, and only then would she return to the den.

That fall, when the pups were old enough to travel, she led her pack a few miles to the east and resettled her family in Lamar Valley. That had been the territory of her ancestors, the Druid Peak Pack, but the Druids had recently fallen apart due to the loss of their alphas, attacks by rival packs and severe cases of mange.

In early October, I spotted the 06 Female and 755 apart from the other Lamar wolves. They were next to a newly killed animal carcass, but it was hard to determine what it was. As 06 Female began to pluck fur from the animal I saw its claws and realized it was a grizzly cub! People on the scene told me that they had seen the two wolves surround the bear. Then 06 Female attacked and killed it. Soon brother 754 joined the alphas, but he and his brother, male 755, were not allowed to feed. Whenever they approached, 06 Female would snarl and lunge. She eventually carried off the remains in her jaws and brought them to nearby pups. After all the times grizzlies had threatened her pups at the den site, it was reasonable to expect that she would kill a cub that had somehow wandered away from its mother.

In late 2010, 06 Female found the old Druid den, the one where her grandmother, Wolf 42, had given birth to her mother back in 2001. After investigating the den, 06 Female cleaned it out and prepared it for her second litter. She returned to the site in April of 2011 and had five pups in it.

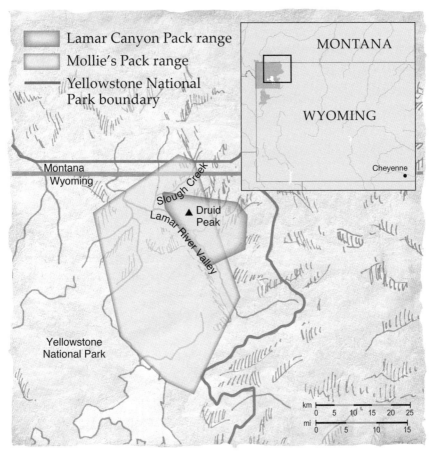

Lamar Canyon Pack range
Mollie's Pack range
Yellowstone National Park boundary

MONTANA

WYOMING

Cheyenne

Montana
Wyoming

Slough Creek

▲ Druid Peak

Lamar River Valley

Yellowstone National Park

km 0 5 10 15 20 25
mi 0 5 10 15

That year I saw her make two solo kills. In late March, pregnant 06 Female spotted a lone nine-month-old elk calf and ran at it. The calf charged forward at her. After deftly dodging the charge, 06 Female stood face to face with the calf. It ran at her again and kicked forward, then kicked down at her. She easily stepped aside, avoiding its flailing hooves, then charged, leapt up and grabbed it by the throat. With her enormous strength she wrestled the calf off its feet and onto the ground while maintaining her grip on its throat. It was dead when she released her grip four minutes later.

In November I encountered her and other pack members near the Lamar River and a five-month-old elk calf that was standing in the water. The pack must have chased it there. About fifteen meters from the calf stood 06 Female, at the edge of the river. She began pacing back and forth along the shore, seemingly trying to figure out how to get at the calf. The two brothers, 754 and 755, were bedded east of the calf, apparently unmotivated to help 06 Female make a kill. Along with them were three of the pack's yearlings and three pups.

Suddenly I heard a splashing sound. Looking back at the river, I observed that 06 Female had plunged into the water and was already attached to the throat of the calf. The calf soon collapsed; the wolf continuing to hold on to its throat. The calf kicked a bit, then all movement stopped.

The prowess 06 Female had as a hunter and as a protector of her pups was matched by her ability to deal with rival wolf packs. In the spring of 2012, 06 Female had another litter of four pups at the old Druid den. At that time, her territory had been invaded by the Mollie's Pack, a much larger group of wolves. At times these rival wolves were seen within a few miles of her den site.

Years before, the ancestors of the Mollie's had controlled Lamar Valley, but they were eventually defeated by 06's ancestors, the Druid wolves, and driven out of Lamar. They settled into a new territory twenty-five miles to the south. In late 2011, the nineteen member Mollie's Pack returned to the Lamar Valley and nearby areas. Outnumbering all of the local packs, they killed several members of the Agate Creek and Blacktail packs. In early February they attacked one of 06 Female's pups, and then left it to chase other members of her pack. The pup survived and later reunited with the other Lamar wolves.

On April 25, about five days after giving birth, I saw sixteen adult wolves from Mollie's Pack run into the dense forest where 06 Female's den was located. For a few minutes all was quiet. Suddenly, seventeen wolves ran out of the trees. In front was 06 Female, running for her life, with all sixteen of the rival wolves right behind her. Hindered by having given birth to four pups a few days earlier, she was rapidly losing ground. To make her situation more dire, she had made the tactical mistake of selecting a route that led to the top of a steep cliff. In a few moments she would be forced to stop and turn to face her pursuers, and outnumbering her sixteen to one, they would easily kill her. Her helpless newborn pups would then die of starvation or due to direct attack by Mollie's wolves.

As her adversaries closed in on her, I became certain she only had a few more moments of life left. But I was wrong, having greatly underestimated her ability to survive. A small gully existed down the face of that cliff, and with deft balance and agility, 06 Female raced down it to the park road, crossed it, then defiantly turned back to look at the Mollie's wolves, who were trying to comprehend what had just happened.

Although 06 Female was safe, the threat to her family was still very much there: the other wolves were between her and the four pups. All the Mollie's wolves had to do was turn around, follow her scent trail back to the den, and kill her pups. At that moment one of 06 Female's adult daughters appeared close to the Mollie's wolves. The daughter, born in that first litter of 2010, was now two years old and had been well trained by her mother, standing in plain sight of the rival pack. The Mollie's wolves immediately spotted her and charged. The daughter ran off, leading the invading pack in a direction away from the den. As the Lamar Canyon Pack's swiftest member, knowing every hill and gully in the den area, she easily got away.

The Mollie's wolves at that point seemed totally disorganized. After running back and forth a few times, they all crossed the park road, swam the Lamar River, left the territory and never returned to 06 Female's den again. As soon as the rival wolves withdrew, 06 Female returned to her den. Several weeks later we saw that all four of her pups had survived the trauma of those events and were in perfect condition.

Three months after the chase, in mid-July, I spotted wolves 06, 754, 755 and three other pack members near a yearling bull elk in the Lamar River. Earlier, the 06 Female and male 754 had chased the bull into the river; then Wolf 755 and the other three wolves joined them. The bull was standing midstream in deep water with a fast current. The alpha wolves both went in the river and swam against the current toward the bull, struggling against the fast moving water. When finally closing in on him, the bull bounded past the pair of wolves into deeper water. Again the wolves swam toward him, but the bull easily rushed past them and returned to his original position. The bull could bound or run through the deep water faster than the two wolves could swim.

The alphas made repeated attempts to reach the bull, but each time he slipped away unharmed. After twenty-eight minutes of exhausting swimming, the two wolves came out of the river, joined the other pack members and rested. The bull, meanwhile, stayed in place in the water.

Alpha male 755 had been with 06 Female for two-and-a-half years by this time and it seemed that he had learned to be a much better hunter by watching and imitating her. In this attack he had matched her determination and persistence in an impressive manner. Male 754 was another story. He was bigger, and likely stronger, than his brother, and he was content to let the alphas do all the work. All the while the alpha pair struggled, Wolf 754 had watched from shore. Once he went into the river but came right back out without any serious effort to assist in attempting to take the bull.

The alphas rested for forty-eight minutes, then the 06 Female plunged back into the river, bounding through the water at the bull. He rushed past her downstream. Immediately the female wolf went after him again. At that point, male 755 entered the river and both wolves swam at the bull, but once again he ran right past the alphas. By now the bull seemed to be tiring. He had been standing in the cold water for hours. He was no longer moving with the speed and vigor he had displayed during earlier bouts with the alphas.

Climbing out of the river, 06 Female climbed up on the bank to rest. However, Wolf 755 kept at it, charging through the water at the bull. Once again the bull started to run past the wolf, but 755 managed to bite into his hindquarters as he went by. The wolf hung on, then lost his grip as the bull reached deeper water. I saw 06 Female running through the water at that point. She grabbed the bull on his left side. Catching up with the bull, Wolf 755 bit into his shoulder. Wolf 06 let go and sunk her teeth into the side of the elk's neck. Together, the pair wrestled the bull down into the water. All this time, the wolves had been forced to fight the bull as they swam beside him, while he had solid footing on the bottom of the river. The lack of leverage put the wolves at a serious disadvantage.

Eventually 06 Female lost her grip providing the bull a means of escape. At that moment big 754, who had been watching the attack from the river bank, jumped in the water, swam to the bull and got a solid bite on his throat. His intervention was the turning point of the attack. The other three adult wolves followed Wolf 754's example, diving into the river and joining the mêlée, and all six pack members bit into the bull as they swam beside him. The combined force of the six was enough to force the bull into shallow water, where they finished him off.

The actions of Wolf 754 at the very end of the attack showed that, like his brother, he had learned to be a better hunter by watching the wise 06 Female. He copied her technique of making the killing bite on the throat and applied it perfectly. It was still true that 06 Female and her mate, Wolf 755 had done most of the work, but brother Wolf 754 proved his value to the pack when the alphas needed extra help most. Using his size and strength, Wolf 754 had bitten the throat of the elk and held on until he was dead.

The next month, in early August, eight of the nine adult Lamar wolves, including 06 Female and brothers 754 and 755, were heading toward a site where a bison had died of natural causes a few days before. The other Lamar Canyon Pack adult was back with the four pups at the den. As the eight Lamar Canyon wolves approached the carcass, they spotted five other wolves at the carcass. I knew that the smaller group was a new pack that consisted of three females from Mollie's Pack and two Blacktail Pack males.

The Lamar Canyon Pack wolves ran at the rival pack with raised tails. When the other wolves spotted them they split up and licked off in different directions. The Lamar Canyon wolves went after one of the black females, Wolf 822. As a young Mollie's adult, she had been with her pack when they had attacked one of 06 Female's pups the previous February. She had also been part of the raiding party that invaded 06's den area in April and chased her to the cliff.

At top speed, Wolf 822 ran north, crossed the park road, and raced up a steep slope. Seven of the eight Lamar Canyon wolves stayed on her route as they pursued her. But Wolf 755 split off, ran along the park road to where the slope was less steep and headed up. He intercepted female 822, grabbed her by the back, pulled her down, and attacked her. Two yearlings ran in and joined the attack. Then the 06 Female arrived and bit the hapless Mollie's Pack wolf on the back of her neck. The other Lamar Canyon Pack wolves arrived with big Wolf 754 bringing in the rear. Grabbing the female, he violently shook his head back and forth. All eight Lamar Canyon wolves bit Wolf 822 at will.

Some of the other members of female 822's pack howled, causing most of the Lamar Canyon wolves to run off in their direction. Soon 06 Female was the only wolf still attacking the Mollie's Pack wolf. Following a series of fierce bites, she paused, looked toward her pack running after the remaining rival wolves, and then left the blood-drenched Wolf 822, joining her pack in the chase.

After 06 Female departed, Wolf 822 eventually stood up, took a few steps, and collapsed. Within an hour she was dead from blood loss and shock. Having managed earlier in the year to avoid many potential confrontations with the much larger Mollie's Pack and surviving two direct attacks, 06 Female and her family had seized the moment to mount a counteroffensive now that the Mollie's Pack wolves were split up and divided, and succeeded in killing a wolf that had been part of those earlier attacks.

The Lamar Canyon Pack, under the leadership of 06 Female, was once again in control of their territory, and the Mollie's Pack wolves and the newly formed pack left them alone. The pack was exceptionally well organized and extremely well functioning. It was led by the most competent wolf in the region as she had repeated demonstrated with her hunting and survival skills in front of her family members. They, in turn, had learned many lessons from her. Both of her males, brothers 754 and 755, had proven themselves as hunters and as defenders of the pack, as had her six adult daughters.

Her four pups were healthy and strong, and they soon started traveling full time with the nine adults. In November of 2012, the thirteen member Lamar Canyon Pack went east from the center of their territory and crossed the Yellowstone National Park border. On November 11 four-and-a-half-year-old Wolf 754 was legally shot in Wyoming. He was taken in a wolf hunting zone that had a quota of eight wolves. Big 754 was the seventh wolf shot.

The pack briefly returned to the Park's Lamar Valley and then revisited the area where Wolf 754 had been killed, possibly searching for him. On December 6, six-and-half-year-old 06 Female was shot and killed close to where Wolf 754 had died. Since she was the eighth wolf taken in that zone, the area was closed to further wolf hunting. The rest of her family would be safe from legal hunting in that part of Wyoming.

Alpha male 755 and his ten sons and daughters later returned to Lamar Valley. His two-year-old daughter, Wolf 776, was now behaving as the pack's alpha female. But the pack soon went back to the area where both 06 Female and male 754 had been killed. I have no way to know if the Lamar Canyon Pack wolves fully understood that their two pack mates were dead and their bodies removed from the area by the hunters who had shot them.

In late January, 755 came back to Lamar Valley by himself, traveled out of his territory to the west and approached other wolf packs. Since all of the adult females in his pack were his own daughters, he was probably looking for a new mate. Yellowstone Wolf Project personnel had observed two other cases where an alpha female had died and the alpha male, having no unrelated females to breed, left the pack to seek out a new mate. In both of those cases, the males died in the attempt to start over.

As of late March, Wolf 755 is still out there, searching for a female, a daunting task for a lone, middle-aged male that has to contend with rival packs and rival males who would resent his intrusion into their territories and likely try to kill him. During the time 755 was back in the park, we received reports that the rest of the Lamar wolves, still living outside the park to the east, had a new, big gray male that was courting Wolf 776 and the other adult females.

The 06 Female was an extraordinary wolf, easily the most famous animal in Yellowstone. She had defiantly prevailed against everything that the natural world had thrown at her. Countless park visitors had seen her during her early independent years, and even more watched her start her own pack and raise three litters of pups. The story of her death was reported worldwide and had a great emotional impact on countless people.

By now, several of her adult daughters are almost certainly pregnant, and the pups that will arrive in the spring of 2013 will be her grandchildren. She trained those daughters well, and they will pass on that training to their pups. Her legacy lives on in her sons and daughters and will live on for many generations to come.

CHAPTER FOURTEEN

Ulrik – a Survivor Among Scandinavian Wolves

Håkan Sand, Camilla Wikenros, Per Ahlqvist, Petter Wabakken and Olof Liberg

WE WERE ALL AMAZED. Could it really be so easy? Eight wolves captured and fitted with radio collars in just four days during our first-ever capture attempt in Scandinavia. And now, late in the afternoon of December 15, 1998 our capture team had darted two wolves in the Leksand Pack from the helicopter, and we, Håkan, Olof and Petter, were heading for the place where we were going to meet up with the helicopter team and start handling the wolves. As Per Ahlqvist brought out the two wolves from the helicopter, we realized that we had captured the alpha female in the pack. She clearly was an adult wolf, and we estimated her to be four-to-five years old. The other wolf was equal in size to the adult female, but obviously a young male. A closer look at his teeth and his front legs revealed that this male actually was a pup, exactly 7.5 months old. As all of us Scandinavian wolf researchers are romantic by nature, he was given the name #98-04, and his mother was named #98-05. Although everyone in the research team was filled with enthusiasm for the past few days' success, at this time none of us could even imagine that this male wolf pup, #98-04, would become our prime provider of ecological insights for the next ten years.

At the inception of the wolf research project in 1998, the Scandinavian wolf population had grown from a handful of individuals in the early 1980's to approximately seventy wolves, with evidence for continued strong, positive growth. The environment was suitable for wolves, with high densities of moose and roe deer and large forested areas with a relatively low density of human inhabitants (one person per square kilometer). However, as in most recolonizing populations of wolves, human attitudes were quite disparate, ranging from pure hate to endless love and care.

Now was the time to start research on wolves using modern technology to focus on individuals. Wolves were already causing strong conflicts with people in the countryside. We were optimistic and convinced that if we just did good research and provided the management and conservation groups with strong data and sound biological information, most of the problems could be resolved. In retrospect it is easy to see how wrong we were about the development of wolf-human conflicts in Scandinavia.

In December 1998 tracking on snow showed that the Leksand Pack consisted of an estimated seven-to-eight wolves in total. In the first week of capture we placed traditional very high frequency (VHF) radio collars on two of those wolves. Although collaring required intensive efforts for obtaining positions via triangulation of the radio signals, the technique offered us better possibilities to track individual wolves than pure tracking on snow. Therefore, we were all eager to start up an intensive study of winter predation as soon as possible—the first of its kind in Scandinavia. The plan was to document the positions of the two wolves at least once per day and combine this information with tracking of the whole pack, thereby finding all prey that the pack had killed. It turned out that this strategy was not a realistic one, despite the excellent manpower of our team. Not only did the wolves travel so far some days that it was practically impossible to keep up with them, they also split up in groups and moved in different directions. Our young male #98-04 seemed to be of a rather independent nature, spending much time on his own or with a few of his siblings. By March 1999, and at an age of ten months, he spent more time on his own than he did with his pack. During this first study we found that he had tried to kill both moose and roe deer, or at least he had followed them at high speed, but we were never able to verify his killing of prey on his own at this young age.

During one of our regular tracking events of #98-04 in March 1999, we discovered that he suddenly suffered from heavy bleeding after crossing a forest road; he was obviously seriously hurt. Backtracking several kilometers did not reveal anything that could explain the sudden appearance of blood. A thin layer of snow from the previous night showed that he had crossed the road with normal speed, and step length ruled out the possibility of a car collision. In fact, only one car had passed this road before us, but after the snow fall. Once #98-04 reached some thirty meters into the clear-cut, after crossing the road, the heavy bleeding had started. His resting sites, not far from the road, showed that he had spent several hours in this small area, while losing a relatively large amount of blood. While we were examining this site, his collar signal indicated that he was just a couple of hundred meters away, obviously not capable of moving as usual. We were finally left with only one likely explanation—that he had been exposed to a poaching attempt from a person in the car passing earlier that same morning when he was crossing the road. After remaining stationary in the area for several days, he finally was able to move more normally. When we resumed tracking him again there were no further signs of blood in his tracks.

This incident may have affected #98-04's attraction for his home territory, because by late March he left his natal territory and became

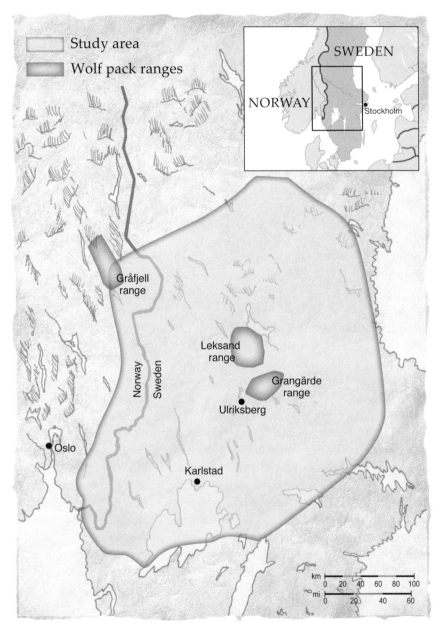

stationary in an area just south-east of the Leksand territory. In this respect he was different from most of his conspecifics in this population who usually dispersed for many hundreds of kilometers before settling and establishing their own territory. Soon we arrived at a good explanation for his rather short dispersal stage. In June 1999 he was observed with a female wolf in the area that we had named the Grangärde territory, after a local, larger village. Although the population at the time was small and the pool of potential mates even smaller, #98-04 had the luck of finding one as soon as he stepped out of his natal area.

During the following summer and winter we closely followed the two wolves in this new territory, using intensive radio tracking combined with tracking on snow in winter, the same combination of techniques we had used in the Leksand territory. In January 2000 we also managed to capture his mate, who turned out to be a four-year-old, 42 kilogram, slightly reddish wolf, #00-04. By this time both wolves were fitted with radio collars. Field studies showed that our young male, together with his female, had gained rather good hunting skills for both moose and roe deer. In the 121 days from November 27 to March 27, these two wolves killed a minimum of two adult moose, fourteen moose calves, and six roe deer. They also visited a number of older carcasses, presumably older kills, but never killed or scavenged any domestic animals, not even during the summer when sheep and cattle were readily available, albeit within fences. Tracking also revealed that the two wolves successfully killed moose, with an attack success rate of approximately twenty-one percent, and that they sometimes followed moose and roe deer for several kilometers before executing a kill. On one occasion both wolves had followed the tracks of one roe deer for nearly fourteen kilometers, but failed to kill it.

Tracking events during winter also revealed that the female was coming into estrus, as shown by blood in her urine. Therefore, in early May 2000, when both wolves showed rather restricted movements, we suspected, and hoped, that a litter was born. If true, our young male #98-04 had become a successful breeder for the first time, at the age of two years. But it was not until October that one of our field workers observed #98-04 and his female with four pups. Now we knew.

Before we had a chance to track the whole pack on snow, we abruptly lost contact with the collared female in mid-November. We routinely searched for her signal during aerial surveys over large expanses of land, including their territory, but without success. The first snow a few weeks later revealed tracks from a total of four wolves, but we could not find tracks from more than one adult scent-marking wolf in the pack, thus confirming that the female, as well as one of the pups, was no longer present in the pack. For an adult, reproducing female to leave her pack is not likely, and for her collar to fail at the same time is even more unlikely. Therefore, we had to assume that she and one of the pups had fallen victim to a poaching attempt. This time the poachers must have been successful, and in succeeding to kill the wolf, most likely instantly destroyed her collar. In retrospect, we have learned by hard evidence that poaching was, and currently is, an important agent of mortality in the Scandinavian wolf population. At that time, in November 2000, we were only able to speculate about the fate of the two missing wolves.

By the start of winter 2000–2001, the Grangärde pack consisted of three pups and #98-04, our collared male. This turned into an opportunity to study how the loss of an alpha female may affect the pattern of predation during winter compared to the previous winter when there were two adult wolves but no pups present. Therefore, we again launched an ambitious winter study, now having an enthusiastic Master's student by the name of Camilla Wikenros as our main field worker. Surprising to us, the pattern of predation did not change much from year one. During the 106 day period the lone male killed fourteen moose calves, seven adult moose and eight roe deer, providing his three pups with a surplus of food. His efforts proved even more successful than the previous winter, with his success-rate on attacks of moose rising to sixty percent. However, the pack was often split up, with one or two of the pups either joining the male or one of the siblings. The pups also spent most of their time at or close to moose carcasses. The adult male was alone on sixty-five percent of all locations recorded and checked in the field, and he spent an average of only one full day on, or in, the close vicinity of each new moose kill. Obviously, #98-04 was a good provider this year, but perhaps he traded his time hunting for less social contact with his offspring.

In early February 2001 Per, with his capture team veterinarian Jon Arnemo and pilot Ulf Grind, was able to capture two of the three pups in the pack. They were both healthy and in good condition with the female pup weighing 31 kilograms and the male 38 kilograms. These two pups both left their natal territory during the following summer, but both were poached within the year, before they had reproduced.

During the summer of 2001, #98-04 was once again on his own, searching for a new mate. He did not have to search for too long. On the first snow the following winter, 2001-2002, we observed him scent-marking his territory together with a female. His territory had shifted slightly towards the south, to an area called the "Ulriksberg." From now on #98-04 also received a more personal name by those of us working closely with him—he now became "Ulrik"—a wolf well-known to both the public and the media because he was now the main provider of our research project, with all kinds of information that seemed to get more and more public attention.

On January 13, 2002 we were able to capture his new and second mate, #02-03. Her age was estimated to be three years, and she weighed 36 kilograms. This was an important capture for our research project, because we did not know how long Ulrik's collar was going to last; it was his fourth year wearing it. Life again looked brighter for Ulrik, and we anticipated his second reproduction during the spring of 2002, but we were disappointed. For some reason Ulrik and his new female did not reproduce, or something happened in the early stage of caring for the pups. They started to roam their total territory a few weeks after the presumed birth time period, and we never found evidence of the birth of pups.

During the rest of the year our research went into a lower intensity mode, with Ulrik and his female regularly followed by triangulation once or twice a week during the snow-free season. As with the year before, the female showed signs of estrus blood in late December 2002. Maybe 2003 would turn out to be a more productive year for Ulrik and his new mate? So far during the winter the two wolves had held on tight to each other while traveling the territory. But during one of these regular location trips on February 27, 2003, the female's signal was suddenly not on the air. This was the first time since her capture that we were not able to record her VHF-signal. Again we followed up by both aerial radio tracking and by checking the tracks of Ulrik on snow, now confirming that there was only one lone wolf in the area. But this was not all. For more than one week we followed as Ulrik roamed over his territory with high intensity, while frequently howling at night, indicating that indeed his female was gone and that he searched intensively for her. Similar to the loss of his former female, the new female's collar was dead at the time of her disappearance. Although we were not able to verify poaching, this seems to be the only reasonable explanation for her sudden disappearance. Apparently, once again, Ulrik had lost his mate due to illegal actions by the wolves' main enemy—humans.

By late winter 2003 we also lost radio contact with Ulrik, but luckily this proved to be caused by technical reasons. His collar had been working for more than four years, and the battery was now depleted. For the rest of the snow period in 2003 we were only able to follow him by regular tracking, and when the snow was gone we had no clue what was going on. We decided that during the following winter a primary objective should be to capture him again to be able to follow up on his life history. Consequently, in January 2004 we started up our capture season by searching for Ulrik in his former territory. Tracking in the beginning of the winter had shown that there was still one adult male present in the area and that this one used the same routes as Ulrik previously did, so we were pretty sure that he was alive and in the area. Somehow he remained out of reach for serious capture attempts the whole week. Not until the last day we had access to the helicopter did we find his fresh tracks. Now the helicopter team did what they were good at. They followed his tracks for more than ten kilometers before catching up with him. Obviously he had learned his lesson from more than five years ago and from previous mates, but, despite this, we captured him a second time late in the afternoon of January 31, the last day of this winter's capture session. At an age of five years, and with a body weight of 45 kilograms, he was not the largest male we had caught, but he was still in good condition. This time we fitted him with a new type of collar based on GPS and GSM for positioning and automatic transfer of information, respectively. We could now follow his where-abouts from our computer in our office and be much more effective with the time spent in the field.

During the following spring in 2004 we received reports from our highly dedicated field crew, Jan Perjons, Göran Jansson and Håkan Björling, that Ulrik again had been observed with another wolf. To confirm this we approached him in June 2004, using his collar to track his whereabouts, and indeed he was accompanied by an un-collared female wolf. GPS positions in May revealed that Ulrik did not display reproductive behavior, indicating that they likely had met sometime after the reproductive season in 2004. Two scats were collected in the territory during the summer, and DNA analyses of those later showed that one originated from Ulrik and the other from a female born in the Gråfjell territory in Norway. When snow emerged in early winter 2004-2005 we assumed that he would be accompanied by the same female, but this time he was alone once again. Maybe the chemistry was not right between the two wolves, or maybe she did not survive in this territory for long; we will likely never know her fate.

That Ulrik was now alone again could also be seen from his move-ments. He went on rather long forays outside his territory and visited at least two other active wolf territories, likely searching for another female, his fourth female in chronological order. At least one of these forays turned out to be rather costly for him. By following up on his GPS coordinates, in combination with snow tracking, visual observation, and a good portion of luck, we obtained a rough picture of what had happened. Two of the trackers that reported directly to us were able to observe how Ulrik was involved in a fight with another male wolf, joined by a female, in this northern territory, later named Lövsjön. That a serious fight had occurred was also verified from tracks of two of the wolves rumbling around, with both wolves receiving wounds that left plenty of blood in their tracks. This rare observation was immediately spread among our trackers; the next day one person was able to get a photograph of two of the wolves out on a frozen lake, close to where the fight had taken place. The photo showed two wolves, likely the male and the female of this territory, one covered with blood over his chest and head. When following the tracks of Ulrik back south to his territory, he also was found to be bleeding rather heavily. No doubt he had been in for a tough fight with the Lövsjön male, likely over access to the female.

It is not unusual for wolves to fight one another over access to females and/or territorial space. On the contrary, it is likely more the norm of the wolves' territorial nature. What turned out to be somewhat more exceptional with this incident is that our DNA analyses later revealed that Ulrik was, in fact, the grandfather of both wolves present in the Lövsjön territory. The analyses showed that they were both born in the Julussa territory in Norway in 2003, that they were siblings, and that their mother was a daughter of Ulrik from his first reproduction in the Grangärde territory in 2000. Thus, she was his third offspring, the one which had not been captured and collared in the winter of 2000-2001. Life is sometimes indeed remarkable, even for wolves.

In May 2005, for unknown reasons, we again lost contact with Ulrik. Scent marks and scat depositions at traditionally used sites indicated that he was still alive and in charge of his territory. Our plan now was that we should follow up on him the next winter and possibly capture him for a third time at the age of six years. When snow came in November 2005 we found his tracks almost instantly, but, to our surprise, this time he wasn't alone. Again he traveled together with another wolf, which later proved to be his fourth mate, who had been born in the Halgån territory in 2004. We decided to go for both Ulrik and his female. On January 27, 2006 we managed to take his female, who was now named #06-02, but Ulrik got away. He had learned how to escape the helicopter by disappearing into a thick, mature forest as soon as the chopper approached. He would only expose himself in open areas when the aircraft was away. Unfortunately for him, our capture crew didn't mind playing the cat-and-mouse game, and, although our budget does not allow for much of this, they finally outwitted him. As before, we were excited to take a closer look at him; he was slightly lighter now, 43 kilograms, than last time in 2004; he had lost one of his front teeth, number 12, and the outermost part of his tail. Apart from that he seemed to still be in good physical condition. We now also understood why we had lost contact with him. His GPS collar showed to have been worn heavily so that the cables connecting the battery with the GPS unit were broken. We issued his third, last, and we hoped, better collar, similar to the one his new female had been outfitted with two days before. Now we were again able to study the details of their movements, and hoped to be able to follow him during the final chapter of his life.

In the spring of 2006, at the age of eight years, and together with his fourth mate, Ulrik fathered the second litter of his life. Data clearly indicated both wolves reduced their movements to a minimum in early May. By this time we had decided that our research also should include visiting all reproducing females within two to three weeks after giving birth in order to count, measure, and take samples from the pups. Accordingly, we approached the assumed den in late May 2006, only to find that it was abandoned. But there was little doubt that this had been the home for the adult pair and a number of pups for a period. Why was the den empty? The GPS/GSM collar data was limited, providing us with data only on their movements up to a couple of days previous to our visit. A few days after our visit to the den we received more data indicating that Ulrik and his female had likely left the den the day before our visit and moved the pups a few kilometers north. In fact, the behavior of using several dens during the first six weeks after reproduction seems to be a standard behavior among Scandinavian wolves, an adaptation allowing them to avoid other predators, such as wolves, brown bears, and humans, and prevent them from killing the pups. However, further data from Ulrik's GPS collar indicated that they cared for pups throughout the summer that same year, and during the following winter a pack of seven wolves could be tracked on several occasions.

During the winters of 2006-2007 and 2007-2008 we again carried out studies of predation with added access to GPS data—hourly positions for eight consecutive weeks from each winter. Instead of trying to track the wolves as much as possible, we regularly checked more than ninety percent of these positions in the field while searching for killed prey. These studies showed that moose were still the main prey, that moose calves were still preferred over adults, and that the pack had access to more kilograms of biomass per day than they possibly could consume. No doubt Ulrik still knew how to handle moose.

During one of these regular tracking events in February 2009, Ulrik and his pack were again exposed to another poaching attempt. Tracks on fresh snow on one of the forest roads revealed that someone had fired a shotgun at the pack from a car. This was discovered by our field crew when evidence in a couple of centimeters of fresh snow revealed what had happened just a few hours before our crew came to the scene of the crime. The pack had been traveling on the forest road while being pursued by the car from behind. The driver had opened the door of his car and leaned out to be able to fire his shotgun towards the pack, which was now standing still at the road looking back at the car. Luckily, the distance was fifty to sixty meters, too long to cause a serious injury to any of the wolves. From the point where the small shots hit the ground just in front of the wolves, they all responded by jumping over the snow wall and running off into the forest with great speed. The police were notified, and we followed up the incident by tracking the pack for many kilometers, but at no place could we find blood or any indication that any one of the wolves was seriously hurt. Once again, Ulrik had succeeded in escaping his worst enemy.

In the summer of 2009 several observations of adult wolves were reported to us by local residents that were concentrated in a small area, indicating that there again was a successful reproduction within the territory. By the following winter the pack consisted of nine wolves. This year, 2010, was also the first year that the authorities launched a licensed hunt in Sweden in order to restrict the growth of the wolf population. Hunters shot two eight-month-old pups in the territory during the hunt in early January 2010, and DNA analyses later confirmed that Ulrik indeed was the father of the two. The length of this wolf's life and the term of his reproductive years were remarkable! There seemed to be no limit to his capacity. Our research showed that Ulrik and his fourth mate reproduced each year from 2006 through 2009, and we were able to follow this pack on GPS collar data up to August 2008, when both Ulrik's and his mate's collars failed. Finally, in 2009 at age eleven years, Ulrik had made his last contribution to future generations.

In the summer of 2010, observations made by our field crew again suggested that there was reproduction going on within Ulrik's territory, and in the winter of 2011 a pack of six wolves was confirmed. DNA analyses of scats also confirmed that Ulrik's fourth mate, #06-02, was still the reproducing female. However, unlike the preceding years, Ulrik was no longer the father of the pups produced. He had by this time been replaced by an adult male from a neighboring territory.

Most likely Ulrik had either died or abdicated from his position as the alpha male during the previous winter, but we have so far not received any evidence of his true fate, and we likely never will.

Ulrik had a remarkable life, longer than, and with more mates than most wolves will have, even if due to circumstances outside his control. His luck and skills in avoiding danger, and his continued search for mates, finally paid off with a total of five successful reproductions in his life and some twenty to twenty-five pups produced, some of which have entered into the reproducing pool of the Scandinavian wolf population. This wolf has by far been the most important contributor to our understanding of wolf ecology in Scandinavia, and has for many of us working with him contributed to some of the most exciting moments in the field. May he now rest in peace.

CHAPTER FIFTEEN

Connection with a Wolf in Yellowstone's Most Remote Region[1]

Douglas W. Smith

ARGUABLY WOLVES LEAD more interesting lives than people, but I am not envious as they don't live long and often have grisly deaths. One recent wolf I have known stands out, and he is alive at this writing!

I first encountered Wolf 760 in 2010, atop the Trident, a massive three-fingered mountain in the Thorofare region of Yellowstone National Park. This is one of the wildest, most unfettered places imaginable in the "lower 48" United States. For some people being in such a remote setting holds an aura of legend. Admittedly, I am lured in by remoteness, partly because so little of it is left. Throw in wolves and I am hooked.

To tell the full story of this particular wolf, some details of the history of the Delta Pack to which he belongs is important in order to provide perspective of his role as an individual within his pack and the population to which he belongs. Frequently these details are not revealed, and thus not known, and usually biologists only deal with the last subject, population status. His story is remarkable because of the challenges of working in such remote areas. I only know some of his story, which makes his life still mysterious—the way wolves should be some say, but I think it is still worth knowing a little, so we are better able to live with them.

The Delta Pack, one of the oldest packs in Yellowstone, are descendants of the Soda Butte Pack released in 1995 on the Northern Range during the original reintroduction of wolves to the national park. After release these wolves headed north and settled for the summer in the Stillwater River, north of Yellowstone National Park drainage, where they successfully raised a single pup. In 1996 they denned on a ranch nearby with much fanfare, but caused little trouble. Though the pack caused no depredations to livestock, social pressure from this ranching community resulted in ranch owners requesting they be removed, which we did. The pack was placed in another acclimation pen built to accommodate them within the park. This second release site was near the remote location they would inhabit and which would become their namesake—the southeast arm of Yellowstone Lake, right where the river flows into the lake forming

---

1   A shorter version of this story was told in the second edition of the book *Decade of the Wolf.*

141

a magnificent and willow-laden delta—hence, the Delta Pack. They were released in October 1996.

After this second release, this time with new pups, they immediately explored and then settled the area from the delta south to the Thorofare region, east up the Thorofare River and into the South Fork of the Shoshone River. At times, they would even travel into the North Fork of the Shoshone River and west up onto Two Ocean Plateau. In their wanderings they covered an expansive territory, the largest of any Yellowstone Park pack, which some years exceeded 1000 square kilometers.

Most Yellowstone wolf packs fail to survive intact beyond ten or twelve years. Seven different wolf packs have existed in one area on the Northern Range, probably a consequence of the higher wolf density there that leads to greater competition for space between neighboring wolf packs. In contrast the Delta Pack can trace their lineage directly back to the 1995. Presently in their nineteenth year, this represents a remarkable run for a Yellowstone pack (only Mollie's Pack has existed as long, and, at this writing, the future of Mollie's is questionable). Apparently settling a territory early during recovery is vital.

Some of this packs' long-term stability may be caused by the exceptionally low overturn of its alpha females. Only three, or possibly four, different females occupied the alpha position in the Delta Pack over its entire history. One indication supporting this is that the pack used only a couple of den locations over this entire period. It is generally acknowledged that the alpha female selects the den and rendezvous sites. A low turnover in breeding females and their tendency to use traditional, well secured den sites, may have led to pup production every year except in 1999, 2009, and 2012. Pack size ranged between four and seventeen, and averaged ten, typical of many Yellowstone packs, but bigger than packs outside the park due to lower conflicts with humans.

From 1999 through 2009 it was anchored by one female, number 126. Her case was enigmatic. She was present within the pack during the entire time and was the presumed breeding female. Yet genetic samplings never turned up any pups identified as hers, suggesting she never bred, or perhaps we never caught her pups. Maybe male wolf number 760 was her son. The genetic results are inconclusive—a puzzle that may never be solved for the Delta Pack. In short, our field data suggests she was the dominant and breeding wolf for a period of years when number 760 was born, yet we cannot genetically link number 126 to him or other offspring, an odd disconnect between field and lab work.

It was the winter of 2010. Winter in Yellowstone adds another meaning to the definition of remote. We were collaring wolves and looking for the Delta Pack. Their huge territory makes it difficult to find them, even when

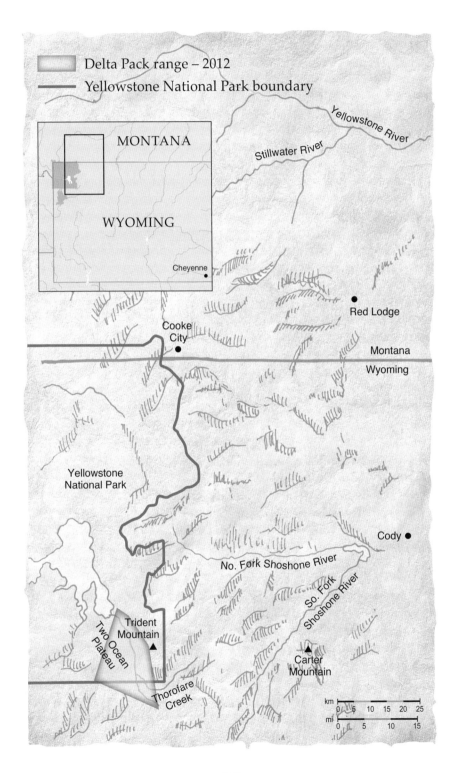

Delta Pack range – 2012
Yellowstone National Park boundary

MONTANA

WYOMING

Cheyenne

Yellowstone River

Stillwater River

Red Lodge

Cooke
City

Montana
Wyoming

Yellowstone
National Park

Cody

No. Fork Shoshone River

So. Fork Shoshone River

Trident
Mountain

Two Ocean Plateau

Carter
Mountain

Thorofare Creek

km
0   5   10   15   20   25
mi
0   5   10   15

some of its members carry functional radio collars. As a further compli-cation, much of their range is in a federally designated wilderness area. We are not allowed to capture wolves there. Consequently, this is one of our most difficult packs to radio track.

On February 21, 2010 Super Cub pilot Roger Stradley found them without the use of radio collars—easily his most impressive feat in nearly twenty years flying Yellowstone wolves. On this occasion Roger was guided to their hideout by a member that wore a radio collar. Immediately upon finding them on the bony flanks of Trident Mountain, he put out the always excited call to me in the helicopter. Helicopter pilot, Bob Hawkins, responded, and we headed toward the wolves, anxious, knowing with more than a little foreboding, what we'd encounter.

When Hawkins first saw the wolves, and more specifically the craggy, rugged terrain they were crossing, he wanted to call things off. "No way are we going to get them in there," he said over the radio intercom. "Let's get out of here." I agreed. There was just no way we could make this work.

At the last minute and on a whim, I asked Bob to hold for a few seconds a safe distance from the wolves so as not to disturb them to observe where they were headed. We fully expected them to go down the mountain, by far their best escape route. But, typical to wolves, they did the unexpected and headed up the mountain pushing through the snow. I couldn't believe it. Just watching gave me goose bumps as these wolves plowed through chest deep snow toward a 10,000 foot mountain summit.

Given that line of travel, I knew if they kept going we might have a chance. The top was flat and open, alpine habitat. Bob began circling the pack from a safe distance, not wanting to push them too hard, just keeping an eye on them. We hovered for a time at the rugged edges of the mountain, along stony cliffs plunging a thousand feet below, me sitting there in the helicopter with the door off, giving me a sensation every time we circled and the ground fell away.

The wolves stayed on course, finally making it all the way to the open summit onto a clean white slate of unbroken snow. The only problem for us was that they'd reached an extreme elevation for a helicopter. The air at these elevations is so thin that the blades of the helicopter don't have much to grab onto. Bob had told me this before, and reminded me again, and even with the high elevation modifications to this copter's tail rotor, he warned me this would be tough going.

"There's not much I can do up here," Bob barked into the intercom. "We'll have to go straight in. If they do anything, I won't be able to stay with them." I knew exactly what he meant. Sometimes when you go in the wolves are full of tricks, cutting this way or that, or even stopping, and once they figure that out, you're out of business. They'll do it every time.

Given that the wolves were right in front of us lumbering through deep snow, I thought we should give it a try. Maybe because they were tired, having just finished a rather heroic bout of mountain climbing, they would not have much extra energy. That being the case they would present easy targets, making shooting easy as they'd line out single file. Bob was able to slide in on the first wolf, and I landed a tranquilizer dart firmly in its hindquarters. This would become our wolf, male number 760.

The time it took to plant a dart into this wolf had allowed its pack mates time to get away. They dropped over the Trident summit and were heading down the other side into the upper reaches of Escarpment Creek. We managed to dart another wolf at the edge of the flat, open plateau before they reached the safety of the trees. Bob swung back and dropped me off with the first darted wolf, our normal way of processing. Then he flew back to where he had dropped the handling crew at the bottom of the mountain. Typically these staging areas were used to lighten the load of the helicopter so it can be as maneuverable as possible while in pursuit of wolves.

I cherish these moments alone with a sedated wolf in the Yellowstone backcountry. I just sit there and take it all in: the wolf, the majestic views, marveling at all the wild country spreading out in all directions as far as I can see. What would all this be without wolves? These are among my most precious moments of the year.

A year passes. Once again we're on the hunt for the Delta Pack. Over the static of the radio there Roger Stradley is again, just as excited, saying he's got them in a good spot up Mountain Creek, not too far from Trident Mountain. He informs us that although they're in a tight spot and it would be tough darting, it's doable. It's one of the snowiest winters in fifty years, and the snow is even deeper than the previous winter. I thought this would help us, as deep snow makes for tough running.

We head over to check it out. One wolf in the pack has a malfunctioning collar. I'm intent on finding this animal and replacing its collar. It was going to be difficult as there were thirteen wolves in the pack; sorting things out would be challenging with wolves running for the forest, and we wouldn't have much time. A couple pups cut away from the trees and into the open snow of a meadow. Bob and I have no trouble getting one of them.

We return and try to find the wolf with the malfunctioning radio in the chaos of scattering wolves beneath us. I make a mistake, one to this day I can't quite get my head around. Somehow I'm fixed on Wolf 760, confusing it for the animal whose collar has quit working. He takes to the creek where ice makes for easier running and a more challenging shot. Smart wolf, but I am able to dart him. Then, as usual, Bob drops me off.

Approaching the darted wolf, laying panting on its side in the snow, I realize what I have done. Here, before me, lays male Wolf 760, and he is big. Really big.

Recovering from the excitement and assessing the situation, I realize that this wolf has grown tremendously in one year. Weighing wolves is something of an inexact science, especially when viewed from above in a flying helicopter! Given that wolves can be holding up to twenty pounds of meat in their stomach doesn't help much. As it happens, the big collared male is slightly unsettled by the tranquilizer and, at one point, vomits. This is not an unusual reaction to tranquilizers. When it happens, we cradle the wolf's head with our arms, making sure to keep its airway clear of any obstructions. In the case of number 760, though, nothing comes up but bile, not a scrap of meat.

Once the ground crew is safely carted in and we begin processing him, I discover he has gained a whopping thirty pounds in one year. No wonder I didn't recognize him! At 148 pounds, he is the largest wolf ever captured in Yellowstone! I am struck by this creature.

Immediately I ask myself, how did he get so big? At the time of his initial capture a year earlier we estimated he was two or three years old based on tooth wear. This meant he was born either in 2006 or 2007. My guess was 2007. Research has shown that wolves are about eighty percent of full size by the end of their first year, but they will keep growing for several years. Having observed so many wolves over the years, I've learned males, especially, seem to go from gangly to bulky between two and three years of age. It just doesn't seem plausible he gained so much weight between three and four years of age.

I also surmise that this large weight gain was a reflection of the excellent foraging conditions in this part of the Yellowstone ecosystem. Quite frankly, wolves from other packs in Yellowstone did not display such weight gains or attain such large size. Unfortunately, we really don't have a good idea what this pack subsists on. We know there are more moose here. Elk abound in summer, deer too, and even an occasional bison. Bighorn sheep are here all year, so prey diversity here may be more than for any other pack in Yellowstone. Chemical signatures of wolf whiskers reveal isotopes unique to prey type. By collecting and analyzing such samples biologists have a way to get at what wolves or other predators' main diet consists of. Samples collected from Delta Pack wolves suggest that this pack eats more moose than any of the other Yellowstone packs. Moose are a large and formidable prey of wolves, and it helps to be large when trying to bring moose down. Perhaps Wolf 760's size was related to, or a result of, his specialized diet.

His great size probably helped him attain alpha status in the Delta Pack. This is unusual, as our Yellowstone data suggests breeder status is matrilineally inherited. Daughters inheriting breeder status from their mothers is far more common than males doing so.

The big male 760 traveled widely, and the only way I could watch him was from the window of Roger's Super Cub. Sometimes he was at the den, other times with the pack on a kill, or perhaps on his own, providing for the pack, I figure. One time I photograph him by a den with pups where he seems somewhat detached, but still attentive (typical dad).

Oddly, the Delta Pack did not have pups in 2012 despite his clear pair bond with an adult female. As a result the pack ranged across the region, exhibiting a winter-like pattern, as no pups tethered them to a den. One time they were sacked out in tall grass under the shade of a lodgepole pine tree at about 8500 feet elevation. It looked so idyllic, a mid-summer slumber somewhere in Yellowstone, I was tempted to ride to the spot on my horse Joker, a several day ride—one way! Another time, with a thin summer coat, he worked his way through a 1988 burn with many downed trees. Tough going, but the wolves seemed to slip through, each wolf picking a different way. Some hopped logs; others went log to log walking down them, and made surprisingly good time.

These bits and pieces of data left much to be interpreted. Why no pups in 2012? Had he really been born to the pack and thus inherited a leadership role? In 2012 he turned five, the average age of death for a Yellowstone wolf. What would happen now? The long, slow, decline? Lose his alpha status? Had his getting-to-be long tenure contributed yet again to the long term stability of this pack? Every time I looked for him, straining forward on the seat in the plane for a look, I wondered if some small clue would reveal itself and flesh out the story. But this wolf, all the other wolves, and this country, don't give up secrets easily.

In 2012, after an especially hot and dry summer choked with smoke from forest fires, the crisp fall air signaled the elk rut. This is also the hardest time of year for a wolf, what I call the seasonal pinch-point because prey are in good shape from a summer feeding on lush forage, and there is no snow to impede escape from pursuing wolves. Prey gets easier to kill with each passing day. Get through this, and winter will bring easier times.

It also means the elk hunting season, and a wolf hunt—the first for the State of Wyoming. Gut piles of elk from human hunters can lure a wolf out of the park—grizzly bears do this too. I understood the need for a hunt, but still I worried about Delta male 760. He was a valuable research animal and an interesting individual.

We flew little during the hunting season due to a combination of factors, so we did not locate the Delta Pack much. On a cold day in early December I climbed into Roger's Super Cub, anxious to learn what we might find. We flew into Thorofare, a favorite haunt of theirs. No luck. We headed east into Open Creek and no luck again. I could see out of the park into the South Fork of the Shoshone River and beyond to Carter Mountain; one of those cold, crisp, calm days in early winter that are hard to come by.

We banked back west, spotting an elk herd in the headwaters of the Thorofare River. Snow had not yet to driven them out of the high country. Tracking our way across the south boundary we slipped into Fox Park, and, just as I was beginning to lose hope, we picked up that beep, there they were, our Delta wolves! Winging in for a closer look, I spotted eleven wolves tightly bunched up under a tree – all of them had made it through the hunting season, number 760 included.

I think of male Wolf 760 because he causes me to wonder about what wolves mean, and really what wildness means. Wolves do not need wilderness to live in. Still wildness and wolves seem inextricably linked. Wolves never do well unless away from people. The conflict is too great. But what is this thing, conflict? Most would say livestock depredation, competition for wild prey, and concern for human safety/health. The last is overblown, so really it is just the first two, and Wolf 760 lives in such remoteness to make livestock a non-issue. But he roams through world-class elk hunting country so the second reason applies. How do we envision hunting? Is it a hunt or is it a crop akin to agriculture? Most of us are recreational hunters, so importantly what type of quarry do we seek? Must wildlife managers manage remote regions like farms, or make parks like Yellowstone and wilderness serve every human need? Doesn't this make it less wild? Aren't these places defined by wolves, grizzlies, bears, cougars, elk, sheep, moose, swans, loons, falcons, eagles? In the absence of these few precious places we'd lose the stories from wolves like number 760 as well as the wild stories, told and untold, of all these other beings that inhabit such wild places.

Fast-forward to 2013 — wolf capture season Yellowstone National Park — Thorofare again; February 3, 2013. Yellowstone Meadows, flat country, deep snow. Delta Pack: sitting ducks. Darting in here would be easy, not like Mountain Creek in 2011 or the Trident in 2010, but number 760 was not a target — his brother number 661 was. But we saw Wolf 760 lumbering along. The pack was resting on an elk kill, and we pushed them out into the treeless meadow. Reluctant to run through deep snow, they mostly ran single file, and it was easy to see the big wolves including number 760, a gray, and his black brother number 661. Dan Stahler was darting and he easily landed a dart in number 661. Once we got to him, we weighed him and, like his brother, he was one of the largest wolves captured in Yellowstone – a whopping 153 pounds! But this wolf did not have an empty belly, so his true weight is unknown. What a pair of brothers, and the largest two wolves caught out of over 450 captures! The fabled Thorofare country of Yellowstone keeps producing stories of wildness and amazement found in few other places in the continental United States.

CHAPTER SIXTEEN

The Vireo Wolf – Life and Death of a Conundrum[1]

John B. Theberge and Mary T. Theberge

WE NEVER LAID EYES on the Vireo wolf, not while he was alive. Phantom-like, he sifted through the Algonquin hills, down by some lonely bog one night, far away on a maple ridge the next. Sometimes he traveled alone, other times with pack mates. Sometimes he was gone so long we thought his radio collar had failed, but then it came back on the air again. We knew his tracks; we heard his howl, and for three years, we repeatedly dialed up his signal from both the air and the ground. Yet he remained a mystery, a conundrum. Gradually it dawned on us that he had a secret. But the Algonquin forests are steeped in ecological conundrums; they hid his secret well.

Even though he eluded us, or maybe because he did that so well, he became one of the most memorable of the 149 wolves that were radio collared during our fourteen-year study in Algonquin Provincial Park, Ontario. Many wolves surprised us, not fitting the classical patterns of behavior and movement, but no wolf so amazed and baffled us. No wolf had pointed to a deep conservation problem like the Vireo wolf, and, in the end, no other wolf confronted us with an issue of evolutionary importance like the Vireo wolf—all sketched out by his remarkable life and death.

The first time we saw him, he was just a pile of fur partially hidden under October leaves. His completely bare skull, the canine teeth worn to stubs, lay on its side at the foot of a majestic old hemlock. By scraping away the leaves we exposed one mandible, a scapula, both femurs, one humerus. His spinal column was intact to the last caudal vertebra, all but the broad atlas that once supported his large head. Some small animal, maybe a pine marten, had dragged its atlas a few meters away, then abandoned it. His radio collar lay on top of his fur, broadcasting its rapid, high-pitched signal to an unhearing and uncaring world, except for us.

He had chosen to die alone in the heart of his territory at the foot of the big hemlock that towered above the hardwoods like a monument. His identity would become etched into its needles as the tree took up his atoms.

---

1 Adapted, in part, from the chapter "New Adaptations, New Species" in *Wolf Country, Eleven Years Tracking Algonquin Wolves*. McClelland & Stewart Publishers, Toronto. 1998.

Five meters away, an iron-stained creek plunged over mossy boulders on its way down through the trees. Its water must have played a requiem, perhaps easing the dying wolf's last mortal minutes. Like other wolves, he had died near an active beaver pond, places where many packs established their rendezvous sites. Had the leaves been off the hardwoods, he would have glimpsed the broad sweep of lowland cradling Wilkins and Robitaille Lakes to the south—the land that had supplied all his needs, echoed his howls, took the impressions of his big feet across its snow-covered lakes.

In the months before his death, we had given the Vireo wolf a lot of attention. He had rewarded us with considerable data, enough that three months earlier it had even predicted his death. His behavior had become wolfishly unacceptable. Sure enough, in mid-October while flying over his territory, graduate student John Pisapio heard his signal on mortality mode.

The Vireo wolf had chosen a remote place to die. We booked a float plane, but low clouds and wind forced us to cancel. Two weeks later we aborted a four-hundred mile trip from our headquarters at the University of Waterloo to retrieve him because of high winds and rain. The following week we tried again, driving logging roads to within five kilometers of John's mark on the map. We portaged our canoes down a steep trail to Vireo Lake and set out. The previous week's snow had melted, but a scattering of large flakes raced us down the lake. Lacy hemlock crowns along the shore bent in the wind, and the ranks of hardwoods swayed on the hills. A flock of common mergansers, oblivious of winter's approach, lifted off the water ahead, and an occasional wind-tossed raven hurtled by. Otherwise, Vireo Lake was stripped of life, ready for winter.

At the end of the lake we hauled up our canoes, took out the map, and plotted a bearing to the carcass about one and two-thirds kilometers away. The wolf's signal came in loud from a hilltop when we were halfway there. As we approached we tuned down the receiver to better distinguish where his collar lay. He was easy to find. We examined and photographed the scene of death, picked up the collar, and packed up his remains into a plastic bag. So ended the record of the life of an unusual wolf.

According to the capture report filed by graduate student Joy Cook on June 1, 1993 he was an adult male weighing thirty-six kilograms—large by Algonquin standards. She named him Jocko 6, believing him to be the sixth wolf we had collared in the Jocko Lake Pack, because the capture site fell three kilometers inside that pack's southern boundary.

Throughout that summer he was located only five times. All but the last were in the same general area where he was collared, but always the radio collared Jocko Lake wolves were away off to the north. His last fix

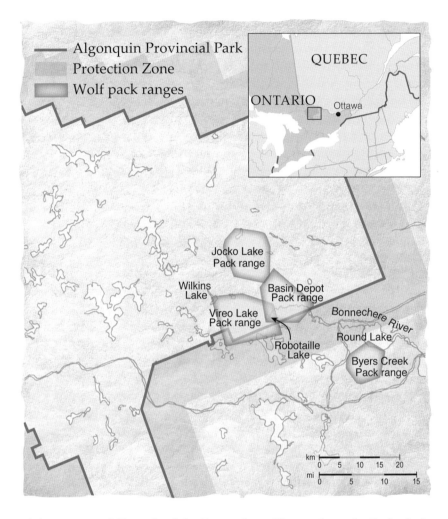

of the summer fell south of the Bonnechere River, where the Jocko Lake Pack never went. Even before that first winter, we suspected he was not really a Jocko Lake wolf. Then, on a blustery January day we picked up his signal from the air outside the park over the Round Lake deer yard, a low snowfall region consisting of an intermingling of forest and farmland. Probably he had followed the last of the migrating deer. Most of the wolf packs with territories in the eastern half (approximately 3,000 square kilometers) of Algonquin Park were migratory, too, staying out of the park all winter with only occasional forays back "home." In the deer yard, the park wolves met the year-round canid residents—various mixtures of coyote-wolf hybrids.

When the Vireo wolf Jocko 6 first went to the deer yard that winter, the Jocko Lake Pack was feeding on a deer out on the ice on Beaverdam

Lake, five kilometers to the north. That evening when we went out to monitor, the Jocko Lake wolves had gone, but to our surprise the Vireo wolf's radio signal showed that he was on the kill. He must have bided his time, waiting in the trees for the pack to depart. For a cross-bearing, we drove to the far shore and, with our headlights off, slowly approached to within two-hundred and fifty meters. We could picture him out there in the dark, wind ruffling the grizzled fur along his broad back as he tugged at the remains of the deer.

Repeatedly our evidence showed that he was a lone wolf. A few days after the Beaverdam Lake incident, we tracked him to a single bedding site in a snowy marsh beside the Bonnechere River. He ran off just before we got there, a disappointment to the photographer from the Ottawa Citizen who accompanied us. Another time we frightened him off a sunny knoll in a south-facing aspen stand where he had been curled up in the snow, basking in microclimate warmth.

He seemed to have an aptitude for finding other packs' kills, which may have been crucial to his survival as a lone wolf. Only four days after taking advantage of the Jocko Lake Pack's kill, he was with a Jack Pine wolf at another deer carcass. At least twice that winter, however, he appeared to have made his own kills. Although old, he was a big, strong wolf.

That winter he traveled extensively, returning four times to the park, often to the vicinity of Robitaille Lake, twenty to twenty-five kilometers west of the deer yard. He did not follow a straight line in these travels, on one occasion roaming deep into the Basin Depot Pack's territory ten kilometers to the north. Once he stayed in the park only two days before returning to the deer yard. After February 6, however, he remained out of the park, roaming extensively throughout the Round Lake area until early March. Then, one week before he returned to the park for the summer, Joy saw him from the air with another wolf. Had he found a mate down in the singles bar, and was it wolf or coyote?

Not until the last day of July 1994 did we learn the answer. The Vireo wolf spent that early summer in the same remote area of the park where he had made his winter excursions, defining his territory to include Robitaille, Wilkins and Vireo lakes. He was around Vireo Lake often enough that we added a new pack name to his identity, and he became Jocko 6 Vireo or, more succinctly, the Vireo wolf. He stayed south far enough to avoid trespassing on the Jocko Lake Pack's land, just as he had the previous summer. Finally, we confirmed that he and his mate had at least two pups in a marshy rendezvous site. They stayed there, howling for us on occasion, until mid-August, the end of the summer records.

Sometime between December 15 and 28, 1994, during the height of the deer migration, the Vireo wolf again traveled out to the farmlands around Round Lake. Often that winter we confirmed the existence of a pack of four. The big male was always one of them. Ninety percent of their fixes fell within a small area covering no more than four square kilometers. Deer were plentiful there, but no more so than throughout much of the deer yard as shown by our track transects. Strangely, the pack's territory was more coyote-sized than wolf-sized.

Also strange was that this winter the Vireo wolf, now with his new pack, stayed in the farmlands without any return trips to the park. His was the only pack that did. A few pockets of deer remained in the park that winter, enticing a few packs to stay on the territory all winter and others to travel back and forth at least once. The land chosen by the four wolves consisted of some pine-poplar hills strung together by marshes and a large cedar swamp. With all its variety, it was good wolf and deer habitat, but it posed a problem for us. Most of it was private property. We had run across the person who owned a central portion of it, and he had little use for wolves, or for us.

Our first encounter with him was along a snowy, one-lane concession road that ended about two kilometers from his farmhouse. One January day, accompanied by a film crew from TVO (Television Ontario), we tracked the Vireo wolf and his pack along the road to an icy overflow where they had cut into the bush. The land on that side of the road was not posted, so we followed their tracks along a creek to an alder tangle where the wolves crossed on thin ice. Normally we would have jumped the creek with ease, but the cameraman and soundman were attached by a two-meter-long cable. To make it across, they would have had to jump in unison. Each man weighed well over two-hundred pounds and carried expensive equipment that added even more weight. We returned to the main road. The landowner had seen our tracks and yelled at us out his truck window to stay off his land. Our attempts to explain that it was not posted seemed to anger him more.

Our second meeting a few days later did little to enhance our reputation. We had found a road-killed deer and were sure the Vireo wolf, always nearby, would find it too. That was the break the TV crew wanted. To improve their chances, producer Loren Miller phoned the Petawawa Military Base not far away and asked for some tank camouflage. The next morning, with the camouflage draped over our truck, we proceeded slowly along the concession road towards the dead deer. Through the tiny holes across the windshield, suddenly, on the narrow road ahead, we saw the same man's truck. He stopped dead, probably thinking he was caught in a military maneuver. We reached him, and Loren got out to attempt to explain. When he realized that no tanks were about to appear and he was not in danger, he gave her the same curt warning to stay off his land.

On three consecutive mornings we drove out to the carcass. The ravens would arrive as first light washed over the snowy scene. They paid little attention to the camouflaged truck, but we had to sit perfectly still or they would detect our movement and fly off. The Vireo wolf had indeed found the carcass and was close by each morning, especially the last morning when his signal placed him in the trees right behind the carcass. Probably he had eaten his fill and was sleeping it off. Once, the ravens all went squawking up from the carcass, and we were able to film the Vireo wolf's legs approaching from behind a big spruce. He stopped just short of the carcass, and then retreated into the trees. To have lived so long in such dangerous surroundings required great stealth. Many people have only glimpsed his legs in the film subsequently shown repeatedly on television.

That winter, 1994-95, back in the Vireo territory in the park, another pair of wolves capitalized on the pack's absence and moved in. We had known about the trespassers since late January. One was Pretty 7, a young female collared the preceding May, who had wandered all summer in the north central part of the park near the Petawawa River and ventured once outside the park almost to the Ottawa River. In early January, after traveling to the edge of the deer yard, she returned to the park and took up residence along the Bonnechere River in the north portion of the Vireo summer territory. One snowy afternoon in mid-March we discovered that she had a mate. We watched them run across a marsh less than one-hundred and fifty meters from the Vireo Pack's previous rendezvous site, and we wondered what would happen when the Vireo Pack returned.

To our surprise, the pack didn't return. In early May 1995, long after all the other park wolves had gone back to the park, the Vireo wolf was still in the farmlands. Anxious to find out if he was alone again, we drove up a muddy road to his pack's usual place. The calls of spring peepers cut the night air. His signal was loud when we got out of the truck to howl. A yippy wolf answered us, followed by long, deep howls on the same bearing as the signal. Then off to the right, about sixty meters from the Vireo wolf and partner, came distinctly coyote-like, nasal, treble yap-howls, accompanied by a lower-pitched, yippy voice. Four animals, as expected, but could the big Vireo wolf be mated to a coyote? Could the pack consist of both species?

We targeted the pack for capture, and over the next few weeks our crews collared the three other pack members: a 20-kilogram lactating female, a slightly larger yearling female, and a more typical 29-kilogram young adult male. Like the howls we had heard, these weights suggested a mixed wolf-coyote pack.

The young adult male surprised us too. If our earlier interpretation had been correct and this Vireo Pack had formed only the previous summer, that wolf should have been no older than a yearling. The explanation came a year later; genetics results confirmed that the young adult was not the big Vireo wolf's son, nor was the yearling female his daughter. So, this could not be his pack of the previous summer.

What had happened? In the fall of 1994, he must have lost his new mate and two pups and again become a lone wolf. Then traveling to the farmlands as he had before, he must have joined this resident farmland pack. We called the farmland pack the Byers Creek Pack, despite the big Vireo wolf's presence in it.

In late May 1995, the Vireo wolf adopted a strangely ambivalent pattern of movement. Repeatedly, one day he was with his farmland family, and a day or two later was back on his territory in the park. Each time he made the switch, he had to travel through another pack's territory. He seemed torn between his new pack and his old lands. We wondered if he could be a member of two packs. He always traveled back to the mid- and southern section of his lands near Vireo, Robitaille, or Wilkins Lakes, a difficult area for us to access. However, we managed to get close enough to howl at him a few times and confirmed with howling and tracks that he was alone. His was a beautiful, deep, resonant howl.

Meanwhile, trespassing Pretty 7 and her mate denned in an old clearing beside the Bonnechere River, the northern part of the Vireo territory. They used a sandy embankment that had been excavated more than a century before to form the cellar of a roadhouse. We kept signal-watch on this fledgling pack. Rarely was Pretty 7 more than a hundred meters from her den. In early July she moved her pups two kilometers west across the Bonnechere River.

One hot July evening, wanting to check on her, we hiked the north shore of the river. Mosquitoes escorted us along. After a while we turned on the receiver and, to our consternation, Pretty 7's signal came in on mortality mode. What could have happened? Could the Vireo male have come back into this northern sector of his territory? We changed channels and, sure enough, for the first time that summer he was there. It was dark by the time we managed to ford the river at a rapids. By flashlight we followed a game trail along the south shore, but soon a complex of beaver ponds blocked us. After groping around in the alders awhile, we were forced to return to the truck and camp for the night.

The next morning we set off early working our way around the ponds and following the signal to the Pretty wolf's rendezvous site at a recently drained beaver pond with new grasses and sedges just starting up. We tracked the signal to a high-and-dry beaver lodge and for a while could not find the collar. Finally, Mary bent over, looked inside the old lodge through a tunnel entrance and saw it lying on the central platform within. Only the collar was there, still bolted up. No blood was on it, no matted hair, but a pair of chip marks along its edges showed where wolf teeth had clamped down on it. There were no signs of a struggle around the lodge. Fresh pup and adult tracks plastered the mud, nothing more. For hours we combed the area, searching in increasingly larger circles from the lodge, finding only scats and bones of beaver and deer.

The collar could have come off in a fight, or even in play, but if it were that loose she would have lost it within the first few days after collaring. All other times we retrieved wolfless collars worn for more than a few days, we were able to confirm that the wolf had died. Pretty 7 had worn her collar for fourteen months. She was alive when observed from the air nine days earlier. If she had been killed just after that, enough time would have elapsed in the summer heat for decay organisms and scavengers to separate her head from her body. How her collar was carried into the beaver lodge with an entrance just large enough for a pup, or a fisher or a fox, but not an adult wolf, remains a mystery.

The Vireo wolf became the prime suspect. After all, Pretty 7 and her mate had been trespassing, even trying to raise pups on his land. Also implicating him was a change in his pattern of movements. After that, never again did he return to his farmland family, the Byers Creek Pack; he simply deserted them and stayed on his old territory. He even pushed beyond his boundaries, first to the east to within a few hundred meters of the Basin Depot wolves, then a few days later to the west, where he was equally close to a male in the Redpole Lake Pack. Perhaps he was looking for scavenging opportunities again.

In August we laid on a few extra flights, anticipating that he would get killed by an adjacent pack, or even possibly by the Pretty female's mate if he was still there. Back in the farmlands, John occasionally heard the Byers Creek Pack howl and suspected it consisted of six animals, not just the remaining three. Had the big Vireo wolf been ousted? He must have died in early September, judging by the leaves partially covering his skeleton. Scavenger beetles, bacteria, and flies had completely cleaned his skull. Judging from an incisor tooth aged by its annular rings, he had lived ten years, making him the second oldest wolf in our study.

His large skull now sits on the window shelf in our home library/office, grimacing down at us, the mystery of his life gone from the empty braincase. At times we look at it and think about wolf social order. A genealogy chart drawn by geneticists Sonya Grewal and Paul Wilson reveals near-irrefutable evidence that the denning Pretty Lake female, that our circumstantial evidence suggests was killed by the big Vireo wolf, was his daughter. Pretty 7 had been caught and collared on a dispersal foray looking for a mate, which explains her extensive movements that summer. Eventually, she returned to her natal territory with her new mate, found it empty, for reasons unknown, and settled down.

Maybe the Vireo wolf attacked her mate and she joined in. Or perhaps she attacked her father and lost, or her mate attacked him and she was forced to choose which wolf to be loyal to, father or mate—we will never know. The event, like whatever motivation drove his strange movements and behavior, remains a secret locked up in the rolling forested hills, the lakes and beaver ponds that once supported his existence. Perhaps his offspring, coyote, wolf or hybrid, are still there.

Our experience with the Vireo and Byers Creek Pack made us ask to what extent coyote genes may be infiltrating into the Algonquin Park wolf population. That question changed the direction of the study and through collaring a mix of wolf-like to coyote-like animals in the farmlands and adjacent Frontenac Axis we discovered the existence of a hybrid soup. Genetic tests from Algonquin Park confirmed these wolves were more closely related to the red wolf than gray wolf. Hybridization with coyotes, of course, spelled the red wolf's near-demise as a species in the eastern United States. We learned that coyote genes were also infiltrating into the Algonquin wolf population.

This gene infiltration was partly the result of park wolves traveling outside Algonquin Park, breeding, and returning to the park, like the Vireo wolf did. As well, coyote-like animals tended to enter the park wherever wolf packs had been annihilated or fragmented by human killing outside the park. And human killing was also the main source of mortality in the supposedly "protected" Algonquin wolf population.

Clearly a protection zone around the park was needed for wolves. Years of lobbying—biopolitics—followed. Hunter and trapper organizations opposed any further wolf protection. But conservation won out, and in 2003 the Ontario government established a permanent protection zone of ten to fifteen kilometers around the entire park. Subsequent research has verified a drop in hybridization within the Park.

Thus the Vireo wolf's life highlighted the fact that wolf persistence in parks and reserves cannot be taken for granted. Even without the hybridization issue, excessive human-caused mortality of trans-boundary packs threatened the Algonquin population's long term viability. Control programs designed to significantly lower wolf populations right up to boundaries of existing parks are on the increase in both western Canada and the United States. Part of winning support for wolves is appreciating their wide range of adaptable behaviors and individual personalities. The wolf still needs advocates.

What about the Vireo wolf's probable hybrid offspring? Are they just aberra-

tions? Hybridization is treated largely as a biological mistake in ecology texts. We learn about the immutability of species, about barriers that exist to prevent closely related species from interbreeding, and that hybridization normally results in biological failure. We are taught that hybrids are sterile, or produce sterile offspring, or have little vigor. Yet, recent research is revealing that in the span of evolutionary time, hybridization has been a significant source of genetic variation contributing in a major way to the diversity of life on Earth. Hybridization is one important way that species innovate, fabricate, adapt.

Wolf-coyote hybrids have demonstrated success in agriculture-forest fragmented landscapes that have been subjected to significant disturbances caused by logging, farming, hunting and trapping. Hybrids come with the more rapid reproductive output of coyotes and an expanded range in size of suitable prey from small to large animals. Maybe the Vireo wolf's life represented evolution in action. With climate change, hybridization may become more common among wildlife species and a more important part of life's resilience.

But at the same time, the Vireo wolf exemplified management action needed to maintain both a viable population and its genetic integrity in a park, where species protection is an overarching goal. In such places, protection must work; invariably for a large-ranging mammal like the wolf, they must be buffered.

CHAPTER SEVENTEEN

A Hybrid's Tale

John F. Benson

I FIDDLED WITH THE TUNER on my telemetry receiver with numb fingers until I had the correct frequency. Then I raised the handheld "rubber-ducky" antenna and slowly rotated it 360 degrees, holding the receiver against my ear. No signal. "Can you hear anything?" whispered Peter Mahoney, my field assistant. Pete was an excellent field biologist with quick wits and sound judgment who had become a valuable partner during our many missions together in the field. I shook my head and tucked the receiver back under my rain coat. It was just above freezing and had been drizzling steadily since we got out of the trucks. At least last night's freeze was keeping the black flies at bay for now. Accompanying Pete and me was Aaron Ketner, an undergraduate student who had grown up just south of Algonquin Provincial Park in Ontario, Canada. Aaron possessed great field instincts and had proved to be a solid addition to the crew. We continued west up a hardwood-covered ridge towards the suspected den site of the wolf-coyote hybrid pack we were tracking.

It was May 16, 2009, the first day of the den season. Over the next month, my crew and I would visit all of the dens of the twelve wolf, coyote, and wolf-coyote hybrid packs I was currently tracking. I was a Ph.D. student in the second of four years spent in the field studying wolf-coyote hybridization dynamics both within, and adjacent to, Algonquin Park. The project had been initiated by my advisor and chief collaborator Dr. Brent Patterson, research scientist with the Ontario Ministry of Natural Resources and provincial wolf research leader. The areas where I conducted my study are inhabited by a very diverse combination of canids including eastern wolves (the dominant wolf inside Algonquin Park), gray wolves (common in northern Ontario), and eastern coyotes (larger versions of the coyotes found in western North America, abundant in southern Ontario). The eastern wolf is thought to be a unique species that evolved in eastern North America, and it is extremely rare. Its current geographic distribution appears to be restricted largely, or entirely, to Algonquin Park and the immediately surrounding areas. My project focused on investigating the behavioral and demographic consequences of hybridization between wolves and coyotes and how hybridization may affect the persistence of eastern wolf populations on the Ontario landscape in the future.

Hybridization is simply interbreeding between different species or distinct populations. Eastern wolves are intermediate in size between larger gray wolves and smaller coyotes, and they readily hybridize with both species in places when they come into contact. Presently much debate centers on the legitimacy of the eastern wolf as a species, made even more confusing by its propensity to hybridize with coyotes and gray wolves. In some cases hybrids are inferior to the parent species that produce them, meaning that the hybrids survive and reproduce poorly relative to the parent species. In other instances, hybrids may survive and reproduce quite successfully, at times even better than the parent species. If one of the parent species is rare, this can sometimes cause a reduction, or even extinction, of the rare parent species as they become replaced by increasingly abundant hybrids. It is in these cases that hybridization can be a very challenging issue for the conservation of rare and threatened species.

It was my job to determine whether the wolves and coyotes on Ontario's contemporary landscape were still genetically and morphologically distinct, or whether hybridization had blurred these distinctions beyond the point where they could be reliably assigned to a single species. Many previous studies had investigated wolf-coyote hybridization using DNA analysis in a lab. Ours was the first study to combine detailed genetic analyses with an intensive field study to better understand the "hows" and the "whys" and "what nows" of hybridization. Brent and I wanted to know if the molecular differences observed in DNA also translated into physical and ecological differences exhibited by the animals, and, in turn, how these differences might affect the ecosystem of which the wolves and coyotes were a part.

So far genetic profiles from the lab lined up very well with the body size measurements I had made in the field and with my impressions of whether captured animals were wolves, coyotes, or hybrids. The two most obvious physical distinctions were their heads and paws. Wolves have big heads with relatively short ears and broad, blocky muzzles. Coyotes have smaller heads, longer ears, and long, narrow muzzles. Wolves have huge paws that balloon out from their narrow lower legs in a way that really catches your eye in contrast to coyotes' narrow legs that transition seamlessly into small paws. As one might expect, hybrids fell out somewhere in between, with intermediate facial and paw characteristics. The more complex questions regarding potential differences and similarities between the behavior and ecology of wolves, coyotes, and hybrids would only be answered by spending many hours in the woods, bogs and frozen lakes of Algonquin and surrounding areas. This was the laboratory where I spent the better part of four years. In the end, I hoped to understand why and where hybridization occurs between wolves and coyotes, and whether there are places or situations where wolves are able to resist hybridizing naturally.

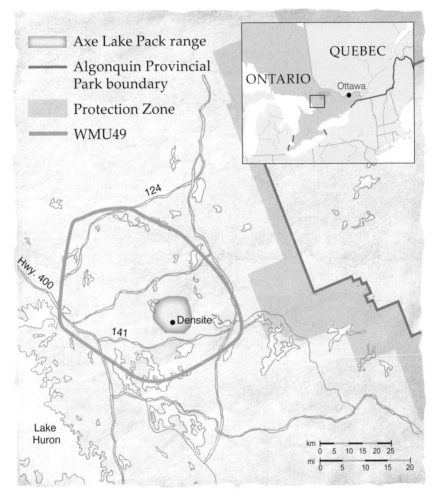

Axe Lake Pack range

Algonquin Provincial Park boundary

Protection Zone

WMU49

QUEBEC

ONTARIO

Ottawa

124

Hwy. 400

141

●Densite

Lake Huron

km
0 5 10 15 20 25

mi
0   5   10   15   20

Canids in this area produce litters of one to seven pups sometime between mid-April and early May. Our goal that chilly and damp May morning was to visit the Axe Lake Pack's den and catch the pups that we believed had been born about four weeks earlier. By catching as many pups as possible and surgically implanting small radio transmitter devices in their abdominal cavities, we would be able to track their movements and survival throughout the rest of their first year. The Axe Lake Pack, like most wolf and coyote packs, was composed of a breeding pair and their offspring. The Axe Lake territory lay about 60 kilometers west of Algonquin Park in Wildlife Management Unit 49, which we referred to simply as "49." The Axe Lake breeding female, ID number 49-09, was a wolf/coyote hybrid whose genetic ancestry came from both eastern wolves and eastern coyotes. Her mate was an eastern coyote.

I continued on through the hardwoods and the dim, raw spring morning. We were climbing and descending a sequential series of ridges, alternating with low and swampy sloughs. When we were about 900 meters from the suspected den site, I flipped on the receiver and was immediately rewarded by the familiar chirping noise of an active telemetry signal. My spirits lifted, and I turned to grin at Pete and Aaron. The signal appeared to be coming from the location of the suspected den site that I had obtained while tracking 49-09 during the previous four weeks. She was wearing a GPS collar that did two important things. First, it transmitted a very high frequency (VHF) radio signal that allowed me to track the animal with an antenna and receiver by tuning into its specific frequency. Second, it collected highly accurate global positioning system (GPS) locations, obtained as the collar communicated with satellites at regular intervals. I received these locations within a few days, after the satellites relayed the information back to earth and delivered them to me as an email message at my field station. Finding 49-09's den had required a combination of the two types of telemetry: GPS (via the satellite technology) and VHF (via the radio signal) tracking.

As the collar was on the pack's breeding female, in theory it should have been easy to find the den simply by plotting the spring GPS locations on a map and waiting until she restricted her movements to a single location, the den, for a period of weeks. The problem: dens are usually underground tunnels or rock caves that block the connection between the satellites and the GPS unit. Thus, the collar stopped collecting and transmitting GPS data as soon as she crawled into the den. When I stopped receiving GPS locations from 49-09 on April 16, I knew she had probably given birth to her pups inside a den. Although the GPS collar is useless inside the den, the VHF signal still transmits loud and clear. Flying over the Axe Lake territory in a small airplane, I had picked up 49-09's signal and guided the pilot with hand motions until he was making a tight circle directly over the point where the signal was strongest. We repeated this several times over the next two weeks and found her in exactly the same spot each time. She was "in the hole," and I had located a potential den site.

Like all female wolves and coyotes, after giving birth she spent most of the first two to three weeks inside the den providing the pups with almost constant nourishment and warmth. After this period she began to make short trips out of the den, probably to stretch her legs and join the rest of the pack on hunting excursions. During this time I received a smattering of locations from the GPS collar. Eventually a couple of GPS locations came in that were very close to my flight locations. Bingo! Now we had a highly accurate GPS location to investigate on the ground.

We huddled within 300 meters of the suspected den site. I told Pete and Aaron to hang back. I would go on ahead to find the den, the way we usually did things. I pointed the antenna at the strongest signal to indicate the direction of the den to them. Then I turned down the volume on the signal and continued on alone. The signal was very steady, indicating that she was not moving. I was standing in a swampy, flooded area between two ridges, now within 100 meters of the suspected den site. The ridge in front of me loomed ominously through the gray and damp morning. From the plane I had guessed the den was located in between two ridges along a relatively wide slough. I assumed the den was just beyond the ridge in front of me. Wolf and coyote dens are usually very close to a water source, and the den was probably burrowed into the bank on one side of the slough or the other. The previous day I had the pilot fly directly down the center of the slough at low altitude while I flipped the telemetry switchbox back and forth. This allowed me to listen to the signal separately from each of the antennas mounted on either wing. The signal had been strongest along the eastern bank. If I was right, this would put her just on the other side of the ridge in front of me.

Given her position nestled below the ridge, and with a stiff breeze blowing out of the west directly into my face, I was pretty confident she had not picked up my scent. The open understory and damp leaf litter from the morning showers allowed my approach to be virtually silent. I took a moment to draw in a deep breath and relish the moment. The previous month's tracking had paid off, the conditions were perfect, and this was the moment of truth! I moved stealthily through the stream and started up the ridge towards the den. On the top of the ridge the signal was booming even louder, although I kept it tuned to an almost inaudible level. I removed the antenna cord from the receiver. The signal continued to pulse directly from the receiver. This only happens when you are practically on top of the animal.

I stole across the ridge-top, passing directly through the spot of a GPS location received from the collar during the previous week, before reaching the edge of a bluff that dropped off to a muddy bank along a wide slough. I noticed a very old beaver dam which had grown over into a convenient moss-covered bridge in case we needed to cross. I jumped off the ridge about ten feet to the bank below and moved towards the bridge while flipping the antenna back-and-forth to either side of the slough. The signal was strong from the far side, but screaming louder when I flipped it back towards the ridge I had just come down.

Then I saw it—a hole somewhere in size between a basketball and car tire, burrowed into the base of the ridge. I pointed the antenna at the hole and the signal roared. My approach had gone well, but maybe a little too well. Most females flush from the den just prior to my arrival. Although

I'd been lucky enough to see a few walk out of the den in front of me and look back at me briefly before disappearing into the bush, I'd never had one still in the den when I arrived. Today I had cornered the collared female in the den!

I walked to the edge of the slough, took the cord and antenna off and walked directly back towards the hole. The signal went from non-existent to a loud thump-thump-thump. No doubt about it, she was in that hole. Canid tracks were all over the bank outside the hole. Many of the older tracks had probably been obliterated by the morning rain but the area outside the den was noticeably trampled down, indicating a lot of recent activity. Several large scats were strewn around the bank with thick beaver hair and small bone fragments.

I put my Rhino dual GPS and Walkie-Talkie unit to my mouth and said, "Pete, Aaron, can you hear me?"

"Yeah John, go ahead," whispered Aaron almost immediately.

"Come to my location, I've got the female cornered in the den. And bring the catch-pole!"

I grinned wolfishly as I imagined the effect these words must have had on their excitement level. The Rhino units automatically sent a GPS location of my current position when radio contact was made between units. All they had to do was hit "GOTO" on their Rhinos and navigate right to me. I turned my headlamp on and stuck my head in the hole. The strong, distinct odor of a wild wolf hit me deep in the back of my sinuses. I couldn't see anything because the hole went up steeply to a big mound of sand that I couldn't see beyond. But, intermittently, I could hear pup noises coming from inside the dark hole, including suckling and occasional squealing and grunting noises. Jackpot!

Aaron had the catch-pole with him; I'd have to wait for the other guys before attempting to deal with the situation. There was no question that 49-09 was aware of my presence. I fell back to give her some room and avoid causing additional stress. Her collar had recently been changed, so there was no value to capturing her. I just wanted the pups. She was probably too scared to come out, but I wanted to give her enough room to make a break for it if she chose to. I retreated to the beaver bridge and crouched down where I could watch and think. As I crouched down I could feel the adrenaline beginning to dissipate slightly, cautiously optimistic that we would succeed. I kept my eyes fixed on the hole in case she tried to carry a pup away in her mouth. If it came down to it, I figured I could probably scare her into abandoning the valuable cargo if I ran right at her. When the other guys arrived, I pointed out the den and briefly recounted my final approach. In their eyes I could see the same exultation that I was feeling. We lived for days like this. Aaron went back up on the ridge and made radio contact with the rest of the crew waiting back in the trucks. He told them to come in and to bring the gear needed for the transmitter surgeries.

As long as 49-09 remained inside the den it would be next to impossible to get at the pups. With the catchpole now in hand I was equipped to deal with her. I placed the catch-pole on the bank in front of the den, adjusted my headlamp, wriggled up through the entrance and stuck my head past the sandy mound. The tunnel dipped slightly. I pushed my body over the mound and down the chamber. Almost immediately it leveled out and there she was! I saw the face of 49-09 staring directly at me from five feet away. Her big yellow eyes gleamed in the light of the headlamp, and I saw the movement of a small gray-brown pup squirming under her left side. I didn't know how many other pups were under her, but the noise sure sounded like more than one. I quickly pulled myself back over the mound and out of the hole onto the bank.

I turned to Pete and Aaron and blurted, "She's right there—and I saw at least one pup!"

Their eyes widened. "Grab the camera from my hip pack!" I demanded. Pete reached into my hip pack on the bank and pulled out the little point-and-shoot digital camera. I grabbed it and wriggled back into the den. The female was in the same position, her eyes fixed directly on mine. I breathed in and out, put the camera up and took a picture. I wormed back out of the den and handed the camera to the guys; in the display window they could see what I had seen.

I went back in with the pole, a five-foot, metal pole with rubber-coated cable extending out of the front forming a circular ring. The ring is closed by pulling on the cable at the far end of the pole through which it extends. The idea is to place the ring around the animal's neck so that you can control its head and keep it from biting you. My plan was to get her head under control, drag her out of the den and then quickly release her. If successful, I assumed she would run away. People are always surprised when I tell them that wolves and coyotes don't stay and fight for their pups. From a cost-benefit standpoint, they recognize humans as bad news and realize that direct encounters will probably end in their death. By remaining to fight, they risk death (not knowing what a softie I am); by retreating they live to breed another year. Presumably, through evolutionary time, individuals that retreated had survived and reproduced better than those that stayed to fight. This meant more offspring inherited flight, as opposed to fight, behavior, allowing this trait to spread in wolf and coyote populations. If Charles Darwin was right about the whole natural selection thing, I would be able round up the pups once she was out of our way.

Easier said than done, as it turned out. I was in an awkward position with my body extended down the tunnel and legs sticking out of the hole;

and she wasn't going without a fight—natural selection be damned! It took a while to get the ring over her head as she snapped at the rubber-coated cable and held it tightly in her powerful jaw. Seeing this convinced me to keep my distance to avoid the wrath of her formidable teeth and massive jaws. I tried to pull the cable-ring back but she clamped even tighter. This happened several times. Realizing the only way to get it back was to stop moving, I waited for her to relax so I could jerk it back from her. This game went on for a while.

Meanwhile, the rest of the crew had arrived. I asked them to keep their voices very low and find a good, level spot to set up the surgery equipment on the far bank where we would reduce disturbance to the den area. While they got busy, I resumed my attempts to coax 49-09 out of the den. The crew was excited and, I suspected, a bit bewildered by the growling and snapping noises coming from the hole from which all they could see were my legs. I was covered in mud by this point, and it wasn't going particularly well. A couple of times I managed to get the cable around her neck, but she managed to pull out before I could tighten it. We had only brought one pole, which was quickly rendered inoperable after sand and grit collected inside the cable shaft. My brand-new, spare catch-pole was sitting back at the field station while the female remained safely tucked away with her pups. Fortunately, the trucks were just over one kilometer away from the den, and it would only be about a fifteen-minute drive to return to the field station and retrieve the new pole.

"Aaron, I need you to go get the other pole. And I need you to really haul ass OK?"

He grinned, "Sure thing boss." That's what I loved about Aaron. You could just tell him what needed to be done and didn't need to bother choosing words carefully. He grabbed his Rhino, adjusted his compass and charged up the ridge. Aaron moved fast in the bush. With the benefit of youth on his side, I knew he would be back soon. While he was gone, I helped the crew finish setting up the surgery station and told Charlene Berkvens, our volunteer veterinarian from the Toronto Zoo, that with any luck we would be able to start processing the pups within an hour. Charlene was one of my favorite vets to work with; she had been a huge help in organizing medical equipment and the tentative schedules of the many vets that would rotate in and out of our crew during the next month. The expertise of Charlene and all the other vets that helped us had been instrumental to our success and allowed us to maintain the highest medical safety standards during the critically important surgeries conducted in our temporary, make-shift clinics.

Even sooner than expected, Aaron reappeared on the ridge-top with the catch-pole. I congratulated him on his speedy journey and went back to work. Things went much smoother this time. I got it around the annoyed hybrid on the first try and tried to move her toward the entrance. She didn't want to come, and she was amazingly strong for her size. Pete stepped up and tried to help me, but he couldn't get any leverage from outside the den, so I waved him back. I started to move her towards the entrance, but she managed to raise her head, wedging her shoulder against the upper lip of the chamber. Wow, I thought, strong and smart! Finally she lowered her head and I managed to pull her out of the hole. I emerged onto the bank with the magnificent grayish-golden bundle of hybrid fury that was 49-09, and she immediately tried to get as far away from me as possible. Not wanting the cable to tighten further around her neck, I moved quickly with her to keep it slack. I felt myself being momentarily dragged by the force of her movement, until I was able to release the cable lock. The cable ring fired open and I flipped it off her head. She shot away down the bank and was out of sight after several bounds. Pete and I glanced at each other briefly as if to say "Wow!" while the crew looked on in amazement. Pete grabbed the telemetry gear to monitor her retreat, and I dove back into the den. I crawled inside and found a pile of seven squirming, grayish-brown four-week-old hybrid wolf pups. Eureka!

Led by Charlene's sure-handed field surgery skills, we successfully implanted a transmitter into each of the pups. As I watched, I wondered what adventures these little rascals might take me on in the upcoming year. We weighed each pup (just under four pounds apiece) and obtained blood samples for the DNA profiles. During the surgeries, 49-09 stayed just out sight, but never left the area, hovering in the woods about 50 to 60 meters away while we processed her pups. The male pup I was holding gazed at me calmly with his deep blue eyes. Although they were a bit growly and snippy at first, after being out of the den for a few minutes the pups had mostly settled down and became pretty docile. When we were finished Charlene and I made sure that each pup was fully recovered. Then I released each pup back into the den. Our work done, we quickly retreated back up the ridge and through the hardwoods to the trucks. It had been an exciting day; I was glad it had gone so smoothly. Now the Axe Lake female, 49-09, would return to her pups to, hopefully, raise them without further disruption.

Almost a year later in early March 2010, I was tracking the Axe Lake Pack on the ground. The pack now consisted of 49-09, her mate, and three of the pups tagged last spring that had stayed through the winter. I was tracking them to document their winter predation patterns. Over the last four days I had spent nearly every hour of daylight snowshoeing across the ridges, swamps, and lakes of their beautiful and remote territory to find moose, deer and beaver carcasses they had killed. I got back to the field station that evening and noticed that I had a voicemail on my cellphone. A trapper from up the road informed me that he had killed one of my wolves, and he asked if I wanted the collar. I wondered which animal it might be, as I knew this trapper operated in several locations throughout "49." As I drove to his house, my mind wandered back to the past several, long and productive days I had spent on the heels of 49-09 and her compatriots. I have found it to be incredibly instructive to spend multiple days in a row tracking a single pack. After a few days of constant tracking, I would begin to feel as if I was almost inside their heads, seeing what they saw and trying to perceive the world as they do.

Arriving at the house, I chatted briefly with the trapper before he led me out to the garage. A sobering jolt went through me as I recognized 49-09, lying dead on the floor in front of me. Instantly the past few days became a distant memory. She looked considerably smaller laying here in a garage then she had when she was looming menacingly in the back of her sandy tunnel-den. Although I had been tracking her intensely all year, I hadn't actually seen her since our tussle in the den almost ten months earlier. After getting some information and weighing her, I removed the collar and walked back to the truck. There were no hard feelings, of course. She had been trapped legally, and I was grateful to recover the collar.

I've grown accustomed to study animals dying, and I recognize that death is an important part of what we are studying. As a conservation biologist my primary interest is in maintaining healthy populations, and this focus generally allows me to avoid becoming attached to individual study animals. Still this one seemed a bit different. As one of the first animals caught in "49," I had been tracking her for almost three years. I was fresh off an unforgettable four days of visiting the most remote corners of her vast and spectacular territory. Her tracks and behavior had served as a looking glass into a fascinating world I was eager to understand. She would no longer be patrolling the rugged hardwood ridges and blustery shores along Axe Lake, and her coyote mate would have to find another partner to join him for his next moose hunt or beaver feast, and with whom to produce next year's litter of blue-eyed contributions to the next generation of Ontario canids. I wondered if his new mate would be a wolf or a coyote, or perhaps another hybrid?

Like it or not, this is the most common way that wolves, coyotes, and hybrids meet their death here in "49," and, indeed, in most unprotected landscapes where humans co-exist with wolves and coyotes. And in some ways I suppose the Axe Lake female's demise had a sort of grim irony. Humans indirectly and unintentionally created the hybrid zone that produced 49-09.

If not for the large-scale habitat conversion and intense persecution of wolves by humans during our westward expansion across North America during the 19th and 20th centuries, coyotes might never have arrived in Ontario. Similarly, the anthropogenic changes to the landscape and ecological communities here in central Ontario have allowed coyotes to become established in an area once dominated exclusively by wolves. Thus, without humans, and our unmatched capacity to change the world around us, it seems unlikely that coyotes and eastern wolves would have come into contact in Canada. Without humans, hybrids like 49-09 probably never would have existed. At the risk of being melodramatic, 49-09 had lived by the sword of humanity and had now died by it as well. It certainly wasn't a feel-good ending, but the death of 49-09 was another piece of valuable information in a study that proved to be an incredibly enlightening window into the mechanisms by which human activities influence hybridization between wolves and coyotes. Through the activities of animals in the Axe Lake Pack and others, we were starting to understand the behavioral ecology of these enigmatic hybrid wolves.

We're still piecing together the puzzle. Body size seems to provide hybrids dietary flexibility not found in larger "pure-bred" wolves, while still allowing them to take large prey. In many ways these hybrids were turning out to be more similar to "real" wolves than expected, as they were effective deer predators and were even capable of killing adult moose on occasion. However the social behavior between wolves and coyotes in the hybrid zone was in stark contrast to other areas where they coexist. Across their historic range, coyotes generally live within wolf territories and often scavenge wolf-killed ungulate carcasses, despite the imminent risk of violent reprisal. Conversely, wolves, coyotes, and hybrids in and around Algonquin do not share home ranges and exhibit very little overlap in time and space. In the hybrid zone, wolves and coyotes are more similar in body size than in other areas, prey on many of the same animals, and likely compete with each other for mating opportunities. This strong competition apparently manifests in rigid territoriality among all canids regardless of their genetic ancestry. We were learning that the wolves, coyotes, and hybrids of "49" defy conventional taxonomic and ecological classification and represent a fascinating example of a predator community experiencing contemporary evolution. The three-species hybrid zone in and around Algonquin is a truly unique study system and one from which we can draw important lessons about wolf conservation in human altered landscapes and, perhaps, gain a broader understanding of the forces influencing hybridization between wildlife species in general.

Chronicles of Resilience

CHAPTER EIGHTEEN

344F: A Remarkable Wolf

Mike Phillips

 HUNDREDS OF TIMES from 1987 through 1994 I put on my flight suit and crawled into the back of the Cessna 172 to radio track red wolves. Throughout most of each flight I could see beneath me a canopy of a heavy forest and reflected light flashing through the hardwoods and pines of the mysterious pocosin wetlands for which the Alligator River National Wildlife Refuge had been established. Pocosin, an Algonquin Indian word meaning "swamp-on-a-hill," are wetlands without obvious drainage ways. Their soils of sandy humus, muck, or peat drain slowly, and flooding is common. These wet soils support a dense, tangled under story of evergreen and deciduous shrubs and an over story dominated by pocosin pine. Canebrake rattlesnakes and water moccasins are common. Pocosin wetlands are formidable places that seem dark and foreboding. They are often called "dismal swamps."

After the local Indians had been subdued by the mid-1700's, settlers rapidly arrived and, through determination fueled by necessity, began a relentless destruction of pocosin wetlands. Ditching, draining and burning has gone on for centuries to make the dismal swamps fit for white man's agriculture and logging, especially of cypress and Atlantic white cedar which were highly prized for their resistance to decay.

The Alligator River National Wildlife Refuge was established in March 1984 across 118,000 acres of mostly mainland Dare County in northeastern North Carolina with the primary purpose of conserving the last best remnant of pocosin wetlands in the United States. The refuge surrounds the 46,000 acre Dare County Bombing Range, an area owned by the Department of Defense. Within the range, the North Carolina Wildlife Resources Commission manages 41,200 acres as game land.

Even before its establishment, the refuge, as well as the adjacent defense land, was considered an ideal location for a red wolf restoration project. It supports abundant prey: white-tailed deer, raccoons and marsh rabbits, but no coyotes and no livestock; it is bounded on three sides by large bodies of water: the Alligator River, Albemarle Sound, Croatan Sound, and Pamlico Sound; and it is sparsely settled by humans. My job from spring 1986 through fall 1994 was to run the project.

Peering from the window of the circling Cessna I saw an occasional logging road break the pocosin canopy affording rare glimpses of the forest floor. These glimpses provided insight into the world of the wetlands and became memories that would last forever. Recollections of a small, black-backed female known as Wolf 344 stand out among all others.

There was no mistaking from the radio signals I heard through my headphones that the two adult red wolves I was tracking, male Wolf 211 and female Wolf 196, were on the move. They had been released together in the refuge about seven months earlier. Over the past couple of weeks they had limited their movements to a small patch of pocosins near the intersection of two rutted and soggy logging roads. Female 196 had been especially attentive to this site, leading me and my teammates to believe that she had established a den.

The effort to establish a population of red wolves at Alligator River represented the first attempt in the history of mankind to restore to the wild a carnivore species that only existed in captivity. Success obviously required the production of pups each and every year. I was quite anxious for the inexorable ticking of this clock of persistence to begin. I had been hired to lead this project, not because of my innate patience, but precisely because I acted urgently. Each and every day my teammates and I set out with urgency to do all we could to ensure that the red wolf rejoined the ranks of wild species.

I saw the two adults easily. Male 211 was a magnificent wolf who tipped the scales at nearly 80 pounds. This made him slightly larger than average. He moved lightly on his feet and with a certainty that grew from his successful transition from life in captivity to life in the wild. His mate, female 196, moved more slowly and with pause. She, too, had established herself successfully in the wild, but today she had another matter on her mind. Trailing only a few feet behind was a small, waddling pup no more than a few weeks old. We reported its presence immediately to members of the larger red wolf recovery team. The red wolf studbook dictated that the pup's name would be Wolf 344. The pup's gender had to be left unas-signed until we captured and physically examined it.

The plane turned to afford us another look, and I grew anxious as 344 navigated what must have been a first encounter with one of the many dilapidated bridges that crossed the refuge's ever-present canals. Retired logging roads, which are common in the refuge, were originally constructed by digging dirt from a long stretch at the forest's edge. These borrow pits quickly filled with water and became canals. As the pilot and I circled for a third time we saw the pup and the female disappear into the pocosins. The long journey for the Alligator River Red Wolf Restoration Project had now begun in earnest. Wolf 344's life would turn in challenging directions for many years. This is the pup's story.

Any historical account of *Canis rufus,* the red wolf, must drift between extremes. This smaller cousin of the gray wolf, *Canis lupus,* was once common throughout the southeastern United States. It took the brunt of the first wave of what would prove to be a multi-century long effort by European settlers and their descendants to exterminate the wolf as an important part of manifest destiny, to settle the continent by wiping wildness from the land. Historical records for wolf bounties paid extend as far back as the mid-1700's. Typical are these from the Tyrell County Courthouse in eastern North Carolina for February 5, 1768:

> Giles Long and Thomas Wilkinson awarded one pound for a certified wolf scalp; Jeremiah Norman awarded two pounds for certified wolf and wild-cat scalps; Davenport Smithwick awarded one pound for a certified wolf scalp.

The war on the wolf lasted over 200 years, and by the early 1900's the red wolf had been rendered ecologically useless. This was followed by near genetic extinction as the last red wolves, unable to find members of their own kind, began breeding with coyotes. By the 1960's the die was cast: the red wolf would go extinct without a miracle.

That miracle came in the form of the 1967 Endangered Species Preservation Act that listed the red wolf as endangered and afforded it federal protection. A recovery program was initiated in the early 1970's under the authority provided by the Endangered Species Act of 1973. Fieldwork quickly confirmed conventional wisdom: red wolves were exceedingly rare and confined to a few areas of coastal Texas salt marshes. Coyotes and red wolf/coyote hybrids were common there.

Fully aware that wild animals in captivity can rapidly lose behavioral traits and capabilities necessary for survival in the wild, the decision, nonetheless, was made to capture and place into captivity the last wild red wolves. It was an act of desperation to save the species, based on the imminence of extinction. Captive breeding to provide a foundation for restoration was an expensive and high-risk endeavor. It was also the red wolf's only chance.

This realization led to the capture of over 400 canids from southeastern Texas and southwestern Louisiana. Forty-three believed to be red wolves were sent to the captive breeding facility outside Tacoma, Washington. The first litters were produced in May 1977. Some pups appeared to be hybrids, so they and their parents were removed from the program. Eventually scientists concluded that only fourteen of the original forty-three were pure red wolves. These animals and their offspring became the last hope for the species.

Female 196 was born in captivity in 1981. She was six when she was

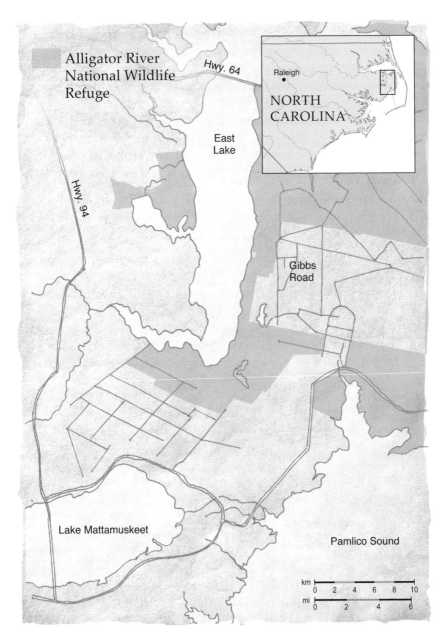

released with male 211 at Alligator River National Wildlife Refuge on October 1, 1987. Scat analysis and inspection of kill sites indicated that they transitioned to a wild lifestyle in a few weeks' time, based on a diet of white-tailed deer, raccoon and marsh rabbit that shared their sixty-square-mile territory along the western flank of the refuge. In early April 1988, over six months after release, female 196 restricted her movements to an area near the center of their territory. Her mate's locations were also centered on this area. My teammates and I knew these restricted movements in April hinted at the production of pups.

We monitored the location every thirteen hours for two weeks to make sure we were aware of any changes in the female's movement patterns. The shift came in mid-May when she struck out again, this time with the pudgy pup, 344, in tow. The pup could not have been more than a few weeks old when I first saw it from the circling Cessna on May 21.

Following abandonment of the den, my teammates and I examined the area. We found a few shallow depressions that had been used by the wolves as day beds. These depressions were located under a thick under story of cane and an over story of pond pine. Broad leafed, evergreen shrubs rounded out the thicket. I'm certain the mother wolf used one of these beds for whelping the pups. Digging a more traditional den would have been disastrous due to the high water table.

For the next month the pudgy pup seemingly shadowed its mother's every move. We saw them several times as they traveled throughout the center of the territory. The alpha male, Wolf 211, was only sometimes present. Curiously, on June 17 we saw the pup alone along the side of a logging road. The mother, Wolf 196, was nearby, but she was not leading the way as was typical. A week later 196 was dead. She was severely emaciated, probably due to a uterine infection, as we discovered in a post-mortem exam. The infection was probably related to birthing. The examination also revealed that she had given birth to up to eight pups. The pudgy pup, 344, was the sole survivor.

After the mother wolf died, the ten-pound pup traveled with its father, male Wolf 211. He had born in captivity in 1982 and had grown to nearly 80 pounds by the time we paired him with female 196 in the autumn of 1986. They remained in an acclimation pen within the refuge for ten months. We surmised that acclimation would allow them to grow accustomed to the smells, sights, and sounds of the refuge, hoping that such familiarity would reduce any tendency to wander after release.

This worked well. Male 211 and female 196 quickly established, and actively defended, a territory through scent marking and physical encounters. The big male, 211, led the effort to prevent other recently released red wolves from establishing themselves in the area. He likely confronted two other males and, through his imposing style, convinced them that moving on was the prudent thing to do. In the eight years that I led the restoration effort, male 211 seemed better suited to life in the wild than any other captive-born and released red wolf I studied.

That capability notwithstanding, the burden of raising pup 344 on his own prompted us to offer help in the form of ten to fifteen pounds of meat about every fifth day. We believed such offerings would increase the odds that the pup would survive. While they typically ate the food we provided, the big male left no stone unturned as he cared for 344. Deer and raccoon were common prey, but on at least two occasions we found where he and the pup had dug up turtles nests and eaten the yolk out of the eggs.

By mid-July an adult female, known to us as Wolf 300, joined the small family. She had traveled as a loner for about a month following the death of her mate, who had been killed by a vehicle. For the next many months male 211 and female 300 restricted their movements to the central portion of his territory. It seemed as though their movements were greatly influenced by the pup, who was reluctant to leave the security of the pocosins.

From the plane on the afternoon of October 18, I spied the two adult wolves as they walked down Gibbs Road, a short and long-ago abandoned logging road that dead ended at the edge of a small clear cut. At one point the big red wolf male, 211, lay down briefly in plain sight. Meanwhile the pup seemed nervous and would not leave the security of the heavily vegetated road shoulder. The adults resumed traveling north on Gibbs Road while the pup reversed course, turning south to the end of the road and disappeared in the confusion of the clear cut.

We tracked the radioed pair of wolves extensively throughout the fall of 1988. In that time we never saw the pup or its tracks, except at the southern end of Gibbs Road, and then only when the adults had been present. The big male 211 and his new consort, female 300, rarely spent extended periods of time there, but they typically returned at least every twenty-four to thirty-six hours to check on the pup.

On October 14 we set out to capture the pup, who was by then about five months old and large enough both for capture by a specially designed foothold trap and to wear a radio collar. On a check of our trap line that very same evening we discovered the pup had managed to step into and pull free from one of the traps. Not wishing to push our luck, we pulled up all the traps and reset four days later. That evening the feisty pup uncovered one of the traps, dragged it out of the hole and then peed on it. We pulled the line the next morning, regrouped and set a third trap line on October 23, only to inadvertently capture the big male, 211.

After removing him from the trap and replacing his radio collar, we placed him in a shipping container at the end of Gibbs Road. We thought he'd be good bait to draw the crafty little pup near our trap line. But the next morning we knew that the confusion of the previous night's activity had impressed the pup to lie low, even with its father in the shipping crate. Determined, we built a small pen for 211, to use him as bait for at least a few more days, and we set more traps.

When we checked the line the next morning we learned the pup had uncovered another trap, this one set blindly in a game trail. This was note-worthy because such trail sets do not rely on bait, and so are typically hard to detect. This pup was seemingly trap-wise beyond what its young life would suggest. On the morning of October 28, feeling roundly schooled by this wise and wary pup, we pulled the trap line and released male 211. All told, we had expended 67 trap nights—one trap night equals one trap out for one night—and 304 man-hours of effort; at least one field biologist monitored the trap line remotely 24 hours per day, attempting to capture the cunning pup. Through the end of the year we infrequently found sign of the pup, but we never managed to see it.

Restoration of endangered species through reintroductions of captive-born animals is an imprecise process, made even more so by the inevitability of random, or so-called stochastic, events. These events cannot be predicted, and they often have profound effects on recovery because of the small size of the population involved. When a wolf population only includes a handful of animals, each one is incalculably valuable. One such stochastic event struck on December 27, 1988 in the form of a raccoon kidney. This kidney would create profoundly challenging consequences for the pup.

Within minutes of killing a raccoon, male 211, father to the wily pup and a supremely capable adult red wolf who had been free-ranging for nearly 15 months, undoubtedly killing countless raccoons, choked to death when the animal's kidney became lodged in his trachea. A more curious death for a wild animal is hard to imagine.

Since the pup was still in the habit of restricting movements to the southern end of Gibbs Road, some four miles from where Wolf 211 died, it never knew what became of his father. The pup only knew that he never came back. Following his death we never again recorded his adult female consort, 300, near Gibbs Road. The pup, however, crafty and trap-wise, was now all alone at the tender age of nine-and-a-half months.

Searching for a young and wary red wolf in the wilds of the largest remaining pocosin wetlands in the U.S. is like searching for the proverbial needle in a haystack. We pressed our search with increasing urgency as the known free-ranging red wolf population dropped to only two animals by mid-March 1989.

In a little over a year we had gone from celebrating our ability to use reintroductions to restore a wolf population to harboring deep and persistent doubts about the likelihood that we would overcome the natural forces aligned against any small population. The young wolf pup figured prominently in our minds as a potent portent of the future. We came to believe that if it could survive, then we would be justified in re-embracing the notion that the species retained sufficient hardiness for life in the wild. Given that the project represented the first of its kind, we were loathe to imagine the wide-ranging consequences of failure. The red wolf pup took on mythic proportions as our sense of the future dangled by a thin thread of reality.

From January through mid-April 1989, we diligently kept an eye out for the pup in the territory established by its parents. We didn't know where else to look. On a few occasions we would detect sign, either tracks or scats, that we believed belonged to the pup, and we set traps in the hopes of capturing it to collect measurements, determine its sex, and attach a radio collar. Each time, the wolf seemingly disappeared or gave our traps a wide berth. We went to great lengths to try anything that was novel that might fall outside the wolf's experience and favor our efforts. Each time we came up short. The pup seemed more like a ghost than a living, breathing animal that had to place one foot in front of the other to get anywhere. For a period of several weeks it simply vanished, conjuring up all kinds of notions that elevated its stature in our mind. It seemed larger than life—other worldly. The pup became the red wolf archetype.

In early April 1989 we detected sign of a single wolf near the pup's old den site. This time we set carefully prepared traps. It was standard practice to boil and carefully set traps cautiously to minimize, if not eliminate, human scent. In a manner unlike anything we had tried in the past, we scattered trap parts along stretches of the roads in the area in an attempt to desensitize the wolf's suspicion of any odor that lingered on our traps. We then set traps with our typical roster of baits and lures and guide sticks that all served to direct a wolf's foot to the pan of the trap to fire the device. We then set other traps without lures and guide sticks, in unconventional sites, with the hope of catching the wolf literally with its guard down.

On the morning of April 16, 1989 we caught the ghostly pup in one of these sneaky sets. At long last we knew that 344 was a female and at 54 pounds, was in great shape. Her coat was full and nearly free of ticks. Her shoulders, back, and hind quarters were well muscled. She was not fat, but she had not been going hungry. Surprisingly, both of her front feet harbored old injuries from foothold traps. We considered it unlikely these resulted from our failed capture attempts months earlier. It seemed far more likely she had twice escaped from traps set for bobcats by local fur trappers.

After quickly assessing her condition and attaching a radio collar, we let her go. She instantly disappeared into tangled, foreboding and mysterious pocosin wetlands. Her capture recharged our sense of purpose and renewed our belief that the first attempt in history to restore a carnivore that had been declared extinct in the wild could succeed.

We tracked female 344 routinely from the ground and the air through the summer and fall of 1989. She fed on rabbits, deer, and raccoons, traveled mostly at night and for the first few months following capture restricted movements to her natal range, the territory originally established by her parents. Starting in November female 344 wandered more widely, perhaps to avoid contact with other adult red wolf pairs that were beginning to infringe on her parents' territory. In early December she left the refuge and traveled south about twenty miles to a pleasant patch of eastern North Carolina known as Mattamuskeet Farms. All 45,000 acres of the area represented a great place for a wolf. There was an abundant supply of food as deer, rabbits, and, surely, raccoons were common, and the farm was ringed by pocosins that made it easy for Wolf 344 to disappear.

Her presence justified our efforts to make Mattamuskeet Farms the site of the first agreement between a landowner and the U.S. Fish and Wildlife Service on behalf of red wolf recovery. Other agreements with the same purpose followed as we expanded the size of the recovery area to advance the species' prospects. Recognition of the importance of private land to the red wolf eventually led to the establishment of the Turner Endangered Species Fund, the largest private effort in the world to redress the extinction crisis by ensuring the persistence of imperiled species and their habitats with an emphasis on private land.

In early 1991, after wandering Mattamuskeet Farms as a lone wolf for a little over a year, female Wolf 344 paired with a two-year old male known as Wolf 392. They remained together for many years and maintained a territory that encompassed about forty square miles. They produced six litters, including at least 17 pups, many of which matured to produce pups of their own. The territory they established would eventually support three packs that included some of their offspring.

Wolf 344's ultimate fate will always remain unknown. She died, of course, maybe not long after we recorded her last telemetry location on the morning of November 21, 1995. For a wolf, seven-and-a-half years is a long time to make a living in the woods with its teeth. We only know that after her transmitter ceased functioning, she just disappeared.

I'm glad for that.

The little wild-born red wolf pup known affectionately as 344F came into the world when the future for her kind was far from certain. If odds matter, the challenges she confronted should have killed her. But she survived, and by doing so affirmed life's tenacity. Nature abhors a vacuum. If there is opportunity, then life will seize it. Female 344 did just that.

Her life was proof positive that significant land-use restrictions were not necessary for red wolves to survive. Many who initially opposed the restoration project did so on the grounds that land-use restrictions would be needed for the effort to succeed. But, hunting and trapping restrictions within the refuge remain unchanged or were relaxed within the first five years of the restoration project. No restrictions were proposed or needed for wolves like 344F that lived all of most of their lives on private land.

Her life also made clear that the original restoration area, the Alligator River National Wildlife Refuge, was too small for restoring a self-sustaining red wolf population. Female 344, and subsequently many others, wandered far afield, establishing territories well outside the boundaries of the refuge. By developing agreements with private landowners that addressed their real and imagined concerns, red wolves were given a fighting chance of survival. After all, female 344 made it clear that a fighting chance was all that was needed.

While at first Wolf 344 seemed otherworldly to us, we eventually realized that she was a somewhat typical red wolf. Rather than deflating, this realization was liberating. It became the basis for our faith in the capacity of most other red wolves to do as she had done—survive. In turn, this faith bolstered our belief that the species could flourish in the wild.

Perhaps most importantly 344's life was irrefutable evidence that restoration is an alternative to extinction. With self-willed nature firmly in the grip of the world's sixth great extinction spasm, such evidence is a useful reminder that we have the power to arrest this crisis.

Since the restoration project's humble beginnings twenty-six years ago, the effort has grown in meaningful ways. As of January 2013 the U.S. Fish and Wildlife Service estimated that the red wolf population included 100 to 120 animals. Some of the wolves are members of 13 known packs. The restoration area has grown to about 1.7 million acres encompassing three additional wildlife refuges, state-owned lands, and private lands. Hybridization with coyotes remains a problem, as does illegal killing of red wolves.

CHAPTER NINETEEN

The Legacy of Big Al, the Little Gal[1]

Richard P. Thiel

WE COULD SEE OUR BAGGIE was up from about thirty yards, a sure indication that we had caught something in our wolf trap. The drag was still firmly implanted in the hole and the trap's chain disappeared into the dense bracken fern jungle along the woods trail. "Damn it!" I exclaimed, certain it was a raccoon or skunk.

Peering out the truck window, U.S. Forest Service volunteer Ron Schultz was unable to see anything. We got out, Ron moving into the ferns while I retrieved the choke restrainer pole from the pickup bed. Ron chuckled.

"What is it?" I asked.

"Don't really know for sure, but it appears to be a timber wolf pup!"

Whatever it was—it was tiny! Pesky deer flies hastened our work. I dropped the loop of the choker over its head and pinned it to the ground. In a few seconds its foot had been removed from the trap, its gigantic paws confirming it was a wolf and not a coyote.

Ron laid the wolf down, placing his hands firmly on its rib cage as I released the choke hold. The pup lay motionless. It was a female weighing a mere 15 pounds, underweight considering it was July 20.

Blood drawn, tag number 099 and 100 inserted into the unflinching wolf's ears, the only thing remaining was to decide whether to place a radio on it. She was a member of the Bootjack Lake Pack, the first newly discovered wolf pack in Wisconsin since winter track surveys two years earlier revealed the presence of five packs in the state. Our initial encounter with the Bootjack Lake Pack occurred the previous February. Woodruff Area Wildlife Manager Chet Botwinski had sent me several reports of wolves. My assistant, Larry Prenn, and I had spent three unsuccessful days cruising fire lanes looking for wolf tracks. Lying ninety miles east of the Minnesota line, where all but one of the state's other packs existed, these four wolves were the first discovered within the Chequamegon National Forest since the wolves' demise three decades earlier.

This pup was really small, and I was reminded of a conversation I had with U.S. Fish and Wildlife Service biologist, Steve Fritts, who advised that pups beneath 25 pounds not be radioed. The radio weighed a little

---

1 Portions of this story are found in Thiel, Richard P. 2001. *Keepers of the Wolves: The Early Years of Wolf Recovery in Wisconsin*. University of Wisconsin Press.

over two pounds, fifteen percent of this pup's weight. But what were our chances of capturing an adult? I decided to collar her.

The collar was fitted as if the pup was an adult by packing the inside with foam so that it fit. Finished, we went through the processing checklist before release. Ron asked, "What are you going to name it?" I reasoned April was the month in which most wolf litters are born. My wife, Deborah, had given birth to our first child, Allison, that very same April. I replied, "Big Al, the Little Gal, in honor of Allison!"

Ron simply released Big Al by lifting his hand off her chest. She lay motionless for about thirty seconds, then jumped to her feet and skedaddled off, the swaying bracken ferns revealing her escape route. We scanned her signal several times that day. By 8 p.m. she had moved about a half mile to the southwest.

Two days later an emaciated, petite, adult female stepped into one of our sets about one-and-a-half miles from where Big Al had been caught. Tooth wear indicated this wolf was middle aged, around five or six years old. She weighed only 48 pounds, was very lightly colored, almost white, and she had hazel colored eyes. No doubt she was Big Al's mother, so I named her Deborah for the mother of our child, Allison.

By the time I returned three weeks later the pack had moved their pups two-and-a-half miles west of where Big Al had been captured. Their new rendezvous site was on a beaver pond that formed the headwaters of Buck Creek.

On a clear evening in mid-August, accompanied by several local agency wildlife officials, I conducted a howl survey near the site, determined to learn how many litter mates Big Al had. Big Al's signal came from the direction of the home site. Deborah was nowhere to be found. Our first volley of vocalizations succeeded: an adult and a pup, presumably Big Al, fired up a response in the vicinity of the beaver pond. We moved further east on the trail, hoping to fool the wolves into thinking that we were wolves on the move. Stopping, I howled three more times. Two wolves at the home site responded in kind. After waiting ten minutes I howled again, eliciting an adult wolf to howl way off to our southeast. Over the next ten or fifteen minutes the two groups of wolves exchanged howls.

About a half an hour later I howled once. Both the pair and the single howled nearby. They were converging on us! We quickly retired into the brush lining the tote trail, hoping that the dying embers of twilight would provide us a view as the wolves walked by.

Presently a howl, deep, and throaty, rising up and falling back down, blasted forth right in front of us. This was swiftly followed by the sound of crunching gravel. Instantly, two wolves howled behind and very near us. I turned on the receiver. The signal pounding in my earphones indicated that one of the wolves behind us was Big Al. A fourth wolf chimed in off to the east. Twigs snapped just behind us and a sharp, raspy howl burst forth! Then all fell silent.

Ten minutes later I turned on the receiver. Big Al's signal was coming in faintly in the direction of the home site. We were humbled by what the wolves taught us. Wolves' senses enabled them to detect our precise location, approach closely, and withdraw silently into their surroundings while we humans sat, arrogantly thinking we had a chance to see them. The show being over, we retreated back to our vehicles. It had been a most rewarding evening.

The next day our pilot located Big Al and Deborah together some six miles west of our encounter. Deborah's absence might be explained by the fact that she may have succeeded in killing a deer earlier, and she had returned to move her pups sometime after we left.

Howling surveys that summer revealed the pack consisted of three adults and two pups, including Big Al and Deborah. This was also confirmed the following winter by several visuals, sightings made from the window of our surveillance aircraft.

One of these was particularly memorable. It was a cold morning in late December. I shared the cabin of the Piper Cub with pilot Ray Marvin. Shortly after passing over the south end of Squaw Lake, I informed Ray we were fast approaching the two radioed wolves. He cut back on the throttle and we began dropping. Conifer trees passed beneath our wings, and the topographical features of this forested landscape began to take shape as we dropped. Ahead of us lay an esker, a steep, sinewy, and winding hill created by melted river waters that had sliced through the continental glaciers some 12,000 years ago, depositing their tons of gravel, stone and boulders in near-vertical assemblages. As we passed the fir-covered esker I heard a sharp "ping." Looking over my right shoulder I spied a wolf sitting on its haunches in a small opening atop the esker. I yelled at Ray. He pushed in the throttle, pulled back on the stick and we banked right, climbing as we circled.

Approaching the esker we saw two wolves in playful chase. One leapt off the top of the mound, flew through the air and landed on its rump on the steep slope. Forelegs outstretched, it slid all the way to the bottom of the hill. Patterns in the snow told us the wolves had been up to this game for quite some time. As one wolf reached the bottom of the slope, the other would launch off and pass by the first, already running back to the top. Near the top of the esker stood a whitish-colored wolf, obviously Deborah, plainly enjoying the sight of her two pups sledding down this remote ski slope. We lingered a bit longer, laughing at the antics of the two pups, before returning to base.

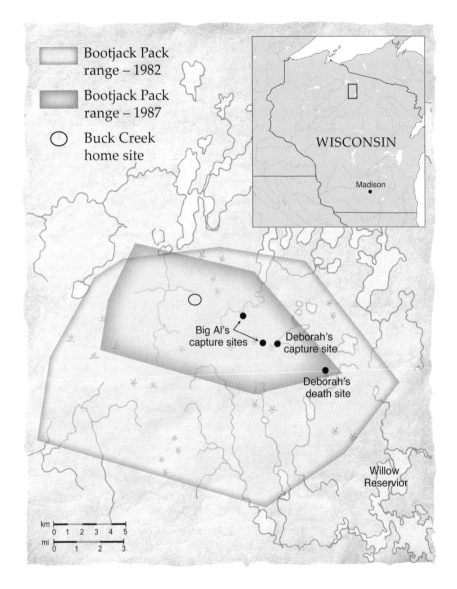

Bootjack Pack
range – 1982

Bootjack Pack
range – 1987

○ Buck Creek
home site

WISCONSIN

Madison

○

Big Al's
capture sites

Deborah's
capture site

Deborah's
death site

Willow
Reservoir

km
0 1 2 3 4 5
mi
0   1   2   3

On January 13 we found bloody urine while trailing the pack, a sure indication that Deborah was in proestrus and would probably breed. A few weeks later Larry and I returned and picked up the trail of four wolves along the Fould's Creek Road three miles west of their summer home site. A nearby raised-leg urination (RLU) contained blood. Deborah was still in heat. The trail led through a dense white cedar swamp. The boughs held much of the snow aloft. We easily followed the trail as it wove around the underbrush. Eventually the wolves' trail led to the tag alder lined Fould's Creek. Here and there the stream surfaced, water gurgling over snow-covered boulders. It wasn't safe to cross. Thankfully, the wolves veered south, staying on the near side of the stream.

Around a bend a very strange spectacle appeared. A jumble of rocks rose vertically twenty-five feet from the stream basin, a remnant spire of the Precambrian Laurentian Shield which lies beneath much of northern Wisconsin deeply buried by a stratum of glacial debris. How this rock column managed to withstand the crushing power of these continental glaciers is beyond imagination.

The trail wound around the alders and led to the rock outcropping. Behind the rock column the wolves' trail was all a jumble and we soon realized the wolves had clambered up the spires before climbing back down to resume their journey. Curious, we scaled the rock, slipping here and there as our bulky insulated boots provided little purchase. At the top we found a half-dozen beds. Ice in the bottoms revealed the wolves had lain here quite some time, providing them an incredible panorama of the Fould's Creek valley sprawled out before them.

But something was awry. A pungent, rancid, oily smell permeated the crisp air. Each of the beds appeared soiled—stained a yellow brown—and embedded within the ice that had formed as the animals' body heat melted the snow were great wads of wolf underfur. A closer inspection revealed the carcasses of hundreds of tiny white bodies with reddish brown heads. What were these things? And what was wrong with the Bootjack wolves?

Pulling out my notebook I knelt down, placing my face within a foot of one bed, counting the tiny organisms frozen into the thin veneer of ice. I selected various one-centimeter square areas within each bed for counts and then estimated the length and width of each bed, scribbling these dimensions into my notebook. Ripping a page from the notebook and folding it carefully, I collected a half dozen of the creatures and stuffed the paper back into the notebook. Back at the hotel that night I calculated at least 540 of these critters lay frozen in a single wolf bed.

En route home that Friday I dropped off the samples with parasitologist Dr. Steven Taft at the University of Wisconsin–Stevens Point Biology Department. A few weeks later he called to inform me they were dog lice, a fairly common hitchhiker among domestic canines that are often found on coyotes as well. As evidenced by the great numbers of shed lice, the stained snow in the wolves' beds, and the smell, the lice had reached epidemic proportions on each of these individual Bootjack Pack wolves. Nonstop itching caused them to scratch, which led to skin lesions, infecting them. This explained the smell and was cause for concern.

The following July we returned to capture another wolf after Schultz reported that Big Al, Deborah and the Bootjack Pack once again occupied the Buck Creek home site. Dan Groebner, a part-time biologist hired to assist in trapping and howling surveys, accompanied us. We set traps on Monday afternoon and caught two wolves in adjacent sets on Wednesday morning. One, Big Al's sibling, a scrawny yearling female covered in lice, weighed a mere 43 pounds. We collared her and named her Carol. The second trap, set by Groebner, contained a feisty, 19 pound male pup also infested with lice. Collaring it, Groebner named this one Ea. Shortly after we pulled out our traps, Schultz ran a howling survey and was rewarded at twilight when three pups ran out of the woods accompanied by an adult.

Budget cuts forced a reduction in flights later in the summer of 1983. In early September Schultz called informing me that Ea's signal hadn't changed position in three flights flown over a two month period. He had discovered its collar lying on top of some bones and matted hair. We had missed a golden opportunity to obtain a fresh carcass and learn its cause of death.

By now we had accumulated enough radio locations of Big Al, Deborah and the newly collared Carol to estimate the size of the Bootjack Pack's territory. Their territory was 100 square miles. Did any pups survive?

Howling surveys in the interim had failed to produce evidence of pups. We suspected the worst, and the radioed wolves were making things difficult for us. Big Al left the territory, exploring the vicinity of the Willow Flowage. Sister Carol slipped even further south, hanging out in the vicinity of Bass Lake. Only Deborah remained. But in early December Big Al reunited with her mother. They were accompanied by a single, uncollared wolf, presumably Big Al's father and mate to Deborah.

During the winter of 1983-84 Big Al continued occasional forays outside the territory near Willow Flowage. Finally, the entire pack was seen reunited in mid-February when Carol returned. As suspected there were no pups. Carol eventually dispersed, and by winter's end the Bootjack Pack was down to Big Al, Deborah and the uncollared wolf.

That spring U.S. Fish and Wildlife research scientist, Dave Mech, told me a newly mutated viral disease, canine parvovirus, had been discovered in Minnesota wolves. The potent virus caused diarrhea, fever and dehydration. It was considered deadly since wolves had no previous exposure to it. He was canvassing antibodies to the disease in wolf blood samples. Since we had routinely provided blood for Mech's blood studies it would be a simple thing to sample banked Wisconsin wolf blood. The news made me suspect the Bootjack Lake Pack's 1983 litter had somehow been exposed and succumbed.

Deborah denned again in 1984. In early June she again moved west to the home site at Buck Creek. All seemed well. But abruptly towards the end of June Deborah's movement patterns changed. She began moving extensively, no longer anchored to Buck Creek. Despite repeated attempts Schultz heard no pups howling in the summer of 1984.

Meanwhile the long awaited parvovirus report arrived. Big Al showed no response. At the time it had been collected she had either been exposed so recently that she didn't have a chance to build up a response, or she simply had never been exposed to parvovirus. Deborah, however, tested positive. Jeff Zuba, a veterinary student at the University of Wisconsin who conducted parvovirus experiments on captive wolves, explained that Deborah was either sickly or had recently recovered from a bout of parvovirus at the time of her capture. Carol, captured a year after Big Al, had by then been exposed to the disease, likely sometime the previous summer when she was a pup. Ea also tested positive, and was likely sick, when the sample had been collected.

Clearly the wolves' immune systems were being heavily taxed. The pack's chronic infestation of body lice over the past six months was a signal. Parasites respond to suppressed immune systems causing further degradation of host immune systems. These wolves were not healthy. Ea's death and the mysterious disappearance of his litter-mates a month following his capture warned of a smoking gun, but in science the absence of a direct link is considered no link at all. Nonetheless, I was becoming very worried about these ominous signs.

The next bad news came in late October when the pilots informed me Big Al had gone missing. In the 1980's batteries within radio transmitters were warrantied with two years of life. The radios on both Deborah and Big Al had already been beeping for over two years. Had Big Al's radio died or had she finally dispersed? At that time I had placed radios on eight yearling wolves in Wisconsin, including Big Al. Three had died. The other four had all dispersed away from their natal pack and then either disappeared or died. Big Al probably dispersed. Either way I would certainly never reencounter her. The fate of the Bootjack Pack could only be determined if Deborah's collar continued to function.

The annual nine-day deer gun season arrived in late November. Although wolves were protected, a minority of hunters occasionally killed them. I considered wolves especially vulnerable each fall as the state's 600,000 deer hunters entered the woods. Luckily the Bootjack Pack's territory was wild, forested terrain with few fire lanes that greatly restricted hunter access. The eastern half lay mostly within Nekoosa-Edwards Paper Mill industrial forest lands gated off to the public. The only significant tract of public lands accessible to deer hunters was the Chequamegon National Forest to the west and a small strip of highly developed private landholdings in Wisconsin's famous northern lakes district on the northeast corner of the pack's territory.

On January 3, 1985 the pilots alerted me that something was odd. In the two December flights following the close of the November deer season Deborah had been located in the same spot. This was not terribly unusual. But the first flight in January showed her at the same location. Ron Schultz, Larry Prenn and I recovered her carcass in the east edge of the territory where there was far more human activity. An elevated deer stand was within thirty yards of her. A bloody hole in her chest cavity told us how she had died.

Still petite at 57 pounds she had regained some weight since her capture, and the pathologist's report concluded she was "in good condition with the exception of tooth wear and a few missing incisors." No lice were reported, so it seemed the Bootjack Pack wolves had shaken that malady.

We gained additional insights into Deborah's life struggles when her bones were removed from the University of Wisconsin Zoology Museum's dermisted beetle colony. The head of her left tibia, the long bone extending below the knee joint, had two irregularly shaped holes. Bone fragments here had been displaced inward. Picking up the bone we heard a rattling noise like a Chilean rain stick. Small bird shot was found within. At some previous time she had a non-fatal encounter with a hunter.

Deborah's reproductive record was not good. Her 1982 litter consisted of two pups and her 1983 litter of three pups was lost by mid-August. She also had three fresh placental scars when necropsied, confirming she had borne a litter of three pups again in 1984. But these had all disappeared by late June.

What was causing this? The Bootjack Pack was one of only four potentially reproductive wolf packs in the State of Wisconsin in 1984. That summer only one of the four Wisconsin packs managed to keep some of its pups alive to winter. And that pack's alpha male had just died from distemper. The statewide population had plummeted to fifteen wolves. Obviously wolf recovery relied on reproductive output and survival of pups.

With Deborah dead I lost radio contact with the Bootjack Pack. Where was I to find them in their 100 square mile territory? Was the unradioed wolf, presumably Deborah's mate and father of Big Al, still around, or had he abandoned this territory to search for safer grounds and a potential mate? Knowledge of the pack's previous winter hangouts gave us a clue where to concentrate winter track surveys.

In late January Schultz connected. But instead of finding one wolf, he found two. And one of these wolves was in estrus! The following summer we attempted, unsuccessfully, to capture one of these wolves after scouring the territory for sign and conducting several howl surveys. Whoever they were, this pair produced no pups that summer. In the winter of 1985-86 only one wolf was detected on numerous track surveys. For all intents and purposes the Bootjack Pack no longer existed, or so it seemed.

On a routine track survey run the following winter, Schultz encountered tracks of a pair of wolves! This fueled hope that pups would once again be produced in the Bootjack Pack. We laid plans to return that summer to trap and collar a wolf. Schultz was in charge of trapping, since I was responsible for running a team developing a state recovery plan for wolves. He called me on the afternoon of August 6 informing me he had managed to capture the breeding female. As he removed the trap from the immobilized wolf he discovered, to his great surprise, that she bore a pair of ear tags: 099 in her left and 100 in her right ear. It was Big Al! Like her mother she weighed a petite 47 pounds. While very thin, she had no lice and appeared in good condition. Two days later Schultz captured and collared a male pup about three miles northwest of where he recaptured Big Al, naming it Sparky.

That September we saw the Bootjack Pack from the window of the surveillance airplane. Lying in an open sphagnum bog beneath us were Big Al, Sparky and two other pups, plus Big Al's mate. By mid-winter one of the pups had disappeared and the pack was down to four members. But Big Al had managed to revive the Bootjack Pack.

The following April Big Al denned in the same area used by her mother, and in July she moved her family to the same home site she grew up in along the headwaters of Buck Creek. There we managed to recapture Sparky, now a 51 pound yearling.

Relying on daytime radio fixes from aircraft left many gaps in our knowledge about how wolves move about within and utilize their varied forested habitats. That August Dan Groebner, now a graduate student at Northern Michigan University, brought in an Earth Watch crew to conduct twenty-four hour monitors on the radioed wolves. Groebner was testing the capability of ground monitoring wolves in heavily forested terrain. He was also interested in learning what wolves did on a daily basis. If his technique worked, it would open up a new view of wolves living in forests.

Groebner's set-up was exquisite. Crews operated out of two vans specially equipped with plotting tables, topographic maps, two-way radios, receivers and an antenna that protruded from the vans' roofs. Vans were parked within a mile of each other to acquire and exchange radio-collar fixes that could then be triangulated, thereby establishing the wolves' locations. When the wolves moved, the vans would stay back, waiting an allotted time so as not to disrupt the wolves' movements. Each crew would then attempt to hop-scotch around ahead of the radioed wolves, timing and plotting their movements as they went. Ranges of radio signals varied, depending on the terrain and the density of trees, but averaged a little less than one mile. Once wolves were on the prowl, these crews had their work cut out for them.

I joined them one evening. Standing on the tote trail leading in towards Buck Creek, I reflected back to an evening in 1982 when we were closely approached by Big Al, the pup, and other members of the Bootjack Pack. Now here I was, listening to the beep—beep—beep staccato of that very same wolf. Only now Big Al, at six years of age, was the Bootjack Pack's alpha female and breeder.

Sparky's signal was not at the home site. Earlier missions by the Earth Watch crews had established that he preferred hanging out along the Fould's Creek drainage. Evidently he wasn't much of a babysitter.

At twilight the pack erupted into a chorus howl, pups with their high, shrill yip-yapping mingled in with the deep throated howls of adult wolves. Then silence. Shortly thereafter Big Al's signal went active. She crossed the road near our parked van heading west. Ten minutes and three miles later she joined Sparky. From the intertwined signals one could visualize the pair coursing up and down Fould's Creek. Around 11 p.m. Big Al ceased moving for a few minutes and then abruptly headed back towards the home site. Likely she had caught a beaver and was now returning to the home site intent on feeding her pups. I considered myself fortunate to have witnessed this intimate view in the day-to-day lives of a wild wolf pack.

On December 5, 1988 we heard Big Al's radio signal for the last time. Sparky's radio continued to function, providing us access to the pack's whereabouts the following winter. From our airplane window we counted the yearling Sparky, three pups, and two adult wolves. Maybe Big Al was one of them. Later that same winter Schultz received a call from a rural resident in the eastern portion of the Bootjack Pack's territory. The person reported a sickly looking wolf hanging around his place. Schultz was able to obtain a glimpse of it. He was certain it was Big Al.

This was the last time Big Al was observed alive.

It is impossible to discern whether Big Al was an ordinary or extraordinary wolf. She survived at least two significant disease outbreaks. These maladies likely stunted her growth and perhaps those of her pack-mates. Small by female wolf standards, she was fully able to hunt, kill and provide.

Big Al revealed some attributes of wolf society not well documented at that time. Following her mother's death only she and a single adult wolf remained. She entered estrus that winter but produced no pups. The following winter the second wolf disappeared and, alone, Big Al maintained the Bootjack territory. The very next winter she was in the company of another wolf, and that summer she produced pups. I believe the pack-mate the winter following her mother's death was her father. By the following winter he was gone. If so, they avoided an incestuous relationship. This cannot be proved or disproved, but the possibility cannot be dismissed.

As the pack's breeding female she used the same den and home site she had herself occupied as a pup. Perhaps her feelings of security as a pup helped her select these same sites for her own offspring. Does this reflect the emergence of tradition?

In Deborah's time the Bootjack Pack claimed a one-hundred square mile territory. By the time of Big Al's reign it had shrunk to around forty square miles. This strategy allows some offspring to claim a corner as their own in beginning their own families. Are these rights of inheritance?

Big Al was a bider wolf, a pup that remains within its natal pack. Most wolves back in the early days of colonization in Wisconsin dispersed. Wracked by disease, reproductive loss, and who knows what other misfortunes, the pack was certainly in bad shape. Did she somehow gauge the odds of becoming an alpha were better by remaining? In the process she saved her natal pack. It exists to this day.

CHAPTER TWENTY

The Old Gray Guy: Genetics and the Wolves of Isle Royale

Rolf Peterson

HIS SPECIAL QUALITIES were evident on our first encounter. This wolf had detected one of our buried foot-hold traps, probably attracted by the scats we had placed nearby, and he had skillfully excavated the entire trap, pulled it out of the hole, leaving it unsprung in the middle of the trail. A young female wolf was in the adjacent trap. The ability to detect and disable buried wolf traps, not seen before on Isle Royale, became a persistent talent among some of the wolves during the following decade. But the contribution of this wolf was far more important and comprehensive than knowledge of how to avoid capture.

As far as I know, I was in close proximity to this wolf only once, and I didn't know at the time his significance. In early May 2001, when we captured his female companion, he was just out of view and very agitated. He was pacing back and forth a few yards in the forest, periodically bursting into a series of barks interspersed with blasts of howling. We decided he was a male because of his voice—low and very loud.

Colleague John Vucetich and I were both shaken by his intimidating presence. The wolf knew we were doing something to his companion and he was upset. It wouldn't have surprised me if he suddenly walked boldly into view and confronted us. This was the first wolf John had live-trapped, and he must have wondered what part of this experience was normal. We hurried to take blood samples, put a radio collar on the young female, and get out of there. The howling ceased as soon as we finished our tasks and left the female to recover from the knockout drugs we'd given her. Soon they were traveling together again, leaving us to ponder the power and influence of an individual wolf.

The young, collared female was easily identified as the alpha female of the Middle Pack that next winter, during the forty-fourth annual winter study of wolves and moose at Isle Royale National Park, a roadless island of 544 square kilometers in Lake Superior, where wolves and moose populations have been monitored annually by researchers beginning in 1959.

But, during the following winter, we were surprised to see the female now accompanied by pups. She had not been pregnant or nursing when we had examined her the previous spring. She was also closely tended by a large alpha male, probably the one that howled at us that spring. Over the next few years, as his pelage lightened with age, we often referred to him as the "Old Gray Guy." But it would be seven more years, long after his death, before we were able to piece together his story.

In 2008, when a decade's supply of fecal DNA samples was finally analyzed, this male became the ninety-third wolf in the Isle Royale wolf chronology. As a result his official identification was M93. Scat collections back-dated his "appearance" in 1997. His DNA was foreign, never before seen among Isle Royale wolves. He became the second most prolific wolf in the population, siring a total of 34 surviving pups in his lifetime. And through this, he conveyed new genetic viability to this isolated wolf population, extending the renowned wolf-moose narrative another ten to fifteen years. The only possible explanation was that he had walked over the fifteen mile ice bridge separating the island from the Canadian shoreline. This may have been the first time since the late 1940's that new genes from the mainland were introduced.

When wolves colonized Isle Royale in the late 1940's, they had been eliminated from much of their original worldwide range. Where not extinct the wolf had been greatly reduced by human persecution. Hence, it was ironic that during this global low point wolves established themselves in a relatively new island national park, Isle Royale, located some fifteen miles from the Canadian shore in the frigid waters of Lake Superior. Some people thought that wolves might resolve a long-simmering problem that had become symptomatic of parks without predators—overabundant ungulates that degrade their habitat and are controlled only by outbreaks of disease and starvation.

Among the people paying close attention to these developments was wildlife biologist Durward Allen. To Allen the island provided the possibility of doing real science that might uncover basic relationships between wolves and their prey in a secure refuge where both predator and prey were not only protected, but also largely unaffected by immigration and emigration. In the early 1950's, when Allen accepted a faculty position at Purdue University, he thought he might finally be able to take advantage of the extraordinary opportunity for research at Isle Royale.

In 1958, after working for years to secure the logistical support of the National Park Service and the financial backing of the National Science Foundation, Allen initiated an unprecedented, ten-year study of wolves and moose at Isle Royale. In the field of wildlife research, nothing that bold had ever been done, and, indeed, such proposals are rare today.

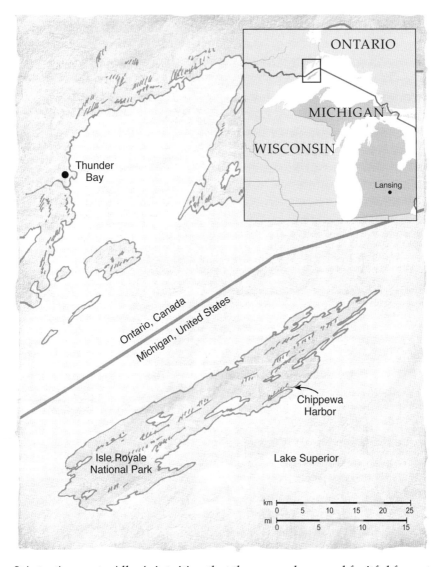

It is testimony to Allen's intuition that the research proved fruitful for not only ten years, but for more than a half century.

In the first round of study, graduate student Dave Mech demonstrated that wolf predation was very selective, concentrating on very young moose and old animals, where there was often evidence of physical deterioration. Allen and Mech published photographs of wolves surrounding moose in National Geographic Magazine in 1964, and people around the world took an interest in the much-maligned wolf. Thus began a makeover in public attitudes that would eventually permit a dramatic recovery of this top carnivore around the world. In the process Allen's outdoor laboratory took on symbolic importance as a wilderness icon, coinciding conveniently in 1964 with the passage of the Wilderness Act by the U.S. Congress.

I became Allen's final graduate student in 1970, which was, in the words of a skeptical chief ranger at Isle Royale, "the twelfth year of a ten-year study." Within a few years, however, dramatic fluctuations in wolves and moose underscored the inadequacy of our understanding of this predator-prey system. Following a sustained increase in moose density, wolves suddenly increased their kill rate in a series of winters with deep snow. During the 1970's, wolf packs proliferated and the wolf population doubled. The moose population plummeted.

The inadvertent introduction in 1981 of a deadly mutant virus, canine parvovirus, by a dog brought illegally into the park, spelled the end of the glory days for wolves, and by 1982 most of the wolves had died. High mortality set the stage for a more insidious change that has dogged the population ever since—loss of genetic variability with the passage of each generation of breeding wolves. Inbreeding, long thought to be a theoretical risk for this small and isolated population began to emerge as a distinct reality.

Anything that affects wolves also affects moose (and vice versa), and the collapse of the wolf population in the 1980's brought on an exponential increase in the moose population, recalling the early 1930's when moose had converted the island into an overused feedlot. That ecological disaster, documented by a young biologist named Adolph Murie, reached its logical outcome in 1934, much as Murie had warned. Most of the moose starved to death during the winter.

An identical scenario unfolded in the 1990's. While the wolf population struggled at its lowest level, just a dozen animals, moose were chronically undernourished. Young moose were severely growth-retarded. Calves that were born survived only because there were so few wolves. The increase in moose seemed unstoppable, until another starvation disaster arrived with the severe winter of 1996. Again, most of the moose perished after denuding the island of all available winter browse.

While the moose population rapidly expanded in the early 1990's, the wolf population seemed to be stuck at a chronically low level. From 1988 to 1993, there were only twelve to fifteen wolves on the island. At the urging of the National Park Service, I initiated live-trapping and radio collaring in 1988 to understand the nature of the high mortality that preceded these population doldrums. However, just about this time mortality rates returned to near average, and it was only much later that we were able to piece together enough information to deduce that parvovirus had brought the wolf population to its knees.

For many years after 1989, parvovirus was not detected on Isle Royale, yet the wolf population did not recover. By the early 1990's, the problem was poor recruitment—pups were either not produced, or they did not survive their first summer. The lack of reproduction was chronicled in the 1990-1991 Annual Report on *Ecological Studies of Wolves on Isle Royale:*

> The decline in wolf reproduction that extended through the 1980's has persisted, as we found no pups among surviving wolves in winter 1991. Six adult female wolves, all potential reproducers, were alive during summer 1990, including four that were radio collared and closely monitored beginning in early May. Yet all radio collared wolves moved widely, and no dens or rendezvous sites were located. Alaska wolf biologist Bob Stephenson quipped, "I've never seen anything like it. If a male and female are paired off, even if conditions are terrible, it seems they always manage to have at least a pup or two."

By 1993 the number of known females had dwindled to three, one in each of three territorial packs. The only female with surviving pups, radio collared in 1988 and known to us as female 450, was at least nine years old. She had a few good years as a reproducing female, preventing the extinction of the population. On January 31, 1995, this female, estimated to be twelve years old, found a recent moose-kill made by a pair of territorial interlopers, including her own son. She killed the foreign female in a spectacularly violent confrontation and then disappeared. She had outlived her radio collar, and we would never learn her fate.

The long-standing territorial West Pack hung on with just two wolves, a male and female. They had last reproduced successfully in 1988. The old male succumbed in the summer of 1994, after a new male moved in from the other end of the island. Even with the new male, only one surviving pup appeared in this pack in 1995. This young wolf, also a male, kept the pack going with a female from the other end of the island, but they never reproduced. In 1998 there were still only two wolves in the West Pack.

Hopes for reproduction turned to the Middle Pack, led by a pair of two-year-olds who reproduced in 1995. The pack flourished briefly, increasing to eight, then nine wolves in 1996 and 1997, respectively. But the collapse of the moose population brought hard times, and the entire population declined to just fourteen wolves in 1998.

Genetic decay from inbreeding became a reasonable hypothesis for the sputtering wolf population. Back in 1988 we had begun collecting DNA samples from the few wolves we handled, and the first thing we learned was that Isle Royale wolves were isolated. All had descended from a single female wolf that had come to the island in the late 1940's.

Public fascination with Isle Royale began to grow during the 1990's as the balance between predator and prey seemed broken. The very real possibility of wolf extinction on Isle Royale generated headlines as well as headaches. In addition to genetic limitations, climate change, evidenced by the lack of an ice bridge to Canada, prevented new wolves from coming to the island. I wrote a book about the wolves of Isle Royale, and, in the final chapter, presented my position on whether the National Park Service should intervene on behalf of the wolves. Using the metaphors of laboratory (I now prefer the term observatory) and cathedral, I argued for consideration of both science and spirit, and assigned highest priority to having a top carnivore to maintain the ecological integrity on the island. I concluded that as long as moose lived on the island wolves should be there for the health of the ecosystem. If wolves needed a little help getting to the island every few decades, so be it.

Starting in 1999, we collected wolf scats, hoping that we would someday be able to identify individual wolves from DNA in the occasional intestinal cells sloughed off in feces. In 2006 Jen Adams, having just finished her Ph.D. on the genetics of red wolves, joined our research team and developed techniques needed to determine the sex and identity of each wolf in the Isle Royale population, after first extracting and amplifying DNA from scats. She made it look easy, but three years and thousands of hours of laboratory work were required to develop a complete pedigree of Isle Royale's wolf population. Her analysis catalogued for each wolf the year of its birth and death, the identity of its parents and its natal pack, whether or not it reproduced, and the identity of its entire offspring. Jen asked me to stop by her office in July 2008, and insisted that I sit down and hear what she'd learned about male 93.

His was a novel male genotype that showed up on Isle Royale in 1999, the first year of scat collections. M93 had a unique genetic signature, possessing three genetic alleles not present in any of the 35 individuals that had been genotyped from skeletal material or blood between 1966 and 1998. Although there had been ice bridges to Isle Royale in 1994, 1996, and 1997, it seemed most likely M93 arrived on Isle Royale in 1997. He then entered the Middle Pack where he sired seven surviving pups in 1997, and this pack began an ascendancy that continued as long as he lived.

Neither John Vucetich nor I, or anyone else, thought to consider that recovery of the wolf population in the late 1990's and 2000's might have been prompted by an immigrant. Occasionally we made passing mention of the "whitish alpha male of Middle Pack," but we attached no significance to this unique pelage. Whitish coloration also began to show up among old wolves in other packs on Isle Royale. None of us guessed what DNA eventually confirmed—the black-and-gray alpha male of the Middle Pack on the cover of the 2001 annual report was the same individual as the stately-looking whitish alpha male on the cover of the 2006 annual report.

Looking back, however, there were some significant hints. In the 1998 annual report we wrote that the Middle Pack had suddenly become the largest pack on the island in almost two decades. That same year it boldly invaded the East Pack territory and killed a moose calf. Even after getting chased out by the East Pack, Middle Pack trespassed again and killed another calf. But we had seen territorial trespassing before.

The DNA analysis also informed us that M93 had taken up with a native female in the Middle Pack in 1998, and this pair reproduced again in 1999, 2000, and 2001. Five of their thirteen pups dispersed and became breeders themselves. By 2001 every territorial pack on the island was led by a wolf that M93 had sired.

The Middle Pack flourished and aggressively acquired more resources. In 1999 we watched them make one major foray into West Pack territory where they killed and consumed two moose. The summer before, the West Pack had contained at least three pups but none of them survived to winter. By 1999 the West Pack was essentially gone, displaced by M93's Middle Pack. The following year, the Middle Pack pushed in the other direction. Their trespass was eventually stopped by the formidable East Pack. But M93 killed a radio collared male that had split off from that pack and formed a pair on the periphery of the territory.

Just a few days later, we followed the running tracks of Middle Pack again heading east, obviously engaged in a chase. The tracks led us to a dramatic scene—the object of the chase was a cowering, half-submerged wolf in the frigid waters of Lake Superior.

"During the next hour we circled overhead. After several minutes of rolling in the snow to dry off, Middle Pack wolves either lay in the snow, watching the victim in the lake, or strutted stiffly back and forth along the shore in front of the hapless wolf. Suddenly, in quick succession, three wolves jumped into shallow water and leaped for the rock where their quarry stood quivering. Confronted by this snarling trio, it fought for its life, snapping furiously toward the lunging pack members. The lone wolf was forced backward into neck-deep water, but it retained its footing and held the attackers at bay; they retreated to shore to shake and roll again in the snow…

We became aware of a new element when the breeding male of the Middle Pack (we now know that this was M93) jumped to the rock to confront the lone wolf. Instead of pressing the attack, however, he slowly wagged his raised tail. Then he circled around to the wolf's side and regarded its hindquarters; the male was interested in courting the stranger, a newly-arrived female in heat. His arousal prompted the alpha female to jump to the rock, along with a helper. A severe attack then followed, and Middle Pack wolves firmly grabbed the female and threw her onto her back in the water. Soon all eleven wolves of the Middle Pack were involved in the melee. In less than a minute, however, the pack retreated and the lone female rose to her feet.

The attacks were repeated again and again, but finally the Middle Pack left the female for dead and continued on its way. A couple of hours later a trailing member of the Middle Pack, a son of Wolf M93, arrived on the scene. When he approached the motionless body of the female, she managed to raise her head slightly, and the male backed off and lay down nearby to watch. Though it would take many days, the female managed to regain her strength and recover from her ordeal, closely tended by her new suitor. They did not reproduce that year, but after recruiting another adult they carved out a territory taken mostly from the East Pack. This newly-formed Chippewa Harbor Pack, started by M93's son and a native female, also flourished. More than a decade later, in 2012, it was Isle Royale's only pack."

The original mate of M93 produced her final litter of pups in 2001. That was the spring in which John and I had first encountered M93. The following winter M93 had a new mate, a female who, we later learned from DNA analyses, had been born in 1998 and was his daughter! For many years John Vucetich and I have discussed this choice of mates. I have to agree with him that M93 consciously chose his own daughter over a number of native females on the island, probably because of genetic fitness—perhaps the other females were too inbred. We have no idea how wolves would make such a judgment, but we know that even American toads in a crowded pool base breeding decisions on genetics. Such close inbreeding was unknown among wild wolves at that time, although it had been documented in captivity. For most wolf biologists, problems arising from inbreeding were only theoretical risks.

M93 and his daughter were an exceptionally successful breeding pair, producing 21 surviving pups between 2002 and 2006. The supremacy of their Middle Pack went unchallenged and they claimed at least half of the island as theirs. M93 was quite a bit older than F58. By now he was showing it, being noticeably whiter. Around 2006 we began referring to him as the "Old Gray Guy." His stomach and lower legs had turned pure white and his dorsal side was light tan.

Circling overhead in the research plane at the end of the winter study in 2006, pilot Don Glaser and John Vucetich observed him mating with his daughter. We never saw him again.

He survived at least until September 2006, when off-duty ranger Karena Schmidt took an end-of-the-season solo hike that started off in Middle Pack country. Walking slowly through a mature maple and yellow birch forest along the Feldtmann trail, wearing an old canvas jacket in the light rain, she heard an annoying sound that she attributed to the jacket rubbing her pack frame. She dropped her pack, adjusted her gear, then shouldered it back up and continued on. The sound repeated itself. This time she was listening more carefully. It was a distinct low "woof"—from a wolf. Apparently the wolf had been paralleling her for a couple of miles, periodically uttering what now seemed like a low warning bark.

Suddenly, a wolf stood facing her, about thirty feet away. The light pelage of Wolf M93 was instantly recognizable. He made no sound, and Karena greeted him, "Hello, Wolf!" as they stared at each other. M93 took one step toward her and she took two steps toward the wolf. Then M93 moved off the trail at an angle, and as he departed she caught sight of several other wolves, some large and some obviously smaller, waiting for M93 to rejoin them. Karena then understood that she had been near, apparently too near, the traveling nursery of the Middle Pack. The ever-vigilant M93 had simply issued a warning.

For the Isle Royale wolf population, the arrival of M93 proved to be pivotal. Between 1998 and 2006 he sired 34 pups and became the second most prolific wolf in the 60-plus-year history of the population. Thanks to M93, the wolf population shook itself free of whatever had held them back in the early 1990s. The population doubled in size, even after most of the moose had died off, and through most of the decade of the 2000's the wolf population appeared to be firmly on its feet once again. Wolf predation resumed its strong top-down control of the moose population, which was increasingly challenged by warmer summers and more winter ticks.

M93's genes did not affect one important symptom of inbreeding in the Isle Royale wolf population. As the population became increasingly inbred, we noted a slow increase in the prevalence of abnormalities in the spines of wolves from Isle Royale—extra vertebrae and asymmetrical vertebrae. After 1994, the spine of every wolf carcass we examined carried these anomalies. This one-hundred percent prevalence is not seen in wolves anywhere else, and outbred populations in mainland situations commonly show a prevalence of less than ten percent. Although his remains were never found, M93's offspring showed spinal anomalies identical to all other wolves on the island.

The genetic fix introduced by M93 was highly successful, but it was temporary. The population will quickly become inbred again. The last wolf that was not a direct descendant of M93 died in 2007. Of four territorial packs on Isle Royale in 2008, the alpha pair of two of them were brother-sister pairs and all were offspring of M93. One of these packs, the Paduka Pack, reproduced once before it disappeared. The alpha female of the other pack, the East Pack, died in early May 2009. One pup was born live before the female died, along with seven unborn pups, when the contractions of her uterus ceased in a condition called uterine inertia. In dogs the condition can be associated with inbreeding, but it can also be caused by low calcium, low blood sugar, hormonal issues, or some other direct cause. This physiological malfunction has not been reported in wolves before, and a cause rooted in genetic history can be suspected.

What might have happened had M93 not ventured across the ice of Lake Superior to settle on Isle Royale? Surely the outcome for the wolf population would probably have been very different. And, given the significance of wolves in the health of the moose population and all the plant species that support them, M93 profoundly impacted the health of the island's ecosystem.

The scientific legacy of M93 is secure. It will be long-lasting and important. By 2010 the wolf population once again entered the doldrums. In 2013 wolves numbered only eight, the lowest number ever counted. In a repeat of the scientific thought process we went through twenty years earlier, we confront the same list of problems that might underlie the sinking fortunes of Isle Royale wolves: disease, food shortage, random demography and genetic decay. The challenge for scientists such as John Vucetich and me, in an observational study where we have not manipulated anything, is to weed through the evidence as it unfolds, seeking to disprove as many hypotheses as we can until we narrow the field down to one or two possibilities. Through this winnowing we eventually gain an understanding into the causes of the ups and downs of wolves and their prey, the moose, on Isle Royale, isolated now more than ever. They have lasted much longer than many ever anticipated, and M93 has shown us the importance of new blood.

CHAPTER TWENTY-ONE

Ernesto: A Wolf in the Agricultural Steppe of Spain

Juan Carlos Blanco and Yolanda Cortés

JUST PERHAPS, as the old wolf prepared to bed down after a night spent searching for food, he perceived something strange in the air: unusual noises, cars moving along normally quiet tracks, voices in remote corners of the woods... Finally, mid-morning, all hell broke loose. The commotion of the dog packs registering in every nook and cranny of the countryside, the shouts of the beaters and the deafening sound of gunshots converted his dream into a nightmare. The members of the wolf pack fled in terror from the hounds; at least three saved themselves by racing like the wind straight back through the line of shooters. But the veteran male, his faculties dulled by old age, failed to detect in time the hunter lining him up in his sights. The good luck which had accompanied him during the almost twelve years of his eventful life finally left him that January 25, 2007. At the end of the beat of an area of scrubland in the north-west of Valladolid Province, the hunters who were gathered around the corpse of an old, dark-furred wolf with worn-down teeth asked themselves if the radio collar it wore could provide information on where it had come from and what it had done in life.

Fortunately, we can provide numerous answers to these questions given that Ernesto, the wolf killed in the hunt, was one of sixteen wolves radio collared between 1997 and 2007 as part of a research project on the species in agricultural habitats financed by the Ministry of the Environment. Ernesto had been radio collared on March 8, 1998, almost nine years before his death, and had been followed until the end of 2002, when the collar's battery finally died. Subsequently, two further years were spent watching his pack's members in the treeless landscapes of the Tierra de Campos region.

Few people would identify the landscapes where Ernesto lived as wolf country. There are no mountains, no woods full of red deer, nor any of the remote areas which characterize many regions inhabited by wolves in the world. This area is almost completely flat and dedicated to agriculture, where the near-endless extension of cereal fields is only interrupted by small woodland pockets, serving as refuge for a very few wild boar, the only ungulate found in the area. In addition, several large four-lane fenced highways have been built in recent times, making it seemingly even less favorable for wolves. And yet, this has been our study area in Spain for many years: the vast cereal plains of Old Castile, an area with ten to forty people per square kilometer in the provinces of Valladolid and Zamora, some two-hundred kilometers northwest of Madrid.

In order to understand the presence of wolves in this region, it is important to know the species' recent history in Spain where it suffered ruthless hounding, followed by a period of recovery. As in the rest of Europe and North America, wolves were viciously persecuted in order to avoid livestock losses. During the twentieth century the Spanish wolf population fell rapidly until the last individuals were left only in the most remote mountain areas of the northwest, out of reach of hunters armed with the guns and poison used to eliminate them elsewhere in Spain. The few Spanish scientists and naturalists voicing alarm over wildlife in the 1960's and 1970's resigned themselves to the inevitable and tragic extinction of the last remaining individuals.

Against all odds, at the end of the 1960's, they found a providential defender, the famous television presenter, Félix Rodríguez de la Fuente, "Félix, Friend of the Animals," as he came to be known throughout the country. He appeared weekly on television screens, captivating the audience with his programs about wildlife and transmitting his contagious enthusiasm, greatly helping to slow the continuing destruction of Spain's fauna and its landscapes. Thanks to his influence, the Hunting Law *(Ley de Caza)* was modified in 1970, and the legal status of wolves changed from being persecuted as vermin when and wherever possible, to being a quarry species, benefitting from a closed season in spring and summer and certain restrictive measures used to hunt them. This allowed wolf populations to increase and expand, extending out from the mountains into the agricultural areas, where their presence had previously been considered impossible.

Many Spaniards have heard of our studies on wolves in agricultural habitats, but very few know that it was Dr. David Mech who provided the kick-start for this project during a visit he made to Spain in 1993. Mech was stunned to discover the presence of wolves in agricultural areas and declared his enormous interest in knowing details about their ecology. In the mid-1990's a great scientific debate had been sparked as wolves spread towards populated regions of Europe and North America. While Mech defended the idea that "wolves are inherently adaptable," other biologists doubted this. Indeed, Gordon Haber asked, "Should Mech's garbage-eating, largely solitary, sunflower-field canids really be regarded as wolves? Or are they the product of a lengthy, subtle process of 'unwolfing?'"

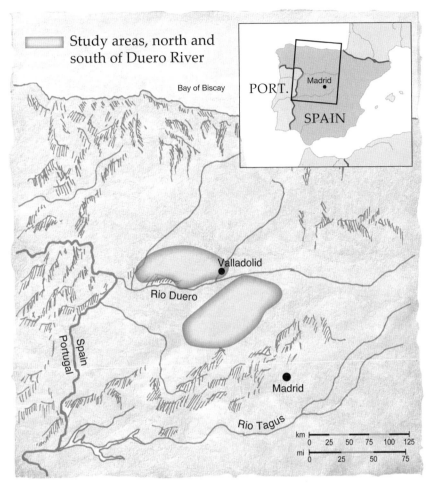

Study areas, north and south of Duero River

At this same time Spain entered the European Union and numerous fenced, four-lane highways were being constructed, cutting through natural areas. Spain's Minister of the Environment at that time was very interested in knowing their potential impact on wolf populations, and the Ministry ended up becoming the project's financer. At this time Juan Carlos was contracted as the expert for wolf and other mammal issues for the Ministry of the Environment, and Yolanda was a Ph.D. candidate at the Complutense University of Madrid. Invited by Dave Mech, Juan Carlos spent five weeks in the summer of 1996 in the Kawishiwi field laboratory in Ely, Minnesota, learning wolf radio marking and study methods from Mike Nelson.

This project commenced in 1997 with double objectives: to collect the first data on the ecology of wolves in agricultural areas, which are apparently so distinct from wolf populations everywhere else in the world, and to evaluate the impact of highways on wolf populations.

Ernesto has always been our favorite wolf. In the cold world of scientific publications, full of technicalities, and as required by scientific convention which considers the establishment of affectionate links to study animals as unseemly, he received the impersonal title of M2 (Male 2). But in this respect we can consider ourselves as sworn sinners, since we have formed a close personal link with each and every single wolf marked. We were delighted when they found mates, celebrated their whelping, and have been saddened on learning of their deaths. Worst of all, we have maintained a special fondness for a smaller number of these wolves, and Ernesto has been the most special of all.

In our defense we should note that we followed six wolves for some time—between four and six years each—which has almost allowed us to cover their entire lives in detail. In addition, Ernesto spent the majority of his life in a treeless agricultural landscape, enabling us to observe him and his pack on a total of seventy-one occasions. We have surprised him at daybreak, returning to his den with a hare in his jaws, trotting over the plains as the first rays of sunlight tinged the stubbled field red. We have seen his mates, and we witnessed how he singlehandedly reared his first group of three pups after his mate disappeared without a trace. Quite simply, if we hadn't become attached to him, we'd be heartless.

Our protagonist was radio collared in a patch of scrubland in eastern Zamora province, just north of the River Duero. He was big, despite weighing a modest 32.5 kilograms, and the wear on his teeth and other physical signs suggested that he was a couple of months short of reaching the age of three. That morning we were particularly blessed by good fortune, since we also captured another wolf almost within a stone's throw away. Our expert eyes, on seeing the proportionately smaller head and more pointed muzzle of this second individual, led us deduce it was a female, and, while waiting for the anesthetic to take effect, we decided to name them Ernesto and Concha, as thanks to two friends who had promoted the project through their consultancy. But when this wolf was finally asleep, and we could calmly contemplate its testicles, we had to recognize our error—Concha had become Concho.

Concho and Ernesto led parallel, though independent, lives for a time. We soon saw that they led an erratic existence, wandering over wide areas without showing any clear site preferences. Concho and Ernesto were floaters, i.e. dispersers. Dispersal is the means by which adult wolves, males as well as females, leave their natal territories and search for a new territory to establish and breed. If this process continues over many months, they convert into floaters. In our study, just over half of our sixteen marked wolves dispersed while their radio collars were functioning. Considering the time they were studied, the annual dispersal rate from packs was around one in four wolves per year. Dispersal tends to be the most difficult period during a wolf's life; mortality rates are higher than at any other time in a wolf's life.

But some wolves have it more difficult than others. Dispersers in habitats where the existing wolf density is almost at that environment's carrying capacity, for example saturated habitats, suffer a higher mortality rate; the survivors take longer to establish themselves, and, when they do, the territory occupied is of lower quality than of those dispersers in areas with lower wolf density. Our study, undertaken on both sides of the River Duero in the Castilla y León, Old Castile, region, has two physically similar areas, differing only in the wolf density present. North of the river wolves have been established for over three decades, and the population appears to be saturated. South of the Duero wolves are recent arrivals; hence, the greater part of the favorable areas were still available for colonization when we started our study.

The three radio marked wolves which dispersed in the low density area south of the river settled in a new territory just a few days after abandoning their natal territories. In addition, their new territories were of similar quality to their areas of origin and the three individuals ended up breeding and forming new packs. In contrast, of the six marked dispersing wolves north of the Duero, two died, two others were lost during the dispersal phase, and in only two cases were we able to confirm settlement and formation of new packs, although these were in poor quality areas. In addition, the dispersal period north of the river, from pack abandonment until establishment in a new area or death, was greater than fourteen months.

Dispersers sometimes cover huge areas looking for a mate and a wolf-free area to settle. They cross roads, enter into areas actively defended by other settled wolves, visit livestock areas guarded by Mastiff dogs that ferociously protect their sheep, and repeatedly cross the numerous hunting estates where many hunters are not exactly wolf-friendly. The eventful lives of these dispersers means they have a much higher likelihood of dying than members of packs in established territories who know to perfection where the food will be, which areas are more dangerous, and where the other packs are. Consequently, the annual mortality rate of dispersers and peripheral wolves—who avoid main pack members and stay at the fringes of pack social center—was two to four times that of pack members, respectively.

When Ernesto wandered the agricultural plains of Zamora and Valladolid, we still hadn't collected all this data, but we had clear motives for being concerned for his survival. Concho had been killed on the road six months after being marked, and Ernesto frequently moved in astonishingly humanized areas. One day we picked up his signal on the edge of a Zamoran village. Indeed the radio collar beeps led us to an abandoned corn field full of building rubble and waste, adjacent to where a flock of sheep fed quietly watched over by a shepherd with numerous noisy dogs. Just two-hundred meters away a small mansion was being built at enormous expense. At that moment we felt it was clear Ernesto had been killed and the collar thrown into the field.

But as we moved to recover the collar, the activity sensor went off, indicating that our wolf was very much alive and kicking. Relieved, and naturally full of curiosity, we drew back and at dusk sat discretely in front of the field. After nightfall the activity sensor again went off, and, by squinting into the near pitch darkness, we were amazed to see how two shadows slunk out of their hiding place and vanished into the night. Ernesto was not only alive, but had bedded down in this implausible spot accompanied by another wolf.

In light of all these dangers, we always feared for Ernesto's life while he was dispersing. None of our wolves died of hunger, disease, or in fights with other wolves, as occurs in other areas of the world. Man was directly, or indirectly, the only cause of mortality among our marked wolves, given that almost all of them were hunted, either legally or illegally, or run over on roads. In our agricultural landscapes, intraspecific competition (with other wolves) displaces some individuals toward areas with higher human population densities, and so increases the probability that they die at the hands of man. Man is the proximate cause of their death, but intraspecific competition is the ultimate causal factor.

During his wanderings Ernesto visited emblematic areas of natural value, but which were equally surprising for a wolf. In July 1998 we discovered him at dawn beside the Laguna Grande de Villafáfila (Zamora) an important flagship site for Spanish naturalists for its populations of aquatic and steppe birds, and also the absolute epitome of the cereal plains, being dead flat and lacking in cover. From the roof of our 4x4 the views extended for several kilometers in all directions, without a single woods to interrupt the bare agri-steppe. Ernesto walked into the water, a saline lake, and drank for half a minute, and afterwards walked slowly across it to the indifference of the avocets and the alarm of the mallards. During other periods, Ernesto wandered the Villafáfila Reserve and bedded down in a small island of vegetation lost in the sea of cereals; his refuge was formed by an ancient holm oak whose cool shade permitted a dense growth of grass and a small pool surrounded by rushes.

Despite our intensive fieldwork, our knowledge of Ernesto's wanderings is incomplete. In his year living as a floater, he roamed over an area covering 1,632 square kilometers, but on more than half of the occasions we tried to locate him we were unsuccessful, suggesting that the real area he covered was perhaps far greater. The area covered extended on both sides of the A-6 highway between Tordesillas (Valladolid) and Villalpando (Zamora), a highway which Ernesto crossed at least thirteen times during that year.

At dusk on November 4, 1998 we watched Ernesto, together with another wolf, leave a corn field adjacent to the highway. At 8:20 p.m. we relocated them, still together, at the end of a raised cattle bridge over the highway. The other wolf separated and disappeared, while Ernesto stayed to hunt rabbits between the broom bushes on top of the bridge, ignoring the passing cars below. In the feeble night light, Germán Garrote, our collaborator, could just make out Ernesto's figure in the short vegetation, making short and very fast runs, interspersed with sudden stops. Finally, at 10:10 p.m. he crossed the highway, using the raised pass, and disappeared.

In fact, the five wolves that could be followed adequately and were marked within fifteen kilometers of the highway were all recorded crossing it using vehicle overpasses. These bridges measure between forty-to-sixty meters in length and eight-to-twelve meters in width. Some are covered with asphalt and others with gravel, but none are adapted for fauna.

Ernesto's familiarity with cars on the highway was also manifest in the way he ignored them while hunting rabbits at night and in close proximity. The highway fence excludes foxes and other predators from the strip of land bordering the asphalt, converting it into a mini-paradise for rabbits, which excavate their burrows here and reach high densities. Ernesto hunted rabbits on the outside of this fence, just ten meters from the vehicles, lights and noise of the highway, one of the principal arterial roads in Spain that supports an average volume of 12,300 vehicles a day.

Surprisingly, while the highways did not constitute a significant barrier for our study wolves, the fifty-to-one-hundred-meter-wide river Duero Artery and several infrastructures along it formed important barriers for our radio collared wolves and delayed wolf expansion for some fifteen years. This suggests that the addition of several small barriers can have synergistic effects, creating a much stronger barrier effect.

In other areas of the world, dispersing individuals are known to avoid contact with wolves of established packs, which can end up killing them, but this is not the case in our study. During his dispersal, Ernesto visited all four corners of each of the three territories held by packs containing marked wolves and even visited one of them in the breeding season, though he stayed for only a few days. One night in July 1998 we found Ernesto howling alongside the cubs of the very same pack in Valladolid where he was to meet his death eight years later, an act normally considered a serious intrusion into the heart of a distinct pack's territory.

Ernesto was not our only marked wolf to display this behavior. One of the options for dispersing wolves is adoption into a pack where a loss had been experienced. This perhaps explains why our radio collared wolves visited neighboring packs—they were checking possibilities. Additionally, in our study area, a large quantity of food in the form of dead livestock was available, which may explain the tolerance of pack members towards outsiders.

Finally, in March 1999 Ernesto began using the same area day after day, the flat and treeless agricultural surroundings in the Tierra de Campos, not far from the village of Medina de Rioseco in Valladolid. After wandering for at least a year, Ernesto had settled fifty kilometers from where he was radio collared, a distance roughly four times less than distances observed by others studying wolves in North America and northern Europe. It is quite probable that the numerous roads and other obstacles are the reasons that dispersers travel shorter distances in these humanized habitats.

In May 1999 his movements became centered on a ditch hidden between barley and flax fields. Now we were convinced that he had established a territory and was breeding, but, given the dense spring vegetation, the wolves were invisible. At that moment we felt the same satisfaction as parents who see their immature and uncertain son suddenly settle down, get married and start a stable life, and we had good reason to be relieved: for Ernesto the dangers that floater wolves face seemed to have passed, and the probabilities of surviving another year multiplied.

Ernesto was one of those few privileged wolves that managed to find his own territory in the saturated area north of the Duero. He had managed to establish himself in an area of extremely poor quality: it was absolutely treeless; it was twenty kilometers from the nearest copse; and he could be spied by hunters from great distances. This obliged him to live making maximum use of the hours of darkness, hidden between crop fields or in the cover provided along tiny, miserable streams which were devoid of water in summer.

Some six months before he definitively settled, Ernesto was in the company of another wolf which must have been his partner. Apparently, they jointly undertook part of their dispersal together and so explored the possibilities of establishing a new territory between those of other packs. They bred immediately after establishing in his new territory. In the month of May, when the fields of Old Castile form a sea of cereals, and the roadsides verges turn red with carpets of poppies, Ernesto started to show strong fidelity to one particular spot, which tends to indicate the presence of a den of wolf pups.

Through a stroke of luck, at 2:15 p.m. on July 12, with the sun pounding down, our collaborator Álvaro de la Puente, while looking for tracks and signs on an agricultural track, noticed three wolf pups resting in the shade of a bush, chewing on sticks. After the inevitable celebration, we set up a program to watch the new family in this flat landscape without disturbing them. From the fragile roof of a ruined farm building, where an irate little owl made short swoops at our heads, we had an ideal viewing point.

At dusk we watched how Ernesto approached the den from over a kilometer and a half away, crossing a road and fallow and cultivated fields, until he reached the flax field where the pups were. They greeted him with enormous enthusiasm, trying to climb on top of him, licking his jowls to stimulate regurgitation of the food he carried in his stomach. From July 13 onwards, when the pups were a little less than two months old, we saw this scene several times at dawn and dusk, but we never saw the breeding female, nor any other adult or sub-adult wolf. It seemed clear that the mother had died sometime before and that Ernesto was rearing them alone.

Following the harvest the crop fields that had hidden the den, which consisted of a large pile of rushes in an almost dry ditch, were laid bare, and Ernesto decided that it was time to transfer the pups to a safer location. On July 19, at 6:30 a.m. we saw Ernesto leave the flax field, looking continuously behind him. He was waiting for his three pups, which followed him with childish lack of discipline, distracted at every step, playing with their siblings and becoming separated from the group. After forty minutes they had barely gone five-hundred meters. At 7:10 a.m., now full daylight, we watched as they started to cross the local road, the pups delayed alarmingly, totally oblivious to the danger they were approaching. At 7:50 a.m. we saw them on the other side of the road crossing some stubble. But now only two pups were following Ernesto. Fearing the third pup had been run over, we checked the verges looking for its body, but found nothing. By 11:00 a.m. Ernesto and the two surviving pups were safely installed in a hemp field four kilometers as the crow flies from the original den.

On July 24 we received a tremendous surprise: while inspecting what we thought was the abandoned den, we flushed the third pup, which ran off through the flax field, suggesting that perhaps it had returned before crossing the road during the transfer. Finally, on July 28, in the half-light of dusk, we were able to make out Ernesto together with the three pups reunited in the hemp field where they had all moved. Apparently Ernesto had been tending his offspring in these two widely separated sites for at least five days.

During the rest of summer and part of autumn we were able to watch the family hidden in a corn field and delighted in watching how the pups grew and acquired the lanky, long-legged look that adolescent wolves show. Ernesto had brought his offspring up alone, and he had worked hard. On various dawn watches we saw how Ernesto arrived at the rendezvous site with a hare between his jaws, trotting in characteristic wolf fashion from several kilometers away. He probably spent every night catching small prey or transporting food in his stomach back to feed the insatiable appetite of his pups.

Ernesto was an excellent rabbit and hare hunter, as we can testify to both from direct observations and through the study of the remains of prey found at rendezvous sites. Ernesto tended to keep his distance from sheep flocks tended by shepherds and defended by ferocious Mastiff dogs, but plenty of sheep remains were also found at the rendezvous sites suggesting perhaps that they were picked up at carrion pits or on the edges of villages. The only ungulates present in these treeless areas are wild boar, and even these are rather scarce. What do wolves in these agricultural areas eat? How can they survive? In order to answer these questions we analyzed more than six-hundred scats collected in the core areas of pack territories. The results indicated that three-quarters of the ingested biomass was of domestic animals, the majority sheep, which the wolves consumed principally as carrion. Less than a quarter of the diet of these plains-dwelling wolves consisted of wild prey, principally rabbits and hares. Wild boar only formed six percent of the diet.

We must stress that the sheep and other domestic animals in our wolves' diet were almost all consumed as carrion. At night, wolves tend to visit carrion pits and other areas where livestock herders dump dead animals, and by this means find the majority of their food. When searching for food, wolves employ the rule of minimum effort and maximum safety, selecting the most vulnerable prey. In these agricultural landscapes dead sheep are easier prey than live ones, especially when the latter are fiercely protected by Mastiff dogs, weighing twice that of a wolf and bearing a spiked collar. Attacks on livestock in our area are infrequent, and livestock farmers show no particular hostility toward wolves. This is because the livestock are almost invariably accompanied by herders. A typical Castilian scene is a flock of 300 to 500 sheep accompanied by a shepherd and his donkey, a few small shepherd dogs, which help to direct the flock, and two or three large Mastiffs which defend against wolves.

This traditional and peculiar form of sheep grazing has had the unintended consequence of minimizing losses from wolf attacks, allowing wolves to colonize this extraordinary habitat. In these areas the shepherds have always accompanied their flocks in the field in order to avoid damage to crops, regardless of the presence of wolves. When wolves returned to the agricultural areas in the 1980's, no change in shepherding habits was necessary, and, in consequence, the impact of wolves on the rural economy has been minimal. The shepherds only needed to acquire Mastiff dogs to protect the sheep during the day and to corral the sheep at night. Under these conditions the wolves cause little damage and are tolerably accepted by the rural community, which explains why wolves have been able to survive in these open flat landscapes where they are so vulnerable.

Had livestock losses been high, nothing would have saved this wolf population. Livestock farmers would have persecuted them relentlessly, legally or not. They would have found their dens in the small clumps of trees or in the corn fields, shot the adults in the open fields, and surrounded them with vehicles. There would be no wolves here.

In contrast, the wolves living in the Cantabrican Mountains of northern Spain, a wild habitat with abundant forest and wild ungulates, cause ten times more damage than those on the agricultural plains. This is the result of the livestock rearing system, where extensive cattle grazing in the mountains from May to October makes them vulnerable to attacks from wolves despite an abundance of natural prey. Survival of these wolves is due to the mountainous terrain, extensive woods in which to hide, and the generous compensation paid out by the regional governments for depredation.

In the spring of 2000 Ernesto was accompanied by an adult female wolf, probably a dispersing individual that found a good opportunity to integrate into this small family. Over the next two years, along with this new breeding female, Ernesto managed to consolidate a strong pack in this area of Tierra de Campos. These wolves were accustomed to remaining unnoticed among the comings and goings of workers in the fields, hunters and shepherds, moving like shadows over the soulless high plains, and disappearing without trace during the day in corn fields and in rush clumps in tiny ditches.

The wolves of these agricultural habitats do not differ in any other way from normal wolves. Our radio collared animals lived in packs of five to ten individuals in territories covering from 150 to 250 square kilometers. Being largely carrion-eating in no way led them to lose their wolf characteristics. Despite the fact that many of these wolves needed to move very little to obtain food, on many nights, after feeding in carrion pits, they walked an average of twenty kilometers, which appeared to be exploratory routes or territorial patrols. Their social and spatial behavior was the same as wolves studied in Minnesota, Alaska and other wild areas of the world, only they have managed to adapt to the unique characteristics of this agriculturally dominated landscape.

To see if our wolves were more solitary than in other areas, we carried out more than 500 "sit and wait" observation sessions, many of them at rendezvous sites, and more than 250 simulated howling trials. This allowed us to make over 270 direct observations of our radio marked individuals and hear them howling on almost 100 occasions, which in turn allowed us to check if they had bred, if they were alone or in company of other wolves, and to define their social status within the pack. Nearly three-quarters of the wolves lived in the heart of the pack, ten percent lived in non-reproductive pairs and only eighteen percent were solitary, dispersers or peripherals.

In March 2002, in the middle of the mating season, one of our collaborators watched three copulation attempts by a large red male with one of the females of the pack. Lying on the ground close by, Ernesto, no longer the dominant male, watched the mating pair until the other male, notably larger, turned and violently bit him. At this stage the radio collar battery was already running out, and it was becoming ever more difficult to locate and record his movements.

That summer we watched these wolves on eight occasions, but only once did we find Ernesto among them. This was on September 8, when the collar had already ceased working. The proud founder of the pack, who used to trot with his body upright, now looked smaller and withdrawn. We observed nothing more of Ernesto until the day he died, almost five years later.

Ernesto's tenure as the breeding male of his pack was a little over three years. In our study the average recorded tenure of six breeders, four females and two males, was four-and-one-half years, and varied between one and seven-and-one-half years. Even for those fortunate wolves that survive to adulthood, disperse successfully and form a pack, the peak of life doesn't last long.

After his dethroning, it is possible that Ernesto started life as a peripheral wolf, living on the fringes of his old pack, but avoiding entering into its nucleus. However, at some unknown point he dispersed again, looking for a new pack to adopt him, which is not uncommon behavior among males. Ernesto finally appeared in the Torozos scrublands to the northwest of Valladolid, which he had explored in depth during his juvenile dispersal and which lay just twenty kilometers from the pack he had founded. Clearly we know nothing about Ernesto's life during those last five years; the last information came from the testaments of the hunters who saw him, together with at least three other wolves, during the legal wolf hunt which ended his life.

Changes also occurred in our study area over this period. After the appearance of mad cow disease (BSE) in Spain at the end of 2000, the carrion pits started to be closed and food availability for the wolves appeared to be declining. If this assumption is correct, the population dynamic parameters could have changed and there could now be fewer loners, smaller pack sizes and a general reduction of the wolf population. These changes make us realize how the environment, for one reason or another, is constantly changing, and that the predictions we made just a few years ago may no longer be valid.

The pack Ernesto founded in the vast Castilian plains continues to breed. At dawn one June morning we discover a female wolf with swollen teats trotting towards us from the horizon. Crossing the cereal fields, the breeze sending out swirling green waves, head held high, she jumps occasionally to get a clearer view of the surroundings above the barley heads, taking in everything around her. Two more wolves enter the field, bordered by a small ditch. Without doubt they are breeding there. The female could even be one of Ernesto's daughters. We imagine the pups as little fluffy black balls, resting on the ditch's soft vegetation. It is more than likely the pack's founder has passed on the genes that give these wolves the audacity and discretion necessary to prosper in these highly humanized habitats.

We pack up the telescopes and leave quietly to avoid disturbing them. The air fills with the song of calandra larks and the verges are radiant with poppies. We wish these recently born wolf pups of the Tierra de Campos all the best they can have and a long life as full of wolf experiences as their special grandfather, Ernesto.

CHAPTER TWENTY-TWO

Brutus

L. David Mech

 I KNEW RIGHT AWAY when the wolf I came to know as Brutus deftly sniffed my gloved hand that he was not your regular, "run-of-the-mill" wolf of the High Arctic. True, many, if not most, wolves in that area, less than 700 miles from the North Pole, tend to be tame to humans. They have seen so few humans, and none they have seen have harmed them in any way. They are 250 miles north of even the nearest Inuit who would hunt them.

But Brutus was far more than tame. I learned over the next several summers that he was blatantly bold. In 2005, for example, Brutus stuck his nose and shoulders under the front of a four-wheeled all-terrain vehicle (ATV) that my companion, Walter Medwid, was sitting on. Walter, at that time Executive Director of the International Wolf Center, had dropped an apple core, and Brutus was intent on snagging it. Walter and I had been perched on our ATV's observing Brutus' pups, as part of a study I had been conducting every summer since 1986 on Ellesmere Island, Canada. Brutus apparently figured that he should get something out of this deal too. Remembering two summers previous when Brutus sniffed my glove, I was not surprised by his current antic, although Walter was suitably impressed, being that this was Walter's first summer with Brutus.

My best guess at Brutus' age when I first encountered him in 2003 was that he was two or three years old. He was with a young female, also tame, and I could see that she was not nursing. Neither wolf had been around the area in 2002, so they apparently had recently pair-bonded. Because they did double-urine mark I hoped they would remain in my study area, the general vicinity of the Eureka Weather Station, and produce pups during the next several years.

And they did! During 2004, they produced four pups, in 2005, three, and in 2006, six. Brutus stood out from the pack during each of these years by his boldness. During my twenty-five summers in this area, I had inter-acted close-up with many tame wolves. In 1987 I had sat surrounded by several pups and their mother, all within ten feet, while we all howled (as seen in National Geographic's video *White Wolf*). Some wolves have slept outside my tent, and others have stuck their noses into it. One pup even untied my bootlace once.

Still, Brutus was bolder than all the others. One time he even frightened me, the first time in my then forty-six years studying wolves that I had been afraid of one. In 2004 when my associate Dean Cluff of the Department of Environmental and Natural Resources, Northwest Territories, Canada, and I were searching for Brutus' den, we took a break, and Brutus found us. As Dean and I were lying on the tundra, I was perched on an elbow, and Brutus sniffed my boot. This was the first time I had ever been off my ATV around Brutus, and I wondered how he would react to the 400 pounds or so of human biomass right down on his level. Sniffing my boot was fine, but when Brutus ambled around behind me where I could not see him, I had second thoughts. I recalled someone's German shepherd several decades before that had nipped at the back of my clothing all the way up to my hair and had actually nipped some of that. I also recalled in 1987 being within a few yards of a muskox calf as several wolves tore at it until it collapsed (also shown in the *White Wolf* video). For a minute or two I became truly frightened.

"You know, Dean, for the first time in my life I am truly afraid of a wolf," I uttered to my companion. I had thought that maybe Brutus would tug at the day pack on my back, and I might jump or whirl around, possibly triggering some predatory move. I knew only too well what a single bite from Brutus could do.

Dean offered little consolation as he lay ten feet away watching Brutus behind me. "All I have is my Leatherman tool" said Dean. I didn't even have anything like that, although, of course, no small tool of any sort would have been sufficient to ward off an attack. Each second Brutus stayed behind me seemed endless until he finally moseyed back around to my side where I could see him. He then strolled some twenty feet from us, lay down and howled. My fear was all for naught, and I ended up feeling foolish. Eventually Dean and I continued our quest, and Brutus departed too.

Brutus remained in the study area throughout 2010, providing me with much good data on several subjects. My companions, who varied over the summers, also benefited from observing and interacting with Brutus and his offspring and pack mates, adding considerably to their knowledge of wolves, as well as to their entertainment.

After my frightened-by-a-wolf incident, Dean and I proceeded to the top of a cliff from which we could spy on Brutus' four pups. When both parents were gone, Dean was even able to sneak up to within a few feet of the pups to observe them closely and take a few close-up photos.

The next year, 2005, was when Walter Medwid and I watched Brutus, his mate, and one of his 2004 pups, now a yearling, at a rendezvous site. We had arrived too late to observe them at their den. I don't think Walter will ever recover from watching Brutus try to fish the apple core from beneath his ATV.

However, in 2006 Brutus pulled his most-interesting stunt. My associates that year were three International Wolf Center board members, Nancy Gibson, Neil Hutt, and Ted Spaulding. For safety's sake I needed at least one companion, and given the isolation of my study area and the high expense of getting there by air, I had to find the right folks each year who could accompany me.

Watching wolves up close is an art. We are clearly bizarre intruders into their world, and around dens, rendezvous sites, and pups, wolves are most sensitive. Long years of studying wolves had taught me that, even before finding the tame wolves in my study area. Also wolves each have a different personality. Some are especially jumpy, others cool and aloof, and a few, like Brutus, are confident and bold, although Brutus was by far the boldest. Most of the time I observed the wolves from atop an ATV, and that usually meant sitting still for many hours, moving slowly when I did move, and getting off the ATV on the side away from the wolves, etc., to keep my intrusiveness minimal. Sometimes one violation of this routine frightened some of the wolves for days.

I had long ago learned that while observing my wolves, I had to keep all my daily gear attached to my ATV, and each year I had to teach my companions my special techniques. During various summers some folks forgot some technique and either scared the wolves, lost gear, or otherwise upset the routine.

The situation for observing in 2006 was ideal. Brutus and his pack occupied a den at which I had spent the most time watching wolves. The den was at the end of a long sandstone outcrop that protruded from a hillside. I knew each good spot to park ATV's to observe the entrance and where the wolves lay from various angles. This particular year, Brutus' pack consisted of seven adults and five pups, a veritable collection of interesting, interacting individuals.

One day, Ted happened to forget one of my basic rules and left his day pack by the side of his ATV rather than on the luggage rack. None of us noticed until I spotted Brutus strolling over for one of his periodic checkups on us. He and his mate, being the parents and guardians of all the others, kept regular track of us, although his mate tended to do so with a wary eye from a distance of twenty yards or so. Brutus would come right up.

My instant command to Ted to pick up his daypack was too late. Brutus merely grasped it and ambled off, just as though we had left him a present. Now Brutus was carrying his present, head held high and Ted's pack dangling from it, toward the rest of the pack. Instantly, all the wolves jumped up, rushed to Brutus and mobbed him. One snatched the pack from him, and ran off with the others chasing it.

"Is there anything irreplaceable in that pack, Ted?" I questioned.

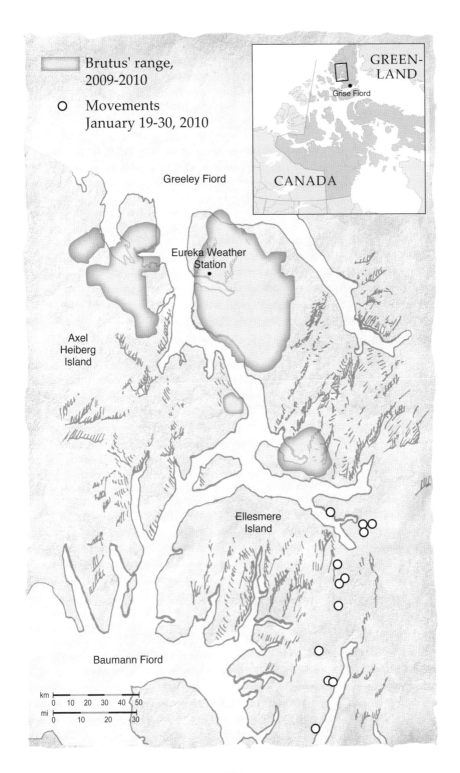

Brutus' range,
2009-2010

○   Movements
    January 19-30, 2010

GREEN-
LAND

Grise Fiord

Greeley Fiord

CANADA

Eureka Weather
Station

Axel
Heiberg
Island

Ellesmere
Island

Baumann Fiord

km
0   10   20   30   40   50
mi
0   10   20   30

My thought was that if there was, we would have to try the unthinkable—extracting the pack from the wolves, an act that might totally destroy the fragile relationship I had with them.

"I think my car keys are in there" replied Ted. Car keys? In his day pack? Here on the High Arctic tundra, 1,000 miles from Alaska, and 2,300 miles from Ted's car?

"No; wait. No; I left them in my luggage back at camp."

"Anything else irreplaceable?"

"Just my M and M's and some peanuts." replied Ted, half in jest, as we all watched the wolf pack play tug-of-war with his pack. I was highly relieved that we could wait until the wolves struck out on their nightly hunt before we retrieved Ted's daypack.

Besides the entertainment, we learned a great deal that summer from Brutus and his wolf pack. This gain in data included some valuable observations of Brutus' pack hunting muskoxen in ways that seemed to indicate the wolves' use of strategy.

Thus it was with great disappointment that in 2007 Brutus was nowhere to be found. The main part of the study area covered a tract of tundra extending almost five miles north of Slidre Fiord, an inlet roughly two miles wide and over fourteen miles long with a river and mud flats at one end that are impossible to cross on foot or with ATV's. Since 1986 I had learned where the wolf dens were, the usual wolf travel routes, good places to find tracks of whatever wolves were frequenting the area. We searched the area high and low in 2007 and found so little wolf sign that we cut our visit short. We could only wonder what might have happened in the past year that Brutus' whole pack of seven adults and five pups were gone.

However, we also realized that the main study area during our summer investigations was really only a fraction of a wolf pack territory—the part used in summer to raise pups. And there was no real need for the wolves to always use the same area each summer to den. In fact, one summer the wolves had denned some fifteen miles from the usual den. Perhaps in 2007 the pack had not produced any pups at all, so were just wandering around their full territory which had to be many times the size of our usual summer study area. Or maybe in 2009 they merely denned somewhere else where we couldn't find them. Could Brutus still be somewhere else?

We were also somewhat dismayed for most of our 2008 stay in the study area. No wolves denned there, but that summer wolves did use the area. We once saw a pack of eight pass through, although no Brutus. In fact, the eight included a nursing female leader that scratched the ground and scent-marked, but no male marked with her. Was Brutus her missing mate? Breeding males don't always accompany their pack, although they usually do. Still, knowing this pack was around but not denning in our area made us wonder where they were denning.

Our question was answered toward the end of our stay. We had several times followed fresh tracks of several wolves, probably of the eight we had seen, along the north side of the fiord, and we had good reason to believe the den was not to the west. However, when the trail to the east reached the end of the fiord, the landscape changed. Steep hills rose along most of the north side of the fiord, kind of forcing the wolves along the shore, but at the end was an open desert north of the mud flats. Thus we lost the tracks there each time. We finally learned that the trail actually led not into the desert area but into the mud flats. Furthermore they seemed to head across the flats to an area inaccessible to us. Was the den, and possibly Brutus, in this area we had never explored?

Using a high-powered spotting scope we searched the hills two miles away across the flats for many hours, and finally we observed a wolf on a couple of different days in the same area. That was probably the new den.

This finding posed a real dilemma for me regarding the future of this long, interesting and productive project. If the wolves had now begun to den in an area inaccessible to me, how could I continue the project? Basic to my annual summer expedition to this distant study area was the assumption that the wolves would be denning with pups in an area where I could observe them daily. After close to twenty-five years of studying wolves there, I needed the study situation to be such that I could continue to efficiently collect enough data to learn something new. Another summer trip occupied with just trying to find the wolves would not suffice. On the other hand, the prospect of having to give up such a unique and productive project was tough to contemplate.

Suddenly, I thought of a possible solution. In my other research in northeastern Minnesota and in Yellowstone, we had been using some new high-tech radio tracking collars that transmitted location data by satellite to my email. Could we perhaps put one or two such collars out here? Logistically it could work. The wolves were tame enough that we could drug one via a syringe pole, a dart pistol, or a blowgun. If we could collar even a single wolf with one of these high-tech collars during my next summer trip, and if it transmitted data for even a few months, we would learn much information I had been wondering about ever since starting this study. How large an area do our wolves use? Where do they range during winter when the pups are large enough to forsake dens and rendezvous sites and roam nomadically with the pack? How large is their year-around territory? How far do wolves travel in the twenty-four-hour darkness of winter? No such information was available for any wolf pack within 1,400 miles.

Dean Cluff, who was with me again in 2008, and who had also been using similar high-tech collars, agreed that we should try collaring a wolf in 2009. This would give the project a whole new impetus and direction. We couldn't wait until July 2009.

When the time came to put our plan into action, we were dismayed that again in 2009 the wolves failed to den in our study area. Thus the possibility of our collaring a wolf would depend on our finding a wolf and that wolf being so tame that we could dart it. We practiced with both a dart pistol and a blowgun, and Dean was a better shot. It would be his job to dart the wolf.

After a few days of tracking, waiting, and watching for wolves, we finally found a pack of five, including a nursing female, and they allowed us to drive our ATV's right up to them. We then saw that one was a large all-white male that looked very familiar. Dean readied his darting equipment, and the large male strolled up to me and sniffed the day pack on my lap—Brutus!

Dean, sitting parallel with me on his ATV, raised the blowgun, and when Brutus finally ambled his way, Dean "poofed," and a dart bounced off Brutus six feet away without fazing him. The second struck, and Brutus went down a few minutes later. What would the other wolves do now as we measured, ear-tagged, and radio collared their 91-pound leader?

Wait around and watch; that's what they did. They all hung around for several hours until Brutus was up and fully functioning along with his brand-new collar. We then followed the whole pack as they made their way eastward along the fiord route where we had followed their tracks last year. Sure enough, Brutus headed across the mud flats. He disappeared over the hills on the other side of the flats some three miles from where we had to stop and watch with a scope and twenty-one miles travel distance from where we had collared him.

Now, if the collar worked as it should, the fun would begin. The collar was programmed to record Brutus' location every twelve hours for at least the next year and to email the data every few days to our computers.

The collar worked wonderfully, and the data poured in. To two very curious wolf biologists who had known Brutus up-close and personal, this stream of twice-daily locations became almost an obsession. Each day as the data came in, we—Dean in Yellowknife, Northwest Territories, Canada, and I in Minnesota—eagerly checked every new move. And we were amply rewarded over the next several months as the area Brutus covered grew larger and larger, helping to answer our questions about where he lived during fall and, eventually, winter.

An extra, very-valuable, bonus came in an email from the weather station. Some of the station crew had photographed Brutus traveling with a pack of more than twenty wolves several times. My count of the wolves in the photo was that there were at least twenty. Now we knew that the locations we received from Brutus' collar recorded the travels of his whole pack.

Almost each email from Brutus yielded new information. My summer study area of almost twenty-five years had been but a tiny part of Brutus' territory. As soon as fiords froze in mid-October, Brutus' pack trekked nearly eight miles across one to an adjacent island. Over winter the wolves made several trips there, traveling as freely in the twenty-four hour darkness as in the light. Eventually their territory covered some 2,594 square miles—one of the largest wolf pack territories known.

Each time Brutus extended his territory, Dean and I marveled to each other by phone or email; and the International Wolf Center hosted a blog with maps about Brutus and the pack's travels, so that anyone could follow them.

Then one day, after a long string of surprising movements, the wolves' locations seemed strange. On January 19, Brutus left the territory that had been neatly outlined by over 370 points and headed south toward the only Inuit, formerly Eskimo, village for thousands of miles.

Although the village was still some 170 miles away, Dean and I both feared that if the wolves got anywhere near the village they would smell food and head there, totally unaware that the inhabitants had a hunting culture. Each day's locations showed that Brutus was on a straight-line trek southward. Thus we emailed the only contact we had in the village of Grise Fiord, population 130, pleading with them not to shoot our radioed wolf and to email us if they saw it. His response was equivocal, but we had hopes that the wolves would veer east to Greenland or west to other islands before reaching the village.

The wolves did not veer east or west, but rather continued bee-lining 100 miles south of their territory. We were pretty certain that it was the whole pack we were monitoring on this trek, because the movements stopped for the right number of locations at a single point indicating a musk-ox kill fed on by not just a single wolf, but by the whole pack.

Then the southward travel stopped, and the wolves turned back to the north, following about the same route that took them south. During their return trip, the wolves traveled straight-line distances of about 25 miles per day back into their territory, arriving at the south border between January 29 and February 1.

We learned much more information about this High Arctic wolf pack throughout those many months of its summer, fall, and winter travels. The next summer of 2010 Dean and I, accompanied by Dan MacNulty on a National Geographic post-doctoral fellowship, explained many of the points where Brutus had stopped for at least two consecutive locations. We visited as many as we could on ATV's and many others by helicopter. Sure enough, we found the remains of several wolf-eaten muskoxen and one Peary caribou.

And, surprise of surprises, we found three active wolf dens, that is with pups, that Brutus had visited the previous year! Had I been studying all these years just one of several dens this pack had maintained each year? If so, that possibility would explain mysterious reports I had received from the Weather Station for each of many winters about a pack of twenty or more wolves showing up. Restricted to one relatively small study area for a few weeks each year, headquartering around a single den had given me one impression about these High Arctic wolves. But Brutus and his high-tech collar filled in many important blanks in my understanding of these wolves.

Then one day in spring 2010, our worst fears were realized. Brutus' locations did not change, day after day after day. Either the wolf had somehow gotten his collar off and it was sitting there on the frozen tundra, or worse, our prize wolf was dead.

The only way to tell was to travel to the location on foot. However, it was April 12, and Dean was 1,300 miles away; I was 2,300 miles away. Still, we had to know what had happened. Fortunately, our friends in the weather station, who had avidly followed Brutus' adventures over the years both by our reports to them and via the International Wolf Center blog, came through for us. The station was only eight miles from the target location. The sun had reappeared in that area in late February, so by April there was enough daylight for the trek.

Rai LeCotey, station supervisor, and a companion made their way by snow machine and hiking to the point in question. By this time they were about as heavily invested intellectually as we were, so imagine their emotions when their GPS led them to some pointed ears sticking up through the snow. They extracted Brutus from his snowy grave and transported him back to the weather station for Dean's later examination in Yellowknife. Brutus was emaciated, and his spleen was enlarged, a good indication that he had cancer. His teeth indicated he was about ten years old, as we had thought.

So, as we all do, Brutus finally reached his end, but not before helping science learn a tremendous amount of new information about arctic wolves. And, as a fitting tribute to his many contributions, Brutus— beautifully mounted—will forever grace the display room in the Eureka Weather Station.

CHAPTER TWENTY-THREE

The Story of Timish

Christoph Promberger

THE RATTLING BUS WAS DRIVING over the bridge above me, belching its exhaust into the cool air of the early summer night. The sky had been clouded all day, but now the dense cover started to break up, and I could see the faint crescent of the moon through the shreds of clouds. The yellow and neon-white street-lights of the exit road to Bucharest reflected on the clouds and gave more light than a cloudless sky would have. Still, it was dark, and without the night vision goggles I wouldn't have seen anything in the river channel, on whose edge I had parked my car. It was one o'clock in the morning, and the few people that had been out for the evening had returned long ago to their homes. This is the city of Brasov in the mid-nineties, its night life hardly developed since Ceausescu's times. Brasov, with its 285,000 inhabitants, is located in the heart of Romania on the north side of the arch of the Carpathian Mountains. Densely populated quarters of the city reach right to the foot of the mountains, and the borderline between the urban area and the wild Carpathian forests are as sharp a contrast as anyone could imagine. Consequently, strange creatures of the night cross the boundaries, protected by the dark—and so did Timish, a five-year-old female wolf that I awaited here under the bridge.

We had caught her a good year earlier in Cheile Rasnoavei, a remote valley some ten kilometers further to the south. A game warden who had been out that evening on a nearby bear-hide had seen her in the trap at the edge of the forest road and quickly went home to call Ovidiu Ionescu, my Romanian partner, to announce our success. She was rather small and not really handsome, but a wolf is a wolf. It was late March and it seemed we had been extremely lucky. Her big belly and her slightly enlarged nipples indicated she was pregnant. What better luck than to radio collar the alpha female of a pack? We equipped her with a Telonics MOD-505 radio collar and let her go.

The next day we received the signal from her collar from the forests above the village of Timisu de Jos, "Lower Timish." As we had made it a habit to name our radio collared wolves after the dominant landmark near which we first relocated them, she was given her name—Timish. Leaving Brasov on the National Road, DN1, towards the south, Timisu de Jos is the next village, not even five minutes away. The DN1 is a winding, two-lane road, which connects Brasov with the capital Bucharest and follows the Timish Valley for its first fifteen kilometers up to a pass at the village of Predeal. On the other side, about sixty kilometers further, the Carpathians flatten out into the Southern Romanian plains containing the capital Bucharest and the Danube Delta. The Carpathian forests stretch on either side of the Timish valley with Postavaru Mountain to the west and Piatra Mare Mountain to the east, both around 2,000 meters altitude.

Timish was not our first radio collared wolf, but up to this moment we had been accustomed to spending the first half of the day driving around just to pick up the signal and the second half of the day attempting to get close enough to the wolves to obtain a somewhat reliable triangulation. Access on forest roads was very limited; the slopes were steep with many narrow side valleys, and the forests were dense. The few humans that moved around these forests were often armed, and the Carpathian wolves had learned to remain secretive and stay out of their way. It was a highlight to hear a pack howling or to find a kill in the winter snow; to actually catch a glimpse of a wolf was a very rare incident.

For this reason it became clear that Timish would be something special: she was within easy reach of us, and the forest she inhabited had more people wandering around than most, which we thought might make her more used to humans. There was a good chance we could spend much more time directly around her and learn a good deal about her behavior in the vicinity of one of Romania's largest cities.

The first weeks following her capture we spent our time mainly on the northeast side of Postavaru Mountain in search of Timish, usually locating her quite quickly, enabling us to learn her favorite spots. Her home range seemed extraordinarily small, but days when we could not find her indicated there was more to discover. Interestingly, we never located her again in Cheile Rasnoavei, where we had caught her, so it seemed we had been lucky and had found her on an extraterritorial stroll. Toward the end of April, her movements focused on the lower part of the Timish Valley. We weren't sure how to take this—would she really have her den in that area, not even three kilometers, as the raven flies, from the edge of Brasov? It seemed like this may be the case, and, on the morning of May 3, we picked up a steady signal from a slope just outside of Timisu de Jos.

With our little Suzuki four-wheel drive I drove there together with Annette Mertens, Masters of Science student from Rome, to check out the situation. We crossed the railroad line Brasov-Bucharest, which runs parallel to the DN1, drove up a forest road four-hundred meters, and ended up at the split of two valleys, Valea Varna Mare and Valea Varna Mica, "Large Varna Valley" and "Little Varna Valley." There was a little log cabin at the split. Two medium-sized dogs came at us barking, and, as we plugged the antenna into the receiver, three lumberjacks peeked at us from the cabin's entrance to see what we were doing. We greeted them, and, just as we picked up a strong signal from the little valley behind the cabin, we passed them, tramping up the little creek. Molly, Annette's German shepherd dog, stayed close to our heels as we quietly moved up the valley. The signal seemed to come more from the left side of the valley, so we decided to stay on the opposite side.

Slowly we hiked up the slope which rose up to our right side, step by step, trying to not make any noise. The forest consisted of over-one-hundred-year-old beech trees with individual fir and spruce interspersed. Where old trees had been taken out or had been blown over from a storm, pockets of young trees immediately emerged under the light cone that created the ecological conditions for the re-growth of the forest. Although the canopy still almost completely covered the sky, there was dense regeneration of beech and silver fir on about a third of the surface. When we reached the top of the slope we met a tiny trail that led us along the ridge dividing the two neighboring valleys.

Fresh bear droppings indicated we were not alone with the wolves in these forests. Many wouldn't be sure whether to take this as good news or bad news. We had become used to the amazing density of brown bears in the Carpathian Forests, which had been a legacy of Ceausescu's hunting pride. Over 5,000 individual bears roamed the Romanian Carpathian Mountains. During the early nineties, this represented almost half of the European bear population west of Russia, despite being less than two percent of the land mass. After a few dozen meters we stumbled over the lower leg bone of a red deer, which was still quite fresh. Apparently, the wolves had already made the area a home.

After traversing four-hundred meters along the trail, we felt we were approximately opposite the position from where we had received the strongest signal from the collar; we sat down next to an old beech, listened and watched. The forest was full of life: chaffinch and red-breasted flycatcher males were competing for their respective females, a black woodpecker warbled his locomotive-like call, and a white-backed woodpecker perched on a small dead beech next to us and hammered the splinters off the tree. From the distance we could hear the traffic from the DN1 and the whistles of the morning train to Bucharest. Otherwise it was quiet; no movement was to be observed around the thicket where we assumed Timish might have given birth to her pups. We sat for a good hour, then left.

Back at the car the lumberjacks were splitting logs for firewood. They asked what we were doing with our antennas and devices up there in the forests. We both felt we couldn't tell the truth without endangering Timish's pups—peasants still weren't all too fond of carnivores, and there was a

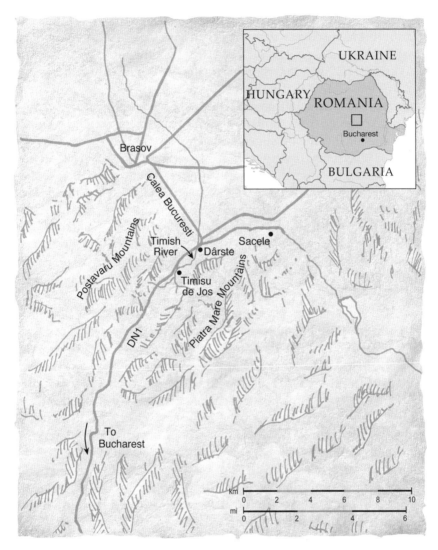

high chance they would go after the pups. I quickly told them we were working for a telecommunication company and needed to check some radio waves from Brasov, requiring us to climb further up the hills. Ion and Sergiu, as they introduced themselves, swallowed this white lie, but warned us of the plentiful bears in the area. We carefully asked whether there would be any other dangerous wildlife around, such as wolves, but they said they hadn't come across any for a few years. This was good news—Timish had managed so far to keep a low profile and to remain under the radar screen.

The next week was rather boring. We monitored the suspected den site almost non-stop, but never saw any movement. Timish obviously must have moved at least down to the creek for a drink from time to time, but she did this so discretely that none of us ever caught a glimpse of her. We still had no idea how many wolves were in this pack.

The loggers' two dogs started to make friends with our dogs, and usually came along when we hiked up to our lookout. One of them was a shaggy gray Carpathian shepherd dog mix; the other was smaller, brownish with some lighter spots. Both had their tails docked and the cartilage of one ear cut, a common superstitious practice in the Romanian countryside believed to make dogs more vicious. Luckily, it hadn't worked, and both were friendly companions. It seemed that, contrary to their masters, they knew very well that there were wolves in the area; they always kept a healthy distance from where we believed the den site would be.

Ten days after Timish's confinement we felt she should be becoming active again. It was 10:00 p.m. when Annette arrived at the loggers' cabin to take over the night shift. The moon was three-quarters full and shone through the beech trees, creating a mystical atmosphere. I had been there all afternoon and evening, but not much had happened. The two dogs from the cabin had disappeared a few hours previous; the loggers had gone to sleep—all was quiet. Molly, Annette's dog, was happy to get out of the car and started running around in circles. I gave directions to Annette and was just about to leave when Annette turned on the receiver; we immediately heard a loud, active signal. Timish was on the prowl again. The signal came right out of the small valley, and it was so strong that Timish must have been very close already. I suggested Annette get Molly back into the car, so Annette quietly whistled to her dog. No Molly in sight. Annette whistled again, and after a while we saw a movement close to the entrance of the valley some fifteen meters away. Timish's signal was extremely strong, so we became worried about the dog, and Annette quietly called her. Molly stopped and looked at us—at least that's what we thought—until Annette was nudged in the hollow of her knee. Molly actually had been hiding behind us, and in front of us was Timish. We froze and held our breath. I was sure the wolf must have heard my hammering heartbeat, but the animal just stood there looking at us. Then she moved on in a slow trot, passed us at the edge of the trees, and disappeared into the darkness. She had been absolutely quiet, and if we hadn't seen her by chance in the moonlight, we would never have realized she was right next to us. It was amazing how relaxed she had been about us; she obviously knew exactly how to handle people.

There were no more thoughts of returning home. Annette and I quietly got back in the car, still monitoring Timish's radio signal. We waited another three minutes until the signal got weaker, then pressed the clutch and let the Suzuki slowly roll down the forest road. We stopped again at the intersection, the signal clearly coming from our left; Timish had been moving to the northeast, which was the direction towards Brasov. We started the engine, crossed the railroad line, and went on the DN1 to the north. After about a kilometer we pulled into the parking lot of a small bar. Jennifer Rush's "Power of Love" boomed out of the building, and a few old Dacia cars indicated there were still some clients inside. On the other side of the road, past the railroad track, the dense forests reached up the steep slopes. The wolf's signal was weak, but she was somewhere around and still active. The signal was bouncing back and forth in the little side valleys, with the direction of the strongest signal changing constantly.

We knew that there was a dirt road up on our side a bit further back in Timisu de Jos, located past a tourist cabin. We thought this might be a good location to provide us with an overlook of the whole east side of Postavaru Mountain, possibly eliminating the bouncing signal and allowing for a better read of Timish's position. We stopped the car above the houses of Timisu de Jos under some huge spruce trees and immediately picked up a much better signal. Thanks to the moonlight we could roughly tell where the den site was, and it seemed she had already gone half the way to the edge of Brasov. She was now only a few hundred meters from the first houses, but what was she looking for? There was a good number of roe deer and red deer in the forests, but we thought they would also keep some distance from the city, its stray dogs, and its inhabitants. Throughout the next half hour, it seemed that Timish slowly continued to move further north. Due to the steep valleys the strength of her signal changed a lot, depending on whether she was on top of a ridge, on the side facing us, or somewhere in the shadow of the hills. At around midnight, when the signal remained weak and we could no longer tell her location, we returned to the DN1 and drove to the edge of Brasov.

We crossed the big bridge over the river and the railroad and stopped the car on the sidewalk. The Timish Valley opened here to the lowlands of Brasov with Sacele village on the east side and Dârste and Noua villages to the west. Over the last thirty years numerous communist-style precast concrete buildings and industrial sites had melted Dârste, Noua, and Brasov down into a single, ugly conglomerate. The Timish River had been forced into a decaying, ten-meter-wide concrete channel. The houses and gardens of Sacele village reached from the other side to the Timish River and formed a four-hundred meter deep barrier between the woods and the meadows to the northeast. Calea Bucuresti, the main four-lane road at the edge of Dârste, led another two kilometers towards the city center.

The signal of the wolf's collar was strong again, but very confusing. Timish seemed to be somewhere in the forests directly above Dârste, but at the same time, the signal came equally strong from the fields. Why was there an echo from a flat surface? We excluded that Timish was in the fields—she would have had to cross the urban areas to get there. For the next two hours, we drove up and down through Dârste and Noua, trying to locate Timish. She was constantly active and moving, but we just couldn't get a sense of where she really was. At three o'clock in the morning, the signal suddenly was gone; it had been very strong for a while and then, within less than two minutes, it disappeared. Eventually, we picked it up again in the Timish Valley; the wolf seemed to be moving back to the den site. By the time we arrived again under the big spruce trees above Timisu de Jos, where we could overlook the whole mountain side, her signal had become steady, which meant she was inactive. We assumed she was nursing her pups. At 4:00 a.m. we finally arrived home, had an early breakfast with a good glass of Scotch, and sat for another hour discussing where the hell she might have been and what she had been doing. Try as we might, we couldn't find an answer to any of these questions.

Throughout the next week Timish repeated these nocturnal excursions three times with exactly the same pattern. As she would move up and down in the forests above Dârste and Noua, the signal would echo from the fields, and it would become impossible to pinpoint where exactly she was. Each time she would spend three to four hours at the edge of Brasov and then return to her den. We were completely puzzled. What was she going for? We had to find out.

During the days we walked up and down the forests above Dârste to see whether there would be any food lying around-- a dumpsite from a slaughterhouse or anything similar. We didn't find anything. Ovidiu asked at the hunter's organization whether they would be aware of something, but they also couldn't imagine what a wolf would find there. The only possible reason for Timish's presence was the Brasov Zoo in Dârste at the edge of the forest. The surrounding fence had many holes, especially on the upper part in the forest, which made it easy for any animal to enter. Inside, we found a container where the animals' food leftovers were deposited, but, except for a few chewed-up bones, there was nothing attractive for a wolf. Did the animals in the zoo maybe attract her? There were a handful of miserable wolves squeezed into a concrete cage of 5 x 3 meters—was that the attraction? We felt that the energy needed to feed her pups would make it unlikely that she would spend her time visiting the caged wolves every other night. How about the two red deer that were kept on a one-hundred-square meter patch nearby? But Timish could have easily jumped the fence into the deer enclosure, so if this was the attraction, why hadn't she killed them yet?

Timish was hardly active during daylight and never left the area of the den, so I decided we would spend more resources following her during the night and no longer monitor her very closely during the day. My plan was to work in two teams, one that would remain under the big spruce trees above Timisu de Jos to scan her movements between the den site and the edge of Brasov, and another team to wait in Dârste to get a better feeling for what she was doing there. In any case, we would have to change our way of living and become nocturnal.

Two of our Romanian wildlife technicians started around 9:00 p.m. under the spruce trees above Timisu de Jos. Annette and I sat in the car at a small meadow next to the bridge, which we christened "small shepherd," where a shepherd kept a few dozen sheep penned together with two dogs. We remained in contact with one another through radios, which operated via relay stations around Brasov, and thus could communicate easily in all of Timish's territory. The first night nothing happened, and we gave up after midnight. Timish had been inactive at the den all evening. The next night Lucian radioed at a quarter past ten that Timish became active and seemed to start moving. Fifteen minutes later Annette and I first received her signal. Except for the few cars that passed on the nearby DN1, all was quiet. The strength of the signal slowly increased and, suddenly, the beeps from the receiver became really strong. It seemed she was coming down over the ridge right behind the small shepherd. If she would continue to the west along the edge of the city, she would indeed get to the zoo. We quickly discussed whether to drive around to get ahead of her.

Before we came to a conclusion, the dogs of the small shepherd started barking. Within seconds the shepherd's yelling joined in. He had been sleeping in a little shelter next to the pen, obviously fully dressed, and jumped out the moment the dogs started to bark. It seemed Timish was attacking the sheep. We made out some movements around the pen, but it was too dark to see any details. The signal indicated she was right there, but after half a minute the sheep dogs went quiet again, and so did the shepherd. If Timish had turned around, she couldn't have gone far, as the signal was still beating strongly out of the receiver. I told Annette to turn the volume of the receiver further down, but she said it was already nearly off. A distant streetlight slightly illuminated the area; from the corner of my eye I saw a stray dog trotting some five meters away over the road and disappear under the bridge. The next moment I was thunderstruck. "Did you see that?" I whispered to Annette. She had also noticed the stray dog, but we now realized this must have been Timish. We jumped out of the car and turned on the antenna. The signal indeed came now from the opposite direction. The wolf had entered into the river channel under the bridge. Timish was going into town!

We had never previously followed the river channel and had no idea where this would lead us. As the railroad track was between us and the channel, we had to try the other side. I started the car, reversed back to the bridge, passed it, and took the first turn into Sacele. Turning down a small dirt road, trying to find a way to the river, I eventually found a three-meter-wide track which followed the river. Wooden fences, which surrounded the small properties, were on one side; the concrete edges of the channel were on the other. There were no streetlights, just a few bulbs dangling at the entrance of some houses which shed a subdued light over the gardens. In the headlights we could see that only about half of the riverbed was covered by water, the other half was gravel, sand, and willows. A lot of garbage was hanging in the willows: plastic bottles, bags, broken tires, and scrap metal – not really a place where you would expect a wolf to hang out.

Timish's signal was getting weaker; it seemed she had made good ground. I reversed the antenna back to the hills and still got a strong beep, the echo of Timish's signal. Here was the answer to our puzzle: we had always mistaken the echo for the true signal and thought the true signal was an echo. After several hundred meters, we had crossed the urban area and reached the fields. Timish had been on a clear mission and was still way ahead of us. This was mostly pasture land, and a minute or two later a sheep camp appeared in the headlights of the Suzuki. Six ferocious dogs stood about thirty meters away in a semi-circle around the sheep pen. Two shepherds appeared in the light, dressed in their traditional "cojoc" (pronounced coshock), which are long sheepskin coats. The cojoc allows shepherds to stay out in rain and snow without getting cold, and many even sleep wrapped in the cojoc in among the sheep to guard them against wolves or bears. We wondered if Timish had been trying to attack the sheep, but although the sheep dogs barked into the night, they didn't seem to be overly-excited or worried. In any case, Timish wasn't too close—the signal was rather weak. The shepherds waved at us, so we stopped for them. We were a bit worried, as they wouldn't have understood how we could follow a wolf in the night and would have interpreted the situation in their own, superstitious way. Luckily, they only asked for a cigarette, and probably thought we were a couple looking for a dark place for a rendezvous.

The dirt road led further towards the southeast corner of Brasov, exactly where Timish's signal came from. The road was bumpy, and we made slow progress. The signal suddenly became stronger again, and it seemed we were getting closer to her. After another half kilometer we stood at the foot of a huge mountain. We were puzzled, but after a while realized we were next to the Brasov garbage dump. Now we understood—this was

Timish's destination on her nocturnal trips. We parked the car on the east side, about two-hundred meters from the dump where we had a good overview. In the dark we could now see the outline of the dump quite well against the lights of the city center. The dump was about five-hundred meters long and thirty meters high. Timish seemed to be quite active, moving back and forth all the time. Every once in a while she stopped briefly, and then she was on the move again. We wondered what she was doing, as it didn't seem she was searching for food in the waste. After two hours she had had enough and descended from the dump, moving back towards the mountains. We assumed we could not keep up with her over the bumpy track, so we went out to the asphalt road on the other side of the dump and drove as fast as we could back to Calea Bucuresti, stopped the car in front of the big bridge, and ran up on it. When we plugged the antenna into the receiver, we immediately received a strong signal, which quickly came closer. We went over on the other side of the bridge, so that Timish couldn't see us against the sky. A few moments later we saw a shadow scurrying over the road, and Timish disappeared again into the forest of the small shepherd.

It was early morning when we arrived home and had breakfast on the balcony of our house. We watched the peasants going to work while we sipped our obligatory glass of whisky and were completely psyched. It was hard to believe what we had witnessed; a wolf in town somehow was beyond imagination. The perception by the public was that wolves needed wilderness to survive. Alaska, Siberia were the places to look for them—the Carpathians would be the only place in Europe where more than a handful of them could live. We biologists knew that wolves were extremely adaptable, but we had still never expected that they would adapt to even an urban environment.

Still, we wondered what Timish had been doing at the dump; it seemed more like she was chasing something than searching for garbage. The next afternoon we were back at the dump and climbed up. There was indeed not much organic waste, but when we walked in our rubber boots over the hill, we found cats, dogs, and lots of rats. Timish obviously had discovered a great hunting ground with easy food.

Throughout the summer, Timish returned almost every night to Brasov. We found her not only on the garbage dump, but also hunting rabbits in the parks, or walking down Calea Bucuresti. We brought a set of night vision goggles, as we felt they would enable us to discover a lot more of Timish's adventures. After 11:00 p.m. Brasov turned into a ghost town—almost no one was around anymore. Timish seemed to realize perfectly when she was safe—where people were unarmed and wouldn't harm her. In June when the pups had grown and didn't need to be fed every few hours, Timish extended her nocturnal excursions into Brasov, often until morning. She crossed roads in the morning rush hour, trotted unnoticed less than ten meters next to bus stops packed with dozens of workers on the way to work, and raided the garbage containers next to the big, precast concrete buildings, together with a dozen brown bears. Due to the high number of stray dogs in Brasov, nobody paid any attention to another shaggy looking carnivore at the edge of the road. Now, with our night vision equipment, we often saw several wolves coming out of the forest at the small shepherd's meadow: a big male, obviously her mate (which Annette called "Alpha Romeo"), and two smaller wolves, presumably yearlings. Once they entered the town, however, they usually split up, and we rarely saw several wolves together.

During early summer we visited the den site only sporadically, as we didn't want to draw too much attention to the area. In late May two little dog pups greeted us at the logger's cabin; when asked, the loggers said the other two dogs had not been seen in more than two weeks. It wasn't hard to imagine what had happened to them. The two new pups didn't last very long either; in mid-June another pair of pups was present. The loggers told us that the pups had obviously been taken by some people, as they were too small to run away. In July, these dogs also disappeared, and the loggers left for the summer. The wolves definitely kept the forests clear of dogs!

In early July, when the pups were about two months old, we couldn't locate Timish anymore in Valea Varna Mare, and it seemed she had moved the pups to another den site. Most of the time she was now in Valea Lamba Mare, a longer and more remote valley about three-and-a-half kilometers further away from Brasov, deep in the mountains. She must have known that with the pups becoming more active, they were no longer safe that close to people. With this relocation, we could finally search for the first den site, locating it where we had expected. It was perfect—the entrance was below a rocky outcrop with a little plateau in front of the rocks where the pups could play, perfectly sheltered by beech thickets on all sides. Two tiny beaten paths led around the rock up to the ridge, still sheltered by young trees. If we wouldn't have specifically searched the thicket, we would have never noticed it.

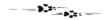

Word about these "downtown wolves" spread quickly among the world of wolf biologists. In the last two decades, wolves in Southern and Eastern Europe had slowly recovered after a long period of intensive persecution. The first individuals showed up in countries such as France, Switzerland, or Germany, challenging the traditional regime of control, cultivation, and human almightiness. So far, they always had been shot in no time, but interest in them was increasing; conservationists saw them as the victims of our battle against nature and the symbol for hope; farmers and hunters saw them as a threat to their economic interests and used the argument that in our dissected landscapes there was no room for wolves to live. Timish and her pack proved that wolves could live almost anywhere, if food was available and people would accept them. The whole discussion about habitat suitability was led ad absurdum. Mike Salisbury from the BBC Natural History Unit, who was just working on a wolf special, had heard of Timish and asked whether there would be any possibility to film her. Just before he was supposed to come in September she stopped her excursions to Brasov. The pack started to move all around Postavaru and Piatra Mare Mountains as they had done in early spring. Their behavior was again what we had considered "normal"—they did what wolves were supposed to do.

During winter, snow tracking indicated that there were two larger wolves, obviously Timish and her mate, and three smaller wolves, likely the pups that had survived. It seemed that the yearlings had left the pack. We never saw any of the wolves, although we tracked them intensively. They were cautious and shy and, when we tried to get closer, they sneaked away long before we could observe them. They were wolves as we knew them, killing deer and wild boar in the forests, and we sometimes wondered whether the nocturnal trips into the urban area last summer weren't just the figments of our imaginations. By late February, Timish was in heat again, and spots of blood in the snow gave hope for another litter in spring.

Two months later we all got excited and monitored her twenty-four hours a day. Once again she spent a lot of time in the lower Timish Valley close to Brasov. Eventually she settled down on the slope just above Dârste, not even three-hundred meters from the first houses of Brasov. She gave birth in a hollow fir tree, but after a few days moved her pups over the ridge back into Valea Varna, close to her previous den. Would she start using the city as a hunting ground again? We monitored her every evening, and on May 18, 1995 she indeed appeared again at the small shepherd's meadow, crossed under the bridge into the river channel, as if she had done this for her whole life, and went straight to her hunting grounds at the dump. During that summer her movements into town were pretty much the blueprint of the previous summer, except that it seemed her insensitivity to humans grew every week. We learned her secret trails and managed to predict her movements. Eventually we could be ahead of her most of the time and await her at various intersections. When had she started going into town; how did she figure that out? Was this already a tradition of the local wolves, passed on from one generation to the next? In any case, the wolves perfectly adapted to the local situation and used the available resources in an ideal manner.

Timish and her mates became stars. Mike Salisbury and his team from BBC came to give filming them a try. Although they brought a starlight sensitive camera with the latest military technology, they were skeptical they would get much footage and thought they would film, at the utmost, a wolf crossing an overgrown dirt road in the outskirts of Brasov from time to time. The two weeks that they stayed with us were the pinnacle of all we had experienced so far. They filmed the wolves every night in the city, on the roads, and in among city dwellers, often from less than ten meters away. Timish and her pack became prominent actors in the legendary BBC Wolf Special.

Although we radio collared over twenty wolves in total, it was Timish who leveraged our project. Two-and-a-half years after we first caught her, we recaptured her to replace the collar. Unfortunately, this was the last time we saw Timish, as her new collar failed after a few weeks; whereas, the old collar still emitted beeps three years later, and she became invisible for us again as she seemed to be for everyone else. Tracks in the snow showed that there were wolves in the area for some additional years, but we could not tell whether or not they were Timish's pack and if they continued their forays to town.

Now, over fifteen years later, the area where Timish and her mates roamed has changed considerably. Huge shopping malls and hypermarkets have been built where the sheep meadows once were; traffic has increased to a point where no wolf could cross Calea Bucuresti anymore without a high risk of being killed; and the little dirt track along the river channel on which we followed Timish on dozens of nights has been converted into a four-lane ring road around Brasov. The small shepherd's meadow is now a housing development with thirty-five new buildings, and the old spruce trees above Timisu de Jos, which we used as shelters to scan the mountain side from Timish's den all the way to Brasov, have been cut to make way for an asphalt road. Wolves have probably long left the area—or maybe not? Timish, the little, unhandsome wolf, has taught us how adaptable her species can be if people let them live, so maybe her ancestors are still roaming unnoticed between the malls and hypermarkets. You never know.

EPILOGUE

AS THE DAUGHTER of a former wolf biologist, I grew up experiencing firsthand the lives detailed within these pages. I howled, tracked and trapped wolves, Care Bear in tow. In second grade, for show and tell, I brandished a gallon-sized plastic bag that contained the sum total remnants of a wolf-killed white-tailed deer fawn. In other words, I cannot help but relate to these stories, and cannot imagine a world without wolves.

The advent of the conservation movement is relatively new in human history. Since the dawn of pastoralism, wolves have largely been seen as vermin, inherently evil. By the time scientific studies commenced in the mid-1900's, populations worldwide had already withered through millennia of intense persecution. Wolves were extinct in my home state of Wisconsin just six years after the birth of my father. That they were returning on their own volition when I was born, just some twenty years later, was due in large part to the concerted efforts of the individuals who authored these pages and to the growing public awareness derived from their research that nature, wildness, and creatures such as wolves have inherent value in and of themselves.

The effort put forth by individual biologists has not been without risks to personal safety, and has certainly, as this book shows, contained at least a modicum of personal discomfort (swarms of flies and mosquitoes, the stench of wolf-bait, cramped quarters within aircraft, to name a few). We are fortunate that such people exist, that such work has been performed. Both species have received a second chance: wolves again grace some of their former haunts and our lives are richer for their presence. This second chance will not be without difficulties. We need to make responsible choices as we continue to move forward in a world that has recognized the intrinsic value of our natural resources. Resources are, by their very definition, finite.

Our decisions, both personal and societal, directly affect how we prioritize the utilization and conservation of these resources. As citizens, we must be aware of the consequences of these decisions and the potential for conflict, and must decide how we deal with conflict once it inevitably arises. As studies into awareness and sentience in organisms other than ourselves progress, we will be further challenged in how we respond to these conflicts and the need for informed discourse will only increase.

Despite these challenges, the future is not without hope. The stories of Ernesto and Timish illustrate the adaptable nature of these animals, capable of surprising even the very people who study them. Their adaptability and resilience is not enough, however. We, as citizens of this planet, need to act as stewards, entrusted with a gift for the future. The first step is to be conscious of these issues. We need to learn from our collective past. We need to care. As editors, we hope this book will be a further step, perhaps even your first, towards understanding and respecting these remarkable animals.

To paraphrase Aldo Leopold, it is inconceivable that an ethical relation to the natural world can exist without love, respect, and admiration, and a high regard for the value of every one of its parts.

— Allison C. Thiel
    with Marianne Strozewski and Richard P. Thiel, Editors

Ahlqvist, Per is a field technician with long experience in capturing wild animals including other large carnivores and ungulates. He has worked at various research projects at the Grimsö Wildlife Research Station at the Swedish University of Agricultural Sciences since the late 1970's. Since 1998 he has been involved and partially responsible for the field activities within the Scandinavian wolf research project.

Benson, John is a Trent University Ph.D. student, serving as field supervisor and lead researcher for Trent University-Ontario, Ministry of Natural Resources research project on Wolf-Coyote Hybridization Dynamics. John's previous work experience included field research with various carnivores (panthers, black bears, etc).

Beyer Jr., Dean E. is employed by Michigan DNR as a wildlife research biologist and is in his fifteenth year coordinating wolf research on the Michigan wolf program.

Blanco, Juan Carlos is a biologist with a Ph.D. in Animal Ecology. He coordinated the first wolf survey in Spain in 1987 and 1988, and since then has been studying wolves and working on wildlife conservation. He has studied the ecology of wolves in agricultural areas, and from 1999 to 2011 prepared and coordinated the National Strategy on Wolves in Spain with the Ministry of the Environment.

Boyd, Diane is presently employed by Montana Fish, Wildlife & Parks. She became involved with wolf recovery efforts in northern Minnesota in the late 1970's under Dave Mech and Steve Fritts. She moved to Montana in 1979 for her graduate research project studying the first wolf to occupy the Glacier National Park area. She has monitored successful recovery of wolves in this region over twenty years as a University of Montana researcher – Wolf Ecology Project field supervisor.

Burch, John began as a research and control trapper under Dave Mech in Minnesota between 1980 and 1985 and was a project biologist with the Denali Wolf Research project, Denali Park Alaska, 1985–1995. From 2002 to present, he has served on the Yukon Charley wolf monitoring project as Wildlife Biologist for Yukon-Charley Rivers National Preserve.

Carbyn, Lu is an Emeritus Research Scientist with the Department of the Environment, Ottawa. He has worked on wolf studies for forty-two years and has served on assignments in Poland and Portugal. From 1989 to 1993 he headed the Canadian Swift Fox Reintroduction program as chairman of the Recovery Team. Lu is currently the Canadian member of the International Union for the Conservation of Nature and Natural Resources (IUCN) Wolf Specialist Group and Canid Group.

Cluff, Dean H. is a wildlife biologist for the Government of the Northwest Territories, North Slave Region, based in Yellowknife. He continues to conduct research and monitoring programs on wolves in the region, but is also active in studies on grizzly bears, black bears, barren-ground caribou, moose, muskox, and bison. Prior to this, Dean worked on a variety of other species including polar bears, coyotes, and beluga whales.

Cortés, Yolanda began studying wolves in 1997, completing her Ph.D. on wolf ecology and conservation in agricultural areas in 2001. Together with J.C. Blanco, she has closely monitored the expansion of the wolf population in Spain and studied the impact of barriers in this process. Recently she has concentrated on minimizing damages to livestock in areas of recent recolonization by wolves.

Dwire, Maggie is currently Assistant Recovery Coordinator for the Mexican Wolf Recovery Program for the U. S. Fish and Wildlife Service, overseeing the captive breeding program and assisting with field work in the recovery of the Mexican wolf.

Hayes, Bob retired in 2001 from Yukon Fish and Wildlife Branch, wolf research and management biologist for the Yukon Territory. Bob supervised and managed field work and coordinated wolf management in the Yukon. He is author of a book on Yukon wolves, and presently facilitates wildlife and habitat conservation initiatives in Yukon communities.

Heilhecker, Ellen is presently a Wildlife Conflict Specialist employed by the Washington Department of Fish and Wildlife. Formerly she served as state Wolf Biologist for the New Mexico Department of Game and Fish on the Mexican Wolf Interagency Field Team.

McIntyre, Rick works with the National Park Service's Yellowstone Wolf Project. For four years he served as Wolf Interpreter, having come from Denali National Park where he worked as a seasonal naturalist over fifteen summers. He is the author of two books on wolves.

Mech, L. David is a Senior Research Scientist, U.S. Geological Survey; Adjunct Professor, University of Minnesota; Vice Chair, International Wolf Center. He has been researching wolves since the late 1950's, beginning as a Ph.D. student under Durward Allen on Isle Royale National Park.

Musiani, Marco is an Associate Professor, Tenured with the Faculties of Environmental Design and Veterinary Medicine at the University of Calgary. Dr Musiani is currently analyzing ecological data on large carnivores and their prey (example, wolves, caribou), which was gathered throughout Northern and Western Canada. He has published books and papers on various theoretical and applied ecology journals, which also include articles on predator ecology, evolution and management.

Peterson, Rolf is the Robbins Chair in Sustainable Management of the Environment, Michigan Technological University. He has been the principle researcher on ecological studies of wolves in Isle Royale National Park, Michigan since the 1970's, determining the relationship between gray wolves and moose in an isolated ecosystem little affected by human activities.

Phillips, Mike has served as Executive Director, Turner Endangered Species Fund since 1997. He formerly held positions as Leader, Yellowstone Wolf Restoration Project, 1994–1997; and Field Projects Coordinator, Red Wolf Recovery Program, 1986–1994. Mike has been a member of all three Mexican Wolf Recovery Teams assembled since 1995.

Promberger, Christoph is manager of several large conservation and re-wilding projects in the Romanian Carpathians. As Project Leader of Munich Wildlife Society, Carpathian Large Carnivore Project he developed, managed and executed research and conservation of a project on wolves, bears, and lynx in the Romanian Carpathian Mountains.

Lonsway, Donald is employed by US Department of Agriculture's Wildlife Services working on the Michigan wolf program, and prior to that he was with Michigan Department of Natural Resources, including annual wolf track surveys, research trapping and collaring, wolf depredation investigation (lethal and nonlethal control), and human, health, and safety issues.

Liberg, Olof is an associate professor in wildlife ecology at Grimsö Wildlife Research Station at the Swedish University of Agricultural Sciences. He has been the coordinator of the Scandinavian wolf research project since its start in 1998. He has worked on population ecology of roe deer and has also a degree in Veterinary science.

Sand, Håkan is Senior Researcher and Assistant Professor, Department of Ecology, Swedish University of Agricultural Sciences, and has led the wolf research project in Sweden since 1998.

Smith, Douglas, Ph.D. is the Project Leader for the Yellowstone Wolf Project, National Park Service. He became involved with studies of wolves and moose on Isle Royale under Rolf Peterson. He has published a wide variety of journal articles and book chapters on beavers and wolves and co-authored two popular books on wolves.

Stahler, Dan is Threatened and Endangered Species Coordinator and Project Biologist for Yellowstone Wolf Project, National Park Service, managing all aspects of Yellowstone's long-term wolf research with Project Leader Doug Smith, as well as handling National Park Service management and monitoring of wolves.

Strozewski, Marianne is retired after teaching secondary English in Tomah, Wisconsin and abroad for over thirty years. She has degrees from U.W. Wisconsin, Eau Claire and Purdue University. When not editing other people's work, she is fabricating stories for her grandchildren. She was Allison's tenth grade English teacher.

Theberge, John was for 30 years a professor of ecology at the University of Waterloo, Ontario, where he specialized in wildlife and wolf research and ecological management of parks, authoring many scientific papers. He has written or co-written two books on wolves. He and his wife continue wolf research in Yellowstone and Arizona.

Theberge, Mary is a researcher, wildlife illustrator and educator who has partnered with her husband in wolf/prey research and co-authored with him several books, scientific papers, and a major monograph on Algonquin wolves.

Thiel, Allison C. works in London as a loss adjustor in the energy sector. She has a degree in mechanical engineering from Michigan Technological University. As the child of a wolf biologist, she had no choice but to know wild wolves and the people who study them.

Thiel, Richard P. is retired from Wisconsin Department of Natural Resources, serving as Wolf Recovery Coordinator from 1980 to 1989, managing field work on the state level. From 1990 to 2011 he coordinated regional wolf monitoring activities while serving as a wildlife educator. He has authored two books on wolves.

Vucetich, John is an associate professor from Michigan Technological University, where he teaches courses in Population Ecology, Wildlife Management, and Environmental Ethics. He is co-director of the Isle Royale Wolf-Moose Project and co-director of the Conservation Ethics Group. He has authored more than 75 scholarly publications on a range of topics, including wolf-prey ecology, extinction risk, population genetics, and environmental philosophy.

Wabbaken, Petter is a researcher at Hedmark University College in Norway and has been a part of the Scandinavian wolf research project since it started in 1998. He is responsible for monitoring of wolves in Norway and has also worked on other large carnivores, including brown bears.

Wikenros, Camilla recently finished her Ph.D. with the Scandinavian wolf research project at Grimsö Wildlife Research Station at the Swedish University of Agricultural Sciences working on ecosystem effect of wolves in Scandinavia.

Wydeven, Adrian is Forest Habitat Coordinator with the Wisconsin Department of Natural Resources, and served as the Carnivore Specialist overseeing the Wisconsin wolf management program between 1990 and 2013. He is editor of a regional book on wolves.

International Wolf Center
Teaching the World about Wolves

THE INTERNATIONAL WOLF CENTER is honored to present this unique collection of wolf stories from the singular perspective of noted field biologists and researchers. We hope that you enjoy these stories with the added appreciation that proceeds from this book will help us serve our mission to advance the survival of wolf populations by teaching about wolves, their relationship to wildlands and the integral role of humans in determining their future.

Your support of this book also draws attention and creates inspiration as more and more people become aware of the complex majesty of this apex predator. Our passion for wolves runs ocean-deep and decades long. We advocate for wolves, through the use of science-based education and outreach. We remain one of the few non-biased, comprehensive resources for students, teachers, outdoor enthusiasts, biologists, naturalists, scientists, researchers, environmentalists, conservationists, and anyone else who values and appreciates wolves and the important role they play in our environment. We encourage you to visit the Center in Ely, Minnesota, and discover the wonder of wolves through our daily programs and the live exhibit wolf pack in their natural habitat.

We invite you to become one of the more than 1.5 million people who annually visit us at www.wolf.org and take advantage of our in-depth on-line resources, read *International Wolf* magazine, or participate in our many interactive classroom experiences.

Our members, now in more than 32 countries, fall on many sides of controversial issues. At a time when polarized debate occupies much real estate in contemporary culture, an organization like the International Wolf Center plays a more valuable role than ever.

We invite your continued support and thank you again for the purchase of this book.

Rob Schultz, Executive Director

WWW.WOLF.ORG

VISIT US   JOIN US